A crime fiction writer, journalist and book editor, Lindy Cameron is the author of four novels: *Golden Relic,* and her Melbourne private investigator series *Blood Guilt, Bleeding Hearts* and *Thicker than Water*. First published in Australia, her PI series is now published in the USA with Bywater Books. Lindy is also the author of *Redback*, the first in a new thriller series, and she contributed true crime essays to both editions of Black Inc.'s *On Murder*. Lindy is a national co-convenor of Sisters in Crime Australia, and editor of its magazine *Stiletto*.

Meaner than Fiction

Edited by Lindy Cameron

The Five Mile Press Pty Ltd
1 Centre Road, Scoresby
Victoria 3179 Australia
Email: publishing@fivemile.com.au
Website: www.fivemile.com.au

First published 2007
Reprinted 2008

Internal design by Sandra Nobes
Typeset by J&M Typesetting
Cover design by Darian Causby
Printed and bound in China

National Library of Australia Cataloguing-in-Publication data:

Cameron, Lindy.
Meaner than fiction.

ISBN 978 1 74178 470 1 (pbk).

1. Crime - Australia. 2. Criminal investigation - Australia. 3. Criminals - Australia. I. Title.

364.994

Contents

Introduction

Justice is blind.

Well, it's supposed to be.

To state the obvious – which, when speaking about the law you really need to do – justice is impartial; it is not supposed to see or imagine any differences in whoever stands before it.

Justice applies equally to all without fear or favour, corruption, avarice or prejudice; and it is there for rich or poor, great or small, and with no exception to race, religion, gender, politics, sexuality, class, education or anything that in the wider community usually distinguishes one person from another.

As the embodiment of the moral force underlining the legal systems of the western world, justice is typically personified as female and depicted as a woman carrying a sword and set of scales, most often bare-breasted and sometimes wearing a blindfold.

The blindfold says to all, 'It does not matter who you are or what you look like or what you're accused of or whether you're innocent as a lamb or guilty as sin – I will judge you fairly according to all the evidence put before me.'

And so, we blindly believe that the law is there to protect us all – despite evidence to the contrary.

The thing is, the legal system and justice are not one and the same; in fact, they often don't even walk into court together. This actuality is compounded by the situation that, regardless of the rhetoric, we live in a world in which there are at least two kinds of justice – one that works, and one that doesn't.

From Charles Dickens and Conan Doyle in Victorian and Edwardian England, through Estelle Blackburn, Helen Reade, Colleen Egan, Andrew Rule, Peter Rees, Kevin Morgan, Karen Kissane and Robin Bowles in modern Australia, to the women who've written the stories in this very collection, writers often feel obliged to do what they do best to shine the cold light of day on the wrongs that afflict not only our society but our legal and justice systems in particular.

'Oh sure,' I hear you say. 'Obliged? Like you don't have your own agenda.'

And you'd be right; of course we do. First and foremost we write to tell a story – it's what we do. But we can and do use our writing to further a cause, to fight the good fight, to expose or seek the truth, or just to lay down an account of what really happened. And whether we do it in literary fiction like Dickens did, disguise it in genre fiction as modern crime writers do, or reveal it in journalism or true crime anthologies like this one, the aim is the same: to instigate change, redress wrongs or, at the very least, get you out there asking questions, perhaps even demanding answers.

I should perhaps warn you that, in this anthology, 'blind' Lady Justice is impaired, not impartial; and she is also deaf and dumb.

The stories herein range from unsolved murders to wrongly convicted 'killers'; from a pervert who secretly filmed his housemates to Victorian-era society's indifference towards an unconventional woman; from a man shot for no good reason to the shame of the Australian Government's Pacific 'solution'.

Within these pages one woman went to jail because 13 years of spousal abuse did not count towards her plea of self-defence. One innocent man was hanged and another wrongly imprisoned on circumstantial nonsense and questionable police conduct; one went to jail because he was a foreign Jew; one because he confessed under duress; and one because an expert twisted the evidence to suit his own theory. Here too one man got off because an expert's dodgy reconstruction threw doubt on his guilt; one walked with a fine because there was no law with which to charge him; and a crazy gunman got a ridiculously short sentence because … well, he just did.

For this anthology I was fortunate indeed to assemble a diverse group of contributors. You will read: experts in their field – forensic pathologist Dr Shelley Robertson, researcher and activist Susan Metcalfe, and academic Lucy Sussex; one professional true crime writer, Robin Bowles; and six writers who usually devote their skills to crime fiction – Kerry Greenwood, PD Martin, Kathryn Deans, Liz Filleul and Leigh Redhead. I too usually write crime fiction because I do so love to make things up.

The title story, and the only reprint in this anthology, is mine and concerns the pointless shooting of Dr Andrew Taylor. His story demonstrates how a major tragedy can lead to radical law reform, but still have no affect on the outcome of actual court cases. The fact that our gun laws were ripped up and rewritten after the Port Arthur massacre in 1996 did not – even one little bit – help Andrew Taylor, who was shot a year later by a nutter who hadn't handed in his guns.

Like all the others here Andrew's story has an unfair ending; although, despite the many murders and suspicious deaths within these pages, his is the only story that features a gun. Mind you, because neither the killer of Elisabeth Membrey nor her body has ever been found, Liz Filleul's account of her murder cannot tell us what weapon was used.

Kathryn Deans' story of what happened to Heather Osland after she finally found the courage to defend herself against a brutal husband is beyond comprehension. It will, along with Kathryn's examples of the strange state of justice in South Australia, raise too many questions about how things work in this country. They and PD Martin's story on the wrongful conviction of Andrew Mallard, and some of the cases in Kerry Greenwood's piece on writers seeking justice, prove the need for Australia's various Innocence Projects, the subject of PD Martin's second story.

Dr Shelley Robertson's piece on just how much of the 'whole truth' doesn't get heard by the jury, because of what is allowed by the court and the rules of evidence, goes a long way to explaining what went awry in Leigh Redhead's story about the pervert who stalked her sister, and Robin Bowles' piece on Bernard Munro's quest to solve the mysterious death of his daughter.

The unfortunate life of Mary Fortune as recounted by Lucy Sussex, and some of the cases in Kerry Greenwood's story, reflect 'the times' – an era in which Charles Dickens could write, in *Oliver Twist*:

[Mr Brownlow says] '… the law supposes that your wife acts under your direction.'

'If the law supposes that,' said Mr Bumble … 'the law is a ass – a idiot. If that's the eye of the law, the law is a bachelor; and the worst

I wish the law is, that his eye may be opened by experience – by experience.'

Thank goodness we live in a country where writers, and other ordinary citizens, can make a stand for innocent people; shine a light on injustice; be a voice for the dead; question the veracity, motives and decisions of the legal powers-that-be; or praise the work of those police, lawyers and judges who try their damnedest to seek the truth in a system that so often works against even them.

Despite the freshly minted fact that under our new sedition laws (designed to protect us from terrorists) we writers can now be jailed by our own government for saying something deemed inappropriate about our own government, we can still stand up for Mohammad Faisal and Mohammed Sagar, as Susan Metcalfe has in this very book.

Blind Lady Justice, so often deaf and dumb, should perhaps also carry an hourglass along with her sword and scales, because for too many people their time runs out while waiting for those scales to balance or the sword to cleave the fact from fiction. Their quest for the truth, for an answer, for justice becomes in itself an example of injustice.

The best we can do is tell you what happened, so it will not be forgotten, so that people beyond the courts will know, so that something good might come from something bad.

Please proceed, but remember, you have been warned: truth is *way* meaner than fiction.

Lindy Cameron

Meaner than Fiction

Lindy Cameron

It was a nice morning. I was wearing runners. I'd just finished seeing a patient and was escorting her back to the front desk. She went through the waiting room; I went, as usual, through the front office.

He was standing on the other side of the counter. He wasn't one of my patients but I recognised him, so I said good morning and asked what I could do for him.

He said, 'I'm very depressed.'

He raised his hand – which was holding a gun; a pistol.

I thought, he's not going to kill himself because he's not pointing the gun at his head.

There was no time to react to what was really happening. The next thing I was on the floor. I didn't feel anything but knew I'd been shot, because of the noise and the fact that I was on the floor. I sat up. There was blood. I'd been shot in the hip. The bullet had gone straight through.

Then he shot me again in the same leg. I tried to drag myself behind a filing cabinet but he kept firing – at the wall, at the cabinet, everywhere; he just kept firing ...

If this were crime *fiction*, in the first person, the narrative would most likely continue with a clichéd balancing act between life and death. As narrator, I'd be trying to hook you with an action-packed or tension-filled flight or fight scenario.

I may well be going down in a hail of bullets, but I'd be telling you all about it as I went.

Actually, if this were crime fiction, I think I'd start again and give the piece more colour by adding all the noise: the screams, the shouting, the Bang! Bang! Bang! of the gunshots and the variety of sounds as each bullet hit something different – a metal filing cabinet, a solid wall, a human body. My human body.

And of course, there'd be the pain – lots of colour there. I mean, I've just been hit by … how many did we get to? Was it two bullets? And let's make them .45 calibre, full metal jackets – for extra oomph and drama.

Okay … so I've just been hit by two bad-arse bullets; the pain alone would have to be enough to kill me. Wouldn't it?

Yeah right; the reader's not silly. Obviously I survive. I have to, in order to tell my tale. I am, after all, the first person. I know, I know; there *are* fictional exceptions. A mystery buff would say: 'Never rule out the dead narrator. All we need here, for a riveting story, is a well-told flashback – to the who, what and why – then the hero can bite the dust, if that's what the author wants. It's been done before. After all, the story is all in the telling; that's what makes it new.'

Flashbacks like those, however, only work if the narrator knows, or can figure out during the re-telling, how they came to be in that predicament. The narrator needs to be able to explain the circumstances that led up to this incident, or there is no story. If the narrator does die in the end, everything else has to turn out right first. And if I die, well … the chances are, in fiction, that I probably deserved it.

On the other hand, if the narrator doesn't have a clue why some nutcase with a gun is on the rampage, then obviously, in fiction, the 'I' of the story has to survive in order to carry out an investigation; to go back to the real beginning, wherever that was, and find out why.

That is the pact that crime fiction writers make with their readers. It's not so much the 'who' but the 'why' that's important. It's not the mystery, but the solution that matters.

And a crime fiction buff cannot be taken for a ride. The motives, of the good and the bad, must be examined, or at least revealed; the outcome must be believable, if only in context; and justice, of some kind, must be seen to be done.

If this were crime fiction it would therefore be my job as the author to provide you with those answers. I would do this because I know that fans of crime fiction don't actually read mysteries or crime novels because they like being confused, baffled or scared; or because they derive a vicarious thrill from the violence. They read it because everything turns out right in the end. Order is brought to the chaos and there is always closure. Compared to that, real life is a bitch.

So if this were crime fiction I, as the author, would now go back to the end of my introduction and after, 'he just kept firing ... ' I would freeze the action there – again – and then delve into a flashback of how I, the narrator, came to find myself in this bizarre and bloody situation.

And if this were crime fiction my editor would, no doubt, suggest I lose the odd reference to the shoes.

But this is not fiction so I will, instead, go back to the start and tell you the truth: that this is a true story, and in real life things rarely end the way they should. This is not my true story, but it does speak for itself, and I don't need to add colour.

On Saturday 12 April 1997 Andrew Taylor, for no other reason than he was a doctor, was – as the press would later say – 'gunned down' by a man who wanted to show someone how he felt. Specifically, he wanted to show a doctor how he felt. Andrew Taylor was the doctor he found. The first and second shots hit Andrew in the right hip.

The Man, armed with a .45 calibre semi-automatic Norinco pistol and two magazines of bullets (a mixture of full metal jackets and jacketed hollow points) fired about nine shots around the small Hastings medical clinic. All were aimed at his one single target; five were direct hits.

The Man ignored the screaming receptionist, over whose head he was firing. He even shouted: 'Shut up, I am not going to kill you.'

He fired and fired and fired. The third shot to hit his target struck Andrew in the left leg, below the knee. The Man emptied one magazine and reloaded. He walked through the crowded waiting room, ignoring all the terrified patients, to follow the doctor into the hall where he had dragged himself. He then shot Andrew Taylor in the back.

This Man just wanted a doctor, any doctor, to recognise, and thereby acknowledge, the pain *he* was in.

But where does a true story like this really begin? Does it start with the story of the victim or the assailant? And whose story should come first?

On 12 April 1997 Andrew Taylor was 39 years old. He was the father of two children, whom he adored, but was separated from his wife. He loved horses, didn't mind a drink or two, was a good doctor who liked being a doctor. He'd been practising at the Hastings Clinic on the Mornington Peninsula for eight years, but had started his working life in Darwin and had done a stint as a doctor in the US Army. On that Saturday, however, he was seriously in the wrong place at the wrong time.

What should you know about the gunman at this stage? Would you like to know that he was a 45-year-old, unemployed, married father of a 15-year-old son? Or is it enough to know that he had his reasons?

He was single-minded. He didn't shoot anyone else. But the fact is, this Man, this gunman, did not know Andrew Taylor personally (although they had met); and he had no specific grievance against him.

So, do you care that the Man thought he had his reasons? Should we care?

If this were crime fiction I could give you the facts, explain the reasons and delve into the motives. I may well be giving you fictional psychology but you would get the best explanation I could invent for an act of random violence.

Crime fiction is the perfect vehicle for exploring legal, political, financial, environmental, social or health issues. In a fictional setting these can all be analysed, investigated, dissected, ridiculed, praised, explained or vilified.

Crime fiction usually has, as its driving force, a moral or honourable heart that ensures that scales get balanced and underdogs have their day. It explores the motives of 'a possible reality', and gives us 'reasons' so we can make sense of the mayhem – both fictional and real.

Crime fiction also gives us strong reliable heroes, the kind we'd want on our side in a tight situation. They walk the mean streets for us and deal with the other side, those bad characters we wouldn't ever want to meet in a dark alley – or, as it turns out, in a well-lit doctor's waiting room.

A crime novel can be a deadly serious excursion into the darkest corners of the human psyche or imagination; it can be a frothy little brain-teasing puzzle designed to amuse; or it can be all manner of things in between. It can haunt or entertain, sometimes it can do both – but it must end the right way or the author will have a very short career.

Crime fiction, finally, is also the home of that whole 'moral of the story' concept. In fact that philosophy is its raison d'être. And we read it because we'd really, really like to believe in that most clichéd of old morals, the one that goes: 'crime does not pay'. We expect it in our crime fiction because it's the only place where it can be relied on to happen. The search for truth or justice in the real world often seems like a pointless exercise; but in crime fiction you are guaranteed at least an answer, or a just or appropriate ending.

I read and write crime fiction for all these reasons. I don't read much true crime, except for the daily newspaper short-form. To be honest I have no idea why people do read true crime. There's more than enough bad stuff going on in the world without delving back into it as a reading hobby. It's hyped up on TV and elaborated on, a little, in the papers under in-your-face headlines, but way too much of it remains unresolved. And how often do we find out what really happened, let alone what happened in the end?

Even when the culprit is safely behind bars we seldom get the full story. We may get all the details of the crime and a blow by blow account of the court case, if there was one, but unless the writer, for part of the story at least, is the culprit then we rarely get to know the *why* of it all. Do we, for instance, know anything about Martin Bryant or Ivan Milat that isn't someone else's opinion? Do we want to? Will the presence of apparent evil in our real lives be more, or less, bearable if we get inside their minds? Or is it enough that a true crime account tells us that it happened, and now it's over? Or, more to the point, that it happened to someone else, and now it's over.

But look at any investigation into an actual crime that gets written as the truest account, and published as *the* book of that true crime. More often than not it will have no proper ending. Why? Because the thing that makes that real-life case interesting is the mystery surrounding the fact that it, probably, has still not been solved.

Where is the satisfaction in reading a mystery that, in a way, is missing its last page? And if you know that before you start, why would you bother? If there's no resolution, no answers, no solution, no closure in what you read – and what you're reading is loaded with bad or evil people, and scary notions or gruesome details – surely that has to leave you dissatisfied, on edge, even fearful.

As the woman across the road from the clinic where Andrew Taylor was shot said, 'I'll be watching very closely at the door for a while. These events seem to touch off copycats.' She was a distant witness to an awful incident that ended badly. She now expects more of the same.

Strangely enough, in fact or fiction, there are things we 'accept' either because, sadly, we do understand them; or because we have no choice, as there will be no further explanation. In the case of murder, or attempted murder, understanding an explanation doesn't mean that we like or condone it, just that we understand the reason. We are not *being* understanding.

If one criminal kills another criminal, we understand the motive. If a criminal maims a punter who owes him big-time, or kills an otherwise-innocent witness to one of his crimes we, strangely, understand that there is a reason.

But, we don't get the serial killer, at all. He is perversely fascinating, but we don't really want to be able to understand him because that might just say something about us. It's the same when a nutter with a gun goes on a killing spree for no apparent reason and with no justifiable – in any sense of the word – target in mind. We frown, we shake our heads, we really don't understand; so we assume he must be mad.

And this is where we sometimes just have to accept the unexplainable, because we have no choice. The 'just plain mad' or 'evil' explanation is quite often acceptable to us – as long as there is closure. Some of us might like to know what made him like that, but mostly we're happy if the mad, evil man gets his just desserts. We want to know that he is dead or locked up. Oh, and we usually also want to know what he looks like; perhaps so we can recognise the face of evil if we pass another like it on the street. This knowledge does not protect us from the bogeyman but it possibly acts as a mojo – of sorts.

So, let's return to Andrew Taylor and the Man who 'had his reasons'. At this stage, whether this is true crime or crime fiction, you'd not only want the doctor to survive but you'd want some sense to be made of this. You've been teased, so you would want to know why the Man felt he had to do what he did, wouldn't you?

What kind of pain must he have been in, you ask, to choose any doctor, supposedly at random, to make a point? Fact or fiction, you'd want to know the why; you'd feel cheated if you didn't get an explanation for this act of violence. But let me warn you now, you won't like the answer; it won't make enough sense.

Andrew Taylor's partner can't, or won't, bring herself to recall the gunman's name. She refers to him as that guy, that bloke, the Man. He is the bogeyman in her life; he doesn't need a name.

Andrew, however, knew exactly who the gunman was, and he remembered most of what happened for the statement that he gave the police at the scene, including the fact that the ambulance guys had wanted to give the wounded gunman priority.

Andrew remembered crawling into the hallway to escape the bullets. He knew the Man had emptied one magazine and reloaded. He knew the Man had come after him, into the hall, that he was 'doing' this to show someone how he felt.

Andrew was in no pain. He could move and there was a lot of his blood everywhere but nothing hurt – not even his legs, which he knew had been hit. He remembered the noise, the blood, the fear; and he recalled rolling onto his back, to face the Man.

He stated afterwards, in an emotional tone that suggested he hated admitting to a moment of weakness, that it was only then, lying on his back in the hall, that he started to plead – for his life, for the Man to stop shooting, for the Man not to kill him, for the chance to speak to his children before …

'That's when I started begging,' he'd said, and he'd sounded embarrassed. Andrew Taylor had nowhere to go. Why would anyone with no way out be self-conscious about asking for mercy?

A gunman was standing right in front of him. Andrew had done nothing, ever, in his whole life, to deserve this. Why the hell shouldn't he beg? Because he was a grown man and men didn't do that? Are men supposed to be brave at all costs and in all situations, even when they've been shot four times and the crazy man with the gun is still coming at them?

He admitted to begging for his life, as if it was a cowardly thing to do.

But then perhaps that was the listener's interpretation. Andrew had certainly seemed more emotional describing that moment than he had with any other part of his account.

But in reality, until then, Andrew Taylor had had a chance. Adrenaline had been pumping furiously through his system to focus his fear on one single thing: to channel all his remaining strength and conscious thought into getting away from the danger. Now, suddenly, he could *not* get away; and most of that precious hormone that keeps the body fighting to survive, against all odds, was probably leaking along with his blood out onto the floor.

The emotion in his voice, when he later explained how he'd rolled over and asked for mercy, was more likely the recognition, after the fact, of the absolute terror of that moment. He knew he'd been scared the whole time, but the fear in that moment was different. That was when his mind was forced to acknowledge the likelihood of untimely, unprepared for, guaranteed mortality.

A huge terrifying mass of fear was suddenly distilled into one pure and perfect bead of time when there was no place to hide from the end; no place to run from sure and certain death at the hand of the Man standing over him with a gun.

If Andrew Taylor saw his life pass before his eyes, he didn't say. If he gave any thought to where he actually was, slipping in his own blood on the corridor floor, the carpeted floor with the red lines that marked the way to the different consulting rooms where he and his colleagues practised ... he didn't say.

So many shots had been fired but, because Andrew felt no pain at all, he didn't realise that the fourth bullet to hit him, the one in the back, had passed through both lungs and exited through his right arm. He wasn't, in fact, even aware that he'd been shot in the back.

He just kept thinking that if he could talk the Man out of firing again, or if he didn't get hit in the head or the heart, he might still have a chance. As a doctor he knew the score: he was still conscious and he could move his legs; yes he was losing blood – a lot of blood – and he was having trouble breathing, but he thought he was okay – until that moment.

So he begged.

Did the Man hear? Did he intend for his last shot to be final – or just the final insult? Was it the worst thing he could think of to do to another man?

He started out, this Man, wanting to show someone how he felt. So what the hell was he doing? How did he feel? What exactly was he on about?

Born and raised in Yugoslavia, of Albanian ancestry, 22-year-old Zuber Vukovic migrated to Australia in 1974. He worked a variety of manual labouring jobs before going back to Yugoslavia in 1979 to get married, returning to Australia 18 months later.

Since his return Zuber Vukovic had, allegedly, worked a grand total of seven days. From 1982 this unemployed (or unemployable) married father of one lived on sickness benefits, then an invalid pension following a workplace accident. He was awarded a $30,000 lump-sum payment, by way of settlement, for that workplace accident; transferred to unemployment benefits; and then made a Transport Accident Commission claim.

Mr Vukovic did have a serious car accident in 1989; he was badly injured and no doubt he did deserve the TAC money he received – but, in his mind, he didn't get enough. Vukovic apparently thought he would receive one million dollars for the injuries he had sustained. He'd been back on a disability pension since the accident, and his case had taken about seven years, during which time he had, allegedly, borrowed money on which to live – on the strength of the one million he expected to get.

When his claim finally went through, in August 1996, Vukovic received only $270,000. It's believed that, after he cleared his debts, he had only a little over $130,000 left. So the Man, who also suffered from anxiety and depression, was now very annoyed.

Or, as a judge later said, his 'already pronounced sense of hostility towards the legal system and the medical profession' was fuelled by his resentment that his claim hadn't been immediately accepted by the TAC, who'd placed him under the surveillance of private investigators, and that settlement had taken so long. The judge added that the delay, however, 'was no doubt contributed to by the fact that you [Vukovic] became paranoid and suspicious about your own lawyers, accusing them of acting against your interests, and changed lawyers many times during the course of the litigation'.

Just over quarter of a million dollars was not enough to live on for the rest of Vukovic's non-working working life, so after fuming over the matter for quite some time he, allegedly, went to see his (latest) solicitor to find out why he hadn't got the million.

Zuber Vukovic may, or may not, have been carrying the Norinco pistol and two magazines of bullets when he demanded to be told why he hadn't got what he wanted but, luckily, his solicitor had a good reason.

Vukovic was informed that the amount awarded in a TAC claim such as his came down to what the doctor's report said. Whatever the doctor said about the condition of the claimant was the thing that decided the amount to be paid.

Vukovic left his solicitor's office. He was really pissed off now but he waited, and he stewed.

Eight months after his TAC claim was settled, on the morning of 12 April 1997, Vukovic told his wife that he had 'just made' a doctor's appointment. He then drove, not to the medical centre, but to his doctor's home.

The front door of this private residence was opened by the doctor's seven-year-old niece who, in answer to Vukovic's question, said her 'father' was not there. The doctor was at home, he was in the shower, but he was spared by a lucky choice of words.

Vukovic then drove into Hastings and went first – for some strange reason – to the medical clinic across the road from the one he actually attended as a patient; the surgery opposite where his own doctor worked in partnership with Andrew Taylor. Vukovic was told by the receptionist there that 'the doctor' was not in at that moment.

Vukovic then crossed the road, entered the Hastings Medical Clinic and asked to see a doctor. As he had no appointment, the receptionist told him there'd be a short wait. He'd been standing by the counter for only a few moments when Andrew Taylor – not his doctor but the next best thing – entered the office, through the door opposite.

Zuber Vukovic raised his gun and shot Andrew Taylor twice in the right hip and once in the left leg below the knee – to show a doctor how he felt. In his car accident he'd been injured in the right hip and the left leg. He didn't actually say the words but the implied message to the entire medical profession was: 'Now you know that my pain is worth a million dollars.'

Why he kept shooting, and still only at the doctor, is a mystery. You'd have to ask the Man himself.

The bad guys in crime fiction always get caught or get what's coming to them, and the good guys always win or find justice – of some kind. That's why we read crime fiction – because there is a suitable end, a just finish, sometimes even a perfect resolution. What goes around, comes around, and there is the closure that we seldom get in real life. That's why it's called fiction.

So, why are you reading this? Do you really want to keep going? You won't like it at all if it doesn't end properly. But, I suppose if you've bought this book and come this far then you're a fan – that sounds wrong – you're a 'reader', of true crime, not crime fiction, so you are accustomed to things not working out. How are your nerves?

If this story were crime fiction – the purpose of which is to restore order, provide a solution, and make sense of, or at least attempt to explain, the dark side of life – then Andrew would have talked the gunman out of bullet number five. Andrew would have had his day in court; he'd have received justice; he, or someone on his behalf, would have secured the proper ending.

Instead, the following, in Dr Taylor's own words, is what actually happened.

It was a nice Saturday morning. I was wearing runners. I'd just come back from the States. I'd taken the kids to Disneyland. It was the second weekend back.

I knew this guy, he wasn't a patient of mine, but I knew him. And I'd just seen a patient, an old lady, and I was walking her out to the waiting room and he was at the front desk.

I said, 'Good morning Mr Vukovic, what can I do for you today? I'll see you soon,' or words to that effect.

And he said, 'I'm very depressed,' and then produced a gun.

Seriously, I thought this is really bad. For some reason I knew he wasn't going to hold it to his head. Just the way he brought it out; because he brought it out towards me, he didn't bring it out towards his own head.

Suddenly, you know, all you see is this gun … and, unbelievably, it went off.

It was that quick. I didn't have time to move anywhere. I just saw it and I think I froze. And it, ah, hit me in the leg and threw me across the room. Other people were screaming.

There was no pain. I only knew I'd been shot because I was on the ground, because I'd seen the gun, and because of the noise. I felt something in the leg, but you couldn't call it pain. There was a sensation; I knew something was wrong with my leg but it wasn't pain, not like a punch in the arm or anything like that.

Then I sat myself straight up and he fired into my leg there again, in the same spot.

There was a filing cabinet near me so I crawled behind it, and as I crawled behind it, he shot me in the other leg below the knee.

There were four or five patients in the waiting room and Kerrie on the front desk. I was the only person he was shooting at *but he was firing over Kerrie and she was screaming. She'd lost it, obviously, but he actually told Kerrie to stop screaming, to shut up, that he wouldn't shoot her.*

I said, 'Call the police, call the police' – which she was obviously doing.

And he just kept firing and firing – I don't know how many bullets, half a dozen I suppose. They were going through the filing cabinet and into the wall.

And I just thought I can't stay here, this is crazy. I sort of threw myself and crawled through the doorway into the hall. It probably wasn't wise to leap out from behind the filing cabinet, where at least he couldn't shoot me in the head, but I just felt I couldn't stay there and let this go on. There was just no way I could stay still and let him keep shooting at my legs like that. I thought I just had to get further away. So I actually exposed myself completely as I leapt across. He could have so easily, even accidentally, shot me in the head at that stage.

I was frightened. You know, you go from 'this is unbelievable, this isn't happening to me', 'to this is real' – like that. Yes, I was very, very scared.

But for some reason I still knew if he didn't shoot me in the head, that I'd be all right – because I'd already survived. Like, I could see both my legs were bleeding, and there was blood everywhere, and there was all the noise and the gun going off, but I'd made it out into the hall.

Then he – I thought he jumped the counter – but he actually came around through the waiting room. I was trying to crawl, sort of on my side, down the hallway. Next thing he's appeared behind me – and I should have just kept crawling.

There was still no pain. My adrenaline levels were red-line, my heart, everything was red-line. I'm sure the pain signals were being sent to my brain, but my brain was just saying, 'We don't have time to deal with that. We got to survive; disconnect those pain terminals for now. We've got more important things to focus on. We have to think clearly; talk; talk to this guy, move those arms.'

He said to me, 'No, you're not dying. I want you to feel the pain I feel,' and then he fired again.

At that stage I just rolled over on to my back and that's when ... I started, that's when I ... I was pleading, 'Please stop, please don't kill me.'

He put the gun up my arse and fired it again.

Then he lay down next to me, put his arm sort of around me, said something about God, and shot himself … through the heart.

I thought he was dead.

Then it was like, right, I knew I'd been badly hurt but I had no idea how bad it actually was.

I was thinking, 'I'm conscious now. Yes, I'm bleeding but that's manageable.' I thought, 'I wonder if I can move my leg, the hip that I've been shot in.' I was able to actually move that, and I moved the other one. But I couldn't breathe very well. I didn't know why. I didn't know, then, that I'd been shot in the back.

I crawled to the oxygen and tried to turn the oxygen on, so I could breathe. That's when Kerrie came to help me. I couldn't turn it, because my hands were slippery with blood. Blood's very slippery. So I was fumbling but Kerrie turned it on, and suddenly I could breathe. Then it was a matter of waiting.

The cops arrived, other doctors from our surgery arrived, the ambulance took ages …

Constables Ian Douglas and Dave Jenkins were the first police officers on the scene. A call had been made to the Hastings Police Station (from the clinic's receptionist) that shots had been fired at the nearby doctor's surgery.

The two officers drove the short distance to the clinic, put on their vests, and made a call to D24 to find out if there was updated information on the whereabouts of the person with the gun. They then approached the front door, with their guns holstered but ready. They could see the receptionist was distraught, but was still on the phone.

'My partner jumped the counter and I went through the waiting room. The people there were frozen in fear,' Constable Douglas said.

'I stepped into the hall where I could see a handgun on the floor and two people lying next to each other. At first, of course, we had no idea who'd done the shooting, but we quickly established that Dr Taylor was the victim and that he was badly wounded. The other guy, the offender, had a hole in his chest.

'I used my vest to cover the weapon, to secure that part of the crime scene. I checked on the condition of the offender, who was still alive, but I took one look at his chest, his eyes, which were rolling all over and, particularly, the exit wound in his back and said, "You're stuffed mate."

'The CIB arrived shortly after us and took charge of the scene, and then the ambos arrived.'

Dr Andrew Taylor was shot for no good reason by someone who was after only him, but did not know him personally. Then, to add insult to injury, when the ambulance finally arrived Andrew was relegated to second in their emergency procedures because the *other* man's single wound was seemingly more serious. Yes, you read that right: the gunman's self-inflicted chest wound gave him priority.

Let's go back to Andrew's account …

The ambulance took ages but the police came right away, and they were great. And Kerrie and our other doctor who'd turned up were being great.

I was saying, 'I think I'm dying,' but in a small part of my brain I knew I'd be all right – if they could get me to a trauma unit in time.

But it was over, the police were there, the immediate danger was gone. I think I just wanted a bit of sympathy and I wanted someone to sit with me. I was saying things like, 'I'm not sure if I'm dying or not, but I've been really badly hurt. I really need to get to hospital quickly.'

Obviously my knowledge as a doctor was still helping my chances of survival. I knew I was conscious, that I hadn't been shot through the heart, and that I was able to talk, so I stood a real chance. Also the fact that I was able to move my legs told me I didn't have spinal damage either.

The only discomfort I was feeling was a quite severe pain in my back. I couldn't get comfortable. I knew that there were bullets all over the floor, so I said, 'I think I'm lying on something. Is there a bullet under me?'

No-one wanted to move me, but I said, 'It's okay. I've actually done a bit of moving just to get here. Don't worry about it.'

I wasn't lying on anything. It was actually the entrance wound from the bullet that had gone in my back and come out my shoulder. I didn't realise that I'd been shot there.

Then there were issues with the ambulance teams and with the helicopter. They, the ambos, were going to take him first because he was the most wounded. One bullet, yeah, but he'd shot himself in the heart. The helicopter could really only take one person and the ambos, after they finally arrived, had already loaded this guy on 'because he was sick'.

Peter, our other doctor, kept saying things like, 'That guy shot this guy; this guy is dying too, of multiple gunshot wounds. That guy might be severely injured but let's not forget what happened here.' But the ambulance guys were saying, 'No, the priority goes to whoever is the most injured.'

I have never forgiven them for that.

I was pretty badly injured; as it turned out I was much more seriously injured than him. But as they said, when they arrived I was conscious. Right; there was a damn good reason for that. Two doctors and a nurse had put a big drip in me, and had run every bottle of fluid we had in the surgery, and the oxygen. So I was being kept alive by intravenous fluid but I was very fast running out of blood – and it was truly time critical.

The ambulance people didn't seem to appreciate that. Fortunately the helicopter guy saw the whole picture. He couldn't believe they wanted him to take the guy who'd done the shooting first, and then come back for the doctor with the multiple gunshot wounds. The pilot said he'd make room for a second person.

That took extra time to configure the helicopter to fit me in as well, and then suddenly we were away. And that's really the last of my clear memories, except for recalling the helicopter landing at the Alfred Hospital and the absolute relief that I was at the trauma centre.

Andrew woke up in the Alfred Hospital four days later.

Of the five bullets to hit him, four had passed right through his body. Two went through the right hip, and one through the left leg. The fourth bullet entered through the left side of his back, passed through both lungs, and exited his right shoulder. On its way out, that bullet travelled though the arch of his aorta; it just missed Andrew's heart, by passing through a gap only marginally bigger than the bullet.

The fifth bullet, the one that Zuber Vukovic fired into Andrew by pushing the end of the barrel into his rectum, grazed the gonadal vessel (but did not penetrate it), surfed around the inside of his pelvis and bounced off into the bowel. Then it took a right turn, towards the pelvis again, and was found lying on the renal artery. If it had taken out that artery, that would have been it.

Dr Andrew Taylor, in one sense, is probably the luckiest man to ever be in the wrong place at the wrong time. So this is good, right? This true crime story has a good ending.

When Andrew woke up in the Alfred Hospital the Wednesday after he'd been shot he knew two things: he was going to be okay, and he'd slept through the worst of it. Once he regained consciousness, however, he couldn't sleep. He recalls watching the second hand of the clock on the wall tick by every second for 24 hours. While still in intensive care he'd close his eyes, then wake violently, as if someone had hit him across the face with a cricket bat. He'd come to with such a jolt that it would hurt, then he'd realise that he'd only been asleep for 15 seconds.

The sleeplessness, he acknowledges, was partly his body fighting the pain, as it worked overtime in survival mode, and partly the whole thing of 'don't go to sleep, you might not wake up'. But his hyper-alert state did give him an 'advantage', because by being awake all the time he could survey his surroundings and make sure he was safe from further harm.

You might think an overwhelming fear of being attacked again is an understandable reaction to being shot five times but there was an even better reason for Andrew's heightened, and unrelenting, alertness. He *needed* to be on guard from the moment he discovered that the gunman, Zuber Vukovic, had not only survived but was in the same hospital.

Andrew now calls it an 'overwhelming paranoia' but given the circumstances it's easy to see why he'd think that Vukovic would want to finish what he started. Andrew asked for a security guard. He told them he was absolutely terrified that Vukovic was going to come and get him.

Andrew was told that the offender was under police guard, that he'd injured himself. Andrew pointed out how vulnerable *he* was; that he couldn't move, he was tied to all the equipment. They told him he'd be safe.

Andrew remembers how wonderful he felt waking up following his first proper sleep. It was three weeks after the shooting, he'd been transferred to another hospital, been given enough 'something' to knock out a water buffalo, and had slept for four consecutive hours.

When I first spoke to Andrew, three years after the shooting, he was still fearful that the Man was going to come after him. And he lives with an awful notion in his mind, one he never thought he'd be capable of – but he can't help it. When he thinks back to when he was lying bleeding in the corridor of his clinic, after the Man had shot himself …

> *I honestly believe if I'd known he was alive – and with what I know now – I believe I could have picked up the gun. I saw him change magazines and although he'd been firing all over the place I knew there was a shitload of bullets left …*
>
> *But I thought he was dead. He looked terrible. He looked dead. I'd seen him shoot himself in the heart, and I actually remember thinking, 'Yeah, that's the right place.' A lot of people, you know, would go for the left side of the chest and would miss because the heart's more in the middle. But unfortunately what he did was he tilted the gun and it actually grazed his heart. But he immediately went unconscious; he went the colour of the fridge. And I thought, yep he's dead.*
>
> *But, if he'd breathed or moaned … I could, yes, I could easily have lived with myself knowing that I'd grabbed that gun. And I wouldn't have missed.*
>
> *That has been the worst thing about this, that this guy is still alive.*

Dr Andrew Taylor was then done over again, by the legal system – eventually.

Technically, the Man – who did not have a gun licence – could have got two years just for possessing an illegal handgun. If the police had picked him up for some reason and had found the gun on him *before* he got to the clinic, Mr Vukovic would have been in deep trouble for that offence alone. (Not to mention for the two 12-gauge shotguns, the imitation automatic pistol and the set of throwing knives that the police found during a search of his home after the shooting.)

Instead, on Saturday 12 April 1997 … wait, let's put this in a wider context.

On Saturday 12 April 1997 – just under one year after the Port Arthur shootings and all the brouhaha over changes to our gun laws – Zuber Vukovic armed himself with an illegal weapon and two magazines of bullets and went around town looking for a doctor to shoot.

He walked into the Hastings Medical Cinic and chose one person to vent his financial disappointments on. During the course of this 'incident' Mr Vukovic emptied one clip and reloaded to continue firing. This Man, carrying and using an unregistered semiautomatic firearm, placed several people in mortal danger and hit his prime, but randomly chosen, target five times.

Then he shot himself in the heart, and missed.

Two days later on 14 April 1997 Zuber Vukovic was processed and charged with attempted murder and remanded in custody (in hospital).

Ian Douglas (now Senior Detective), one of the first officers on the scene, later said, 'We really thought the offender was as good as dead. Didn't think he had a hope of surviving. But a few months later there he was in the box at the committal hearing. I couldn't believe that he was standing there as healthy as anything.'

At that committal hearing Zuber Vukovic was remanded to stand trial. The Man allegedly refused to plead guilty to a charge of attempted murder, so he then spent a year on remand, while the situation was deliberated on or sorted out by his defence, or the Director of Public Prosecutions, or the court, or a group of astrologers. Sorry. Obviously a trial date had to be set, because the accused would not plead guilty and accept a sentence.

Then, at the end of that first year, Andrew Taylor was informed that if 'Mr Vukovic' was charged with 'intentionally causing serious injury' instead, the matter could be dealt with more quickly. The difference in the sentences was something like 12 to 15 years for attempted murder, and a maximum of 12 years for the serious injury charge.

As a victim of crime Andrew Taylor could get no compensation *at all* until Zuber Vukovic was convicted of something. Twelve months had already passed. Andrew was still on the mend and he'd been unable to work for the first three months. He was a partner in a business that cost money to run, and which, if he couldn't work full time, wasn't making him anything either. And he had his own medical costs – the ones incurred through having been shot five times – which included things like ambulance bills, helicopter bills, hospital and rehab bills.

Andrew said, 'Fine, intentional serious injury is good enough.' He thought his case would have to be regarded at the severe end of the sentencing scale, and, as there was little difference in the penalty between that and the minimum for attempted murder, Andrew figured it would do.

Then somebody, somewhere along the line, would not agree to, give, or accept a guilty plea on the charge of intentionally causing serious injury. So, strangely, another 12 months passed in which nothing happened, at least as far as Andrew was concerned. What Vukovic's legal team and/or the DPP were doing was anybody's guess. The Man spent all that time in the Melbourne Remand Centre, still unconvicted.

Two years after the shooting Andrew Taylor finally got his day in Court – until he got there.

On the day, having travelled up to Melbourne for what he thought was going to be a trial, before a jury, Andrew was informed that Mr Vukovic was suddenly going to plead guilty to 'intentionally causing serious injury'.

With a guilty plea there was no need for a trial. So there was no real court case; no actual evidence was given. The full story of what really happened on that Saturday morning two years before did not get told to the judge, let alone a jury.

Andrew wanted to say, 'You bastards. Why didn't you do this a year ago? Why did you make me waste another day of my life – because of this Man? Why did you make us all wonder if we'd have to stand up in court and give evidence? What crappy bastards you all are.' He didn't say that, but he *really* wanted to.

If what happened to me was not attempted murder, then what the hell is? Okay, so in his car accident the guy suffered a fractured right hip and a broken left leg. He now has a metal hip, walks with a limp, didn't get enough compo and that's why he wanted to show a doctor how he felt.

That was the first three bullets; that's why he shot me in the legs. And if he'd stopped there, you could say, 'Well, yeah, it was just intentional injury.' But he didn't stop there, so how can it be anything else but attempted murder? At the very least he deserves the maximum for intentional injury.

Bad as he was though, I think the courts were worse. He is a very bad man, but he's screwed in the head. The courts' behaviour, however … I mean these are rational, intelligent people with time and a system of justice that's been going forever but which, in reality, seems designed only to suit them, the lawyers – and no-one else.

In court that day the defence people wanted me to sit down with them and talk. I said, 'I don't know what you've been told, but this is the situation: this guy had a gun, tried two other doctors, couldn't find them so he came and shot me. He had two magazines with bullets. This was clearly not a guy who was going out to commit suicide in a public place. This is a very bad man.'

None of the truth came out in court. None of how I got shot came out. I'd made a statement in hospital, you know when I had drips and morphine coming and going in me. It was like a one-page statement, to the effect: 'He came in, I said hello, he shot me in the legs, I tried to get away, he shot me a couple more times, then he shot himself.'

All they talked about in court was that statement. They never asked if there was anything else I wanted to say, only if I wanted to add to that statement. I was never asked to go over what actually happened.

In the brief time in court the defence people made me feel that it was my fault I got shot, that I deserved to be shot. They're very sneaky.

At one stage I made a comment like, 'The best thing that could happen to this guy would be that he disappear; that he'd go to jail and disappear', to which one of his lawyers said something like, 'You still seem very bitter.'

I replied, 'This man shot me up the arse, excuse me if I take it personally.'

On May 28 1999, in the Supreme Court of Victoria, Justice Eames said: 'Zuber Vukovic, you have pleaded guilty to a charge of intentionally causing serious injury to Andrew Clifford Taylor, a medical practitioner who was shot five times by you at his medical clinic … on 12 April 1997. You have been in custody since that day and it is now my task to pass sentence on you for that offence.'

He went on to say, 'The explanation for this appalling crime is to be found not only in the deficiencies of your own personality, character and intellect, but also – as the facts themselves would inevitably suggest – in the fact that you were suffering mental illness at the time the offence was committed … '

[However] 'I reject the suggestion that you went to the clinic for the sole purpose of shooting yourself … You intended to shoot any medical practitioner who had the misfortune to be present at the clinic upon your arrival. In my opinion, the evidence is quite overwhelming that by arming yourself as you did, and by taking as much ammunition as you did, you intended to shoot a medical practitioner that day.

'What these facts demonstrate is that at the time of this offence you were a very dangerous man.'

Zuber Vukovic was sentenced to six years with a minimum of four, minus, of course, the two and a bit years (or 777 days) he'd already served in remand. In his summing-up the judge implied that in his opinion a longer jail term would not help the prisoner to reform, while adding – quite illogically it seemed to Andrew – that he anticipated that the Man, if placed under undue stress, would probably re-offend.

What the hell happened to the possible 12 years for 'intentionally causing serious injury'? And what on earth does that say about our court and prison systems? It seems that prison won't reform this bad guy, but that's okay because the court will put him back inside when – not if – *when* he does it again.

But a conviction was finally made. Andrew Taylor, as a Victim of Crime was then 'awarded' $50,000. Andrew said the 'Victims of Crime guy' was the only decent legal person he met during the whole course of his so-called case.

'It was the only time I was treated with any respect,' Andrew said. 'The guy acknowledged my "suffering", told me that $50,000 was the maximum I could get, and that I would get it; no question about it. And then he apologised that it had taken two years to come through.'

What is wrong with the end of this story? This was a well-respected doctor who'd been shot, and nearly killed, by a man who was simply pissed off because he hadn't got enough compensation for his car accident. As far as the Man was concerned, $270,000 – or more than five times the amount that Andrew received as a victim of his later crime – was not enough for the leg injuries he'd received in an accident. Zuber Vukovic had not been crippled by those injuries – he had walked around the clinic that day shooting at Andrew Taylor.

To add insult to the injury, a patient waiting – quite safely as it turned out – in one of the consulting rooms while all the shooting was going on also claimed compensation.

Some of the people in the waiting room, through which the armed and angry man had walked, claimed victim status and were awarded a few thousand each. Andrew's receptionist, over whose head the gunman had fired, did not claim compensation.

But this patient, who escaped through the back door and (allegedly) didn't see a single flying bullet and probably no blood, claimed victim compensation for stress over the incident. And how much did he receive, this opportunist who had not been shot at, let alone hit by five bullets, and who had lost nothing? You guessed it: $50,000. He claimed he had helped save Andrew's life but no official bothered to check with Andrew or the people who did stay, whether this was so. It wasn't.

But, I hear you say, with a conviction Andrew could take out civil action and sue the Man – the offender, the perpetrator – for damages. Of course he could! But Zuber Vukovic had been right about one thing: the TAC compensation wasn't nearly enough to live on – not when you've got lawyers to pay. The $130,000 (or whatever was left after his other debts were paid) had disappeared down the gurgler in legal fees, eaten up by the 777 days he'd already spent in remand for shooting someone because a bit over a quarter of a million hadn't been enough. There was nothing left.

And that is just one more thing that Andrew doesn't understand. Why did he have to pursue a civil action at all, when the judge in his case could have awarded him damages? It hardly seems fair that Vukovic's legal team – the criminal's representatives – were paid but Andrew, the victim, got nothing at all from the court.

Oh, there's one last truly curious thing about this whole bizarre so-called court case. At no time during any of the proceedings did anyone from the Office of Public Prosecutions ever contact, question or consult Andrew Taylor. The office responsible for prosecuting Zuber Vukovic for shooting someone never spoke to the person he shot.

Good grief! If this were crime fiction I'd fix this absurd situation by looking up the word justice in the dictionary and applying the concept of it to this mess. I could try my hand at fictional law reform, but then I'd have to market my novel as fantasy crime.

On the other hand, although I wouldn't be able to rectify the situation with better laws, in fiction I could work creatively with the existing ones by applying a simple one-two-three accounting system based on fair play.

If the sentence for possessing an illegal handgun is two years (Victorian Firearms Act 1996) then that penalty would be my baseline. And if that particular charge is applicable to an unlicensed someone caught with an unregistered handgun in their own home, then all the other real laws about carrying the aforementioned weapon around town in a huff would automatically increase the sentence. After all, there must be some kind of intent in that act alone. And, speaking of acts, let's just take a look at some of the other weapons charges we could apply – one on top of the other.

According to the Victorian Firearms Act 1996:

- It is an offence (licensed gun owner or not) to possess, carry or use a firearm on private property – without consent. Penalty: one year.
- It is an offence to carry or use a firearm in certain places. For example, a person must not carry a loaded firearm or use a firearm in a town or populous place or on any thoroughfare or place open to or used by the public for passage with vehicles. Penalty: one year.
- It is an offence to damage property with a firearm. Penalty: two years.
- A person who is carrying or using a handgun must ensure that the firearm is carried and used in a manner that is secure and is not dangerous. Penalty: two years.
- A person who is carrying or using ammunition must ensure that the ammunition is carried and used in a manner that is secure and is not dangerous. Penalty: one year.

What have we racked up here so far? A gunman like the Man in Andrew Taylor's case would already be looking at an automatic nine years in jail.

In my fictional world the offender's 'intent' with that weapon would then be considered by a judge who would make a statement, not about gun control, but about gun use. The Man, in my book, would get two months for each bullet fired, and six months for every bullet that hits a human being. Our Man is now looking at about 14 years.

Then legal, and moral, issues such as 'intentionally causing serious injury' versus attempted murder, (and others unrelated to this example, such as manslaughter versus murder) would be addressed – separately.

I would also devise a similar fictional accounting system to the compensation awarded to the victims in the case. If a man who was not personally threatened, and who escaped completely unhurt from any kind of danger, gets $50,000 compo, then that is the bottom line. The people in the waiting room would then get twice that; and the receptionist, in the actual line of fire, would get another $50,000. The actual victim, Andrew Taylor, would then start from an automatic baseline entitlement of $150,000 plus, let's see, $10,000 for every bullet that hit him, compensation for medical costs, etc ...

You do the sums. Isn't fiction wonderful!

When Andrew first told me his story – only a year after the conviction, but three since the shooting – he was already waiting and dreading the day when the Man was released. Six years, with a minimum of four, meant that if he'd been 'good enough' in jail – or, as the judge advised, if he undertook psych treatment and maintained proper levels of medication – then that day was fast approaching.

Andrew was still worried the gunman would come looking for him. The terror engendered by the Man on that day in 1997 was as vivid as ever. Andrew's sense of not being safe was partly the residual fear of the actual attack, that lives loudly and colourfully in his memory, and partly the fact that the Man might indeed seek him out. It wasn't likely but it was possible. Andrew wondered, for instance, whether the Man would blame him all over again – but this time specifically.

Given the logic of the first attack, however, if the Man did again seek someone else to blame for his own circumstances then it was more likely that he'd visit his legal team. Sure, they managed to get him only four (to six) years but in the meantime they took *all* the rest of his money. And that was the trigger in the first place. It was money, or rather not enough money, that set this whole disaster in motion.

There are probably a few other things you should know about Dr Andrew Taylor. He obviously, though some would say luckily or even miraculously, recovered from his wounds. The *Herald Sun* paid him $300 for an interview; he gave that money to the Mt Eliza Hospital. The philanthropist Richard Pratt, on hearing about the case, gave him $10,000. That money was given to the Frankston Hospital – as a donation; it was not used to pay any bills.

Andrew has since found love and happiness with an old friend who rang him late one night to find out if he'd survived the shooting that she'd heard about, and they now have a son. And Andrew is still a good doctor *and* he has a fine sense of humour. He can even joke about some aspects of his ordeal that day.

> *Now, the ambulance took ages. The police came right away as did one of the other doctors. In fact everyone got there before the ambulance. You know, Boy Scouts came, the Jehovah's Witnesses were there; and then Amway arrived and said, 'I see you've got some time on your hands, and you're obviously going to need some soap powder …'*

Andrew Taylor remembers every single thing about that day: he remembers the noise, the blood, the gun, the fear, the bullets, the screaming, the Man, the fact that there was no pain – everything; including the odd little fact that he was wearing runners. He is also, understandably, angry about the ending of his true crime story; because this is how it ends …

It doesn't.

Postscript

Zuber Vukovic was released from prison in February 2003 after serving nearly six years.

The Truth, the Whole Truth, and Nothing But the Truth

Shelley Robertson

'I swear by almighty God ... that the evidence I shall give ... to the court in this case ... shall be the truth ... the whole truth ... and nothing but the truth.' This, as everyone knows, is the oath that witnesses giving evidence in our courts swear, with the Bible upheld in their right hand.

It sounds reasonable, doesn't it? Of course we expect a witness to tell the truth. After all, there are penalties, and charges such as perjury, that can be laid against witnesses who tell lies. And how can we expect a jury to reach a proper decision if they are given a pack of lies?

So a witness is obliged to tell the truth. But does the jury really hear the whole truth and nothing but the truth?

The answer is 'No'.

Members of a jury hear only what the court and the rules of evidence allow them to hear. This means that pieces of evidence, often quite important pieces, are withheld from them. That evidence thereby plays no role in enabling the jury to reach a verdict.

This fact has always made me more than a little uncomfortable, as I regularly give evidence in court, usually pertaining to cases of murder. I take the oath when I step into the witness box, knowing that I speak for the victims after having performed an autopsy on their remains. I establish their cause of death, document their injuries and interpret the patterns of injury, results of toxicological analysis and other relevant material.

I would like to think that the jury can have all the available information, that is, 'the whole truth'. But this doesn't always happen. I'll give some examples.

Voir Dire

This is a French term, translated literally as 'to see, to speak'. In legal terminology, it means a 'case within a case'.

The *voir dire* usually takes place in the early stages of a trial, and the jury is not present. Witnesses give their evidence before the judge and counsel (both prosecution and defence), who may then argue and finally reach agreement with the judge as to which part of the evidence given by each witness can be heard by the jury, and which bits must be left out.

This is an example of evidence deliberately withheld from the jury. It poses an ethical dilemma for the witness who has just sworn an oath to '… tell the whole truth … ' but is now told to omit some of their testimony, some of the evidence.

I experienced this in a case where a slightly built female was accused of murdering a male who was physically much larger than herself. I had performed the autopsy investigation on the male and was required to give evidence of my findings at the trial. As part of the autopsy, I had collected specimens from the deceased and sent these to the laboratory for analysis, looking for traces of alcohol, drugs or poisons.

The results were quite interesting, as a number of drugs were identified in the male's blood. Most of these, I ascertained, had been prescribed for the deceased so one would expect to find them in his blood. But there was one exception: a 'sleeping pill', one that would cause considerable drowsiness. This particular medication was no longer freely available as it had been withdrawn from the market. When it was available, it was only obtained by prescription, and there was no record of it ever having been prescribed for the deceased.

It all seemed pretty straightforward to me. The murderer had given him the sleeping drug, rendering him incapable of offering much resistance, and then killed him.

So, did I present this information to the jury? No. At *voir dire*, it was decided that too much uncertainty surrounded the issue of the sleeping drug. There was no direct evidence to prove that the accused had given him the drug. So, rather than let the jury hear about the drug and draw its own conclusions as to its relevance, the evidence was left out.

This was hard enough for me to deal with, the deliberate exclusion of part of my evidence, but it got worse. When the trial proceeded before the jury, the defence barrister pointed to the accused seated in the dock, and asked, 'Do you really believe that my client, this small frail female, could have overpowered a large able-bodied male to bring about his death?'

I almost choked in the witness stand. I wanted to shout, 'But he wasn't able-bodied! He'd been drugged,' but of course I couldn't do that. *I* would be held in contempt of court and a retrial would have ensued. So much for the jury hearing 'the whole truth'.

Too Prejudicial

There are things that the jury doesn't get to see or hear, on the grounds that they are 'too prejudicial' towards the accused. A common example – strange as it may seem – is crime scene photographs.

Take the average murder scene (if there is such a thing), which is never a pretty sight. The centrepiece is a dead body, often with horrific injuries and lying in a pool of blood. There may be signs of a struggle, with smashed furniture and household goods strewn everywhere. Blood may be spattered around the room, on furniture, walls, ceilings and light fittings. A weapon stained with blood and human tissue may be lying near the body.

Police crime-scene examiners carefully document and photograph the scene, usually before the body is moved or the scene disturbed in any way. This forms an accurate record of the crime, and the photos are used in the investigation of the murder. The theory is that they should also be shown to the jury, as an accurate representation of what took place.

The practice, however, differs from the theory. Defence counsel is able to eliminate some or all of these photographs from the evidence presented to the jury, on the basis that the pictures are so awful that the jurors will lose objectivity and, therefore, the ability to consider the evidence impartially.

Similarly, during the autopsy investigation all the injuries, and any other features that the pathologist thinks are relevant, are meticulously photographed. Although the forensic pathologist also describes each injury and may include charts and diagrams in the written report, the old saying, 'a picture is worth a thousand words' is particularly applicable to our work.

I have often stood in the witness box valiantly tying to explain the exact site, dimensions and nature of an injury. My autopsy report is written using medical terminology and I must 'translate' this into ordinary language so the jury can understand it.

All the while I'm doing this, I am thinking, 'Now let's just have a look at photograph number 46, which shows the injury clearly.' But my prompt remains unspoken, because the jury won't ever get to see photograph number 46 as the injuries are too horrific and there is so much blood around.

The absurdity of this was highlighted in a very high-profile murder trial in Victoria. A huge effort had been undertaken by police, forensic scientists and prosecutors to bring the perpetrators to trial. Everyone involved was anxious not to do anything that could possibly compromise that trial. As part of that I had several pre-trial conferences with the prosecuting barrister, and at the last one he sprung his surprise.

'You want me to take what to court?' was my incredulous response.

The prosecutor was adamant. As the police photographs of the bullet injuries to the victim were just too awful, they would not be shown to the jury. Instead, the man responsible for prosecuting the perpetrators wanted me to use what was, effectively, a stand-in.

I was to bring to court an articulated skeleton (used for teaching purposes) that I would take into the witness box and use to demonstrate the injuries and the path of the bullets.

The skeleton sat next to me in the back of an unmarked police car as we were driven to court. There was slight difficulty getting him out of the car and into the courtroom without the popular press having the opportunity to photograph us all. It was a bit crowded in the witness box, where I used coloured knitting needles to point out the path of the bullets through the skeleton, but in the end it all went very smoothly.

Courtrooms are sometimes described as theatres, but I felt that we were taking the theatrical a bit too far, especially when perfectly adequate photographs showed the bullet path. Well yes, counsel, the photographs *were* prejudicial, but what happened to the victim was also prejudicial.

I believe that the jury has the right to see the crime in all of its awfulness, not just a sanitised version. In this case, however, the jury seemed to get the picture and the perpetrators were convicted.

Ultimate Issue

The role of an expert witness is to assist the court in matters that are beyond what is expected to be the day-to-day experience of ordinary persons (i.e. members of the jury). Expert witnesses may have expertise in areas such as science, engineering, document examination, DNA technology, fingerprints or, as in my case, forensic medicine and pathology.

An expert witness can give evidence that would not be admissible if given by a material witness (for example, someone who saw a crime being committed). Experts can give hearsay evidence and they can give opinions.

Expert witnesses are also subject to all the tactics in the defence barrister's armory. These tactics are designed to discredit the witness before the jury, the idea being that if the witness is such an unreliable, confused and possibly biased person, none of the evidence that they give should be taken seriously. This often results in quite an ordeal for the expert who, after all, does not have a vested interest in the outcome of the case. Our evidence is impartial, based on scientific principles, and given to assist the court – except, with reference to the latter, when it comes to 'ultimate issue'.

The ultimate issue rule of evidence prevents expert witnesses giving 'opinions' to the court, when that opinion forms the crux of the decision to be made by the jury; in other words, when the defendant's guilt or innocence depends on that particular piece of opinion evidence.

One very frustrating, both personally and professionally, example of the operation of this rule occurred in a case of alleged child abuse, resulting in the death of a little girl. There were really only two explanations as to how the toddler could possibly have sustained the injuries that caused her death.

One scenario, put forward by the accused, was that the injuries occurred while the child was playing alone; that is, they were the result of an accident. The other, more realistic scenario was that the accused had deliberately inflicted the injuries.

I had performed the autopsy on the child and documented all her injuries. My opinion was based on many years of experience in forensic pathology, referral to medical literature and discussion with colleagues. Stated simply, these injuries could not have been accidentally inflicted in the way the accused described. Another clinical expert in paediatric injuries independently came to the same conclusion.

We were both called upon to give expert evidence regarding the little girl's pattern of injuries, but neither of us was allowed to convey our opinions to the jury because of the ultimate issue rule. The explanation for this was that if the members of the jury accepted our opinions, they *had* to find the defendant 'guilty', so our evidence was the ultimate issue.

The end result in this case was a 'not guilty' verdict, and a man went unpunished for the murder of a tiny child.

Previous Convictions and Similar Fact Evidence

The jury must not hear evidence relating to the accused's previous convictions, even if they are for offences similar to the one for which he or she is currently standing trial. The only exception to this rule is that of 'similar fact evidence', but this often proves difficult for the prosecution to be allowed to present to the court.

To use it, the previous crime must very closely imitate the current one. The similarities need to be more than just, for example, the use of a similar weapon. The similarities must relate to the details of the way in which the crime was carried out. If the judge allows similar fact evidence to be heard, it is only then that a jury may learn of the accused's previous crimes. Otherwise, they are not to know of any previous convictions until after a verdict has been reached.

The judge may take previous convictions into account when deciding on the appropriate sentence for the accused, when they're convicted. (If they're convicted.) At the end of a trial, after reaching a 'guilty' verdict, stunned jury members have listened in horror to the accused's list of prior convictions being read out by the judge. They have often just spent many agonising hours trying to decide if this particular individual is actually capable of carrying out the terrible deed of which he or she is accused, so you can imagine how they would feel on learning that the person has already done something like it several times before.

This insistence that the jury not know of an accused's criminal past is a matter taken very seriously by the court system. Trials have had to be aborted, for instance, due to zealous media reporting of a specific case. The judge has to presume that the jury, having seen or heard prejudicial material regarding the accused, will or even might allow this to cloud their judgment.

I was giving evidence in a trial where the accused appeared as a very neatly dressed young man. He was escorted into the courtroom by police officers, as usually happens, and took his seat in the dock. The jury did not know that only minutes earlier the accused was in handcuffs, having been delivered to the courthouse in an armoured van with heavily armed guards. You see, this accused was not the mild-mannered conservative young man that he appeared to be. He was, in fact, a dangerous career criminal already serving a prison sentence for armed robbery. But the jury could not know about this.

The judge almost ordered a retrial when video footage of the accused's arrival in court was shown on television news reports. The judge was concerned that if members of the jury knew that the accused was a convicted and dangerous criminal, they would automatically find him guilty of the current charge, without considering the evidence.

But is this really a fair assessment of the jury's capacity? If our legal system encompasses 'trial by jury', then surely the '12 ordinary men and women' should be able to hear some adverse information about the accused, just as they are able to hear favourable reports about them. It doesn't seem fair that good character references for the accused are admissible, but prior bad actions are not.

Right to Remain Silent

Lots of people give evidence at a murder trial. There may be eyewitnesses who actually saw the crime, persons who saw events leading up to or following the crime, or persons giving alibis for the accused. There are police officers involved in investigating the crime and arresting the accused; and there are crime scene analysts, forensic scientists, forensic pathologists and other experts. The list is long.

And when the trial comes, we all take our place in the witness box, raise the Bible in our right hands and take the oath to tell the truth. We are subject to rigorous cross-examination by opposing counsel.

But did you notice that someone was missing from the above list? Yes, the accused. Unless he or she volunteers to give evidence, the accused has the right to remain silent, and the jury cannot draw any adverse inferences from that silence.

This rule, along with the privilege against self-incrimination, was designed to afford the accused some protection against police harassment or the production of forced confessions. The onus is placed on the prosecution to prove the guilt of the accused, independent of his or her evidence. However, the rule gives an unfair advantage to the accused.

Many times during the course of cross-examination, usually when I am being attacked and berated by defence counsel, I have glanced across the courtroom at the defendant sitting mutely in the dock. And, while battling to maintain my professional integrity as a witness, I have wondered, 'Why doesn't he have to go through this? Why is he so special that he doesn't have to answer any questions put to him?' But that is how our legal system works.

A particular case that I was involved in highlights the absurdity of this rule. The case was that of a very nasty murder, followed by dismemberment of the body. The resulting parts were then wrapped in plastic to form packages that were buried separately at various sites.

Once the packages had all been located, the grisly business of opening them and trying to determine what had taken place began. The cause of death was not a problem. Even though the remains were quite badly decomposed, it was impossible to miss the crossbow bolt that still protruded from the chest region.

One issue, however, was trying to determine what type of implement had been used to carry out the dismemberment. After giving evidence regarding my autopsy findings I was cross-examined by counsel for the accused. When questioned I had said that, in my opinion, the dismembering could have been carried out using a bandsaw, such as that used by butchers.

'Well, Doctor,' boomed the barrister, 'are you sure it was a bandsaw, or could it have been a large knife or perhaps an axe?'

I groaned inwardly, envisioning the hours of cross-examination to come, as we painstakingly canvassed each and every possibility. I caught sight of the defendant, silently seated in the dock, and thought, 'Why don't you just ask him what he used?'

That, of course, didn't happen. He remained silent – because he could, and, although he was ultimately convicted, we may never know just what it was he used to cut up the body. My money is still on the bandsaw.

This is how our legal system operates. It is called an 'adversarial system' because evidence is presented by one side and tested by the other, before a judge and jury. The judge makes directions as to the way in which the jury must apply the law but it is the members of the jury who determine the verdict: guilty or not guilty.

I'm sure we would all like to think that the system has sufficient faith in its jurors to allow them to reach a decision after they have heard all the relevant material, but this is not the case. Legal rules prevent certain pieces of evidence being presented to the jury.

Perhaps the oath taken by witnesses should be changed to reflect this. It could go something like this: 'I swear by almighty God … that the evidence I shall give … to the court in this case … shall be the truth … those bits of the truth that I'm allowed to give … and nothing but the truth.'

Australia's Pacific Borderlands

A Bridge Broken at Both Ends

Susan Metcalfe

Mohammed Sagar cannot go back to where he came from, he cannot go forward to a new life; he is trapped in one of Australia's offshore borderlands where the forbidden, and the mostly forgotten, are contained.

For more than five years he has lived in an Australian detention camp for asylum seekers, in the tiny Pacific country of Nauru. Daily he must negotiate his life in a void of displacement and separation from his family, in a tiny country with little relevance to his own culture.

Over the past few years I have become inescapably entwined in the stories of many asylum seekers and refugees housed by the Australian Government in Nauru. But with none more deeply than the two Iraqis, Mohammad Faisal and Mohammed Sagar, left behind after the resettlement or return of more than 1500 people processed under Australia's Pacific Solution.

Faisal is now receiving psychiatric treatment in Australia; Sagar remains alone in Nauru.

The men left Iraq when it was under the rule of Saddam Hussein; both faced persecution and neither can return. Faisal and Sagar both left behind mothers who loved them deeply and families who were at the centre of their lives. Families are as important in Iraqi culture as they are anywhere else in the world, so the decision to flee could not have been made lightly. If their lives had been different, they would both probably be married with children by now but fate decided otherwise.

For more than a year, barely a day has passed when I have not had contact with one or both of these men. On most days their situation has felt impossible to affect, and the way forward has been blocked on all fronts. But one thing I have learnt, in the face of injustice or in difficult times, is that if you just keep going, keep pressing ahead, something will eventually change.

Australia's border has come to signify the limits of our identity, both cultural and moral. It mediates our capacity for hospitality and compassion to outsiders; it records the extent to which we are able to manage our fears.

Ever since the Norwegian freighter the *Tampa* rescued 438 asylum seekers at sea in the midst of the Australian election campaign in 2001, 'border control' has been the mantra of the Howard Government. 'We' are protected on one side of the border from 'them' on the other side.

Gloria Anzaldua's description of the US–Mexico border, where the desperate try to cross to a better life, resonates with Australia's use of offshore processing as a legal and moral black hole:

> una herida abierta *where the third world grates against the first and bleeds. And before a scab forms it hemorrhages again, the lifeblood of two worlds merging to form a third country – a border culture ... A borderland is a vague and undetermined place created by the emotional residue of an unnatural boundary ... The prohibited and forbidden are its inhabitants.*

Regardless of how compelling the stories of people fleeing persecution may be, their fates are bound by each nation's sovereignty. People are free, if they can, to leave their homeland where they have feared for their life. But where are they free to find sanctuary? And what happens to those who remain trapped between the border of the land they have left and the hope of new life in a peaceful country?

In 2001 Mohammad Faisal left Indonesia with more than 228 strangers on a rickety fishing boat called the *Aceng.* On Friday 7 September the *Aceng* was intercepted by the Australian Navy near

Ashmore Reef, a shelf edge atoll 610 kilometres north of Broome. After a number of unsuccessful attempts to force the boat back to Indonesia, the navy finally transferred the passengers to the *HMAS Manoora* the next day. On the *Manoora* they joined 438 other asylum seekers being taken to Nauru after their rescue by the *Tampa*.

It was to be a month before people finally disembarked from the overloaded *Manoora*. Their journey had been tense and conditions difficult on a ship equipped to carry only 450 troops. Finally landing in Nauru, Faisal and the others faced makeshift conditions as the camps were being set up. Everyone was suffering, particularly the women and children and some of the men who were especially vulnerable.

Mohammed Sagar's boat, the *Olong*, arrived in our waters on Friday 6 October 2001 and was intercepted at sea en route to Christmas Island. The navy made numerous attempts to turn the rickety boat back to Indonesia; gun shots were even fired across the bow to encourage the men, women and children to change course.

The *Olong* became well known at the time because of the Australian Government's accusations that people on the boat had thrown their children into the water. Philip Ruddock, then Immigration Minister, claimed that 'a number of children have been thrown overboard, clearly planned and premeditated'. John Howard said that these were not the type of people he wanted in Australia, and Defence Minister Peter Reith produced photos he claimed were of children who had been thrown into the water by their parents.

But no children were ever thrown from that boat and no-one had ever given advice to the Government that they had been. Amongst the many findings of a Senate inquiry into the incident in 2002 was that Defence Minister Peter Reith had 'engaged in the deliberate misleading of the Australian public concerning a matter of intense political interest during an election period'. Peter Reith alone took the fall for the Government and there was never sufficient evidence to implicate Howard or Ruddock in the deception.

Eventually on Sunday 8 October, with the boat starting to break apart and sink at sea, the 223 passengers on the *Olong* were transferred to the *HMAS Adelaide*. They were taken first to Christmas Island and then to Australia's other new detention camp being set up in Manus Island, Papua New Guinea. In 2002 Sagar was transferred to Nauru where he has remained.

Until recently, the Australian Government has been keen to ignore Faisal and Sagar indefinitely – their justification, simply, that the men are threats to Australia's national security. What exactly this means is unclear, but it is enough to squash debate and deny the humanity of the two men involved.

The current Immigration Minister, Amanda Vanstone, has even been known to challenge the Labor Party to 'make her day' if they would like to suggest that men with adverse security assessments should be brought to Australia. No worries there, as that's a call the Labor Party would not make for fear of political annihilation.

October – November 2006

From my hotel room in Nauru, this current chapter of my life seems as endless and fathomless as the ocean only metres away. The needs of my own personal life, put on hold for too long now, are breathing down my neck. But I am committed for as long as it takes for these men to gain their freedom – they do not deserve what has happened to them and we are all in this for the long haul.

As I write this, Mohammed Sagar remains here in Nauru, his future uncertain, his inner life in turmoil. More than five years of struggle and there are still no answers to any of his questions.

Why did this happen to him? I admit I don't have the answers; I am in the dark like most others. But I do bear witness to the moral crime and injustice committed in my name as an Australian.

I have also come to Nauru, this time, to visit a newly arrived group of seven Burmese men and I am already daunted by the prospect of the cycle beginning again. Sitting with the new men inside the camp, I find it hard to explain why Mohammed Sagar is still here after five years. I know the details of his situation so well but it still makes no sense to me.

Nauru is an unusual country with barely the population of many small Australian country towns. About 10,000 people (I don't think anyone keeps count) live on a 22-kilometre dot in the Pacific Ocean. The island has some natural beauty near the coast and around the lagoon in the district of Bauda, but years of phosphate mining have left scars in the landscape. Nauru is most famous for its rise to and fall from the heights of great wealth.

On all my visits I have found Nauruans to be overwhelmingly friendly and kind. I feel sad that they have reached such financial depths and now struggle to feed their children; sad too that they now rely on income and jobs created by housing Australia's asylum seekers.

Back in Australia, just before this trip, I left Faisal struggling with life in a Brisbane hospital and a still-uncertain future. Faisal became suicidal in August 2006 and had to be evacuated out of Nauru. His conditions in Australia, however, are even more restrictive than they had been in Nauru, prompting his intermittent urges to return to that 'no man's land'.

At least in Nauru he had a level of freedom; he had some caring friends; and he had his dogs – puppies he had lovingly cared for when they were abandoned by their mother. He remembers Nauru as a comfort zone that is perhaps more inviting in memory than when it was his life – and in Nauru he had no future. At least in Australia he now, finally, has access to some sort of legal process.

It is 9pm in Nauru when I knock on Sagar's door for a visit. After all the time I have known him he has finally found something to feed me. I am a vegetarian and allergic to wheat, so his choices are limited. We sit down with a dish of beans and egg, the idea of the combination unsettling me at first. But the mouthful I bravely taste is surprisingly good and one that I am sure I can revisit.

As we eat, we talk about his situation and I ask him about his family. But the subject is too painful – five years of separation is nearly unbearable. He tells me that when he speaks to his mother on the phone he is frustrated that he cannot explain why he is still in Nauru, and he worries about her. His family obligations weigh heavily on his mind but there's nothing he can do; he is powerless to help even himself.

We talk too about the politics dominating most of the Australian Government's decisions. Sagar knows more about the intricacies of Australian politics than many Australians, but perhaps he has seen the worst we have to offer. It makes me sad for my country that we have shown such an ugly face to the world.

I know that these two men Sagar and Faisal will forgive us, but surely there are others who won't. The head of Australia's Federal Police, Mick Keelty, makes a similar point:

> *The worry there is that whatever we do in the treatment of terrorism, in the treatment of people's rights, in the treatment of people as human beings, we cannot do anything that might encourage or inspire others to take on the cause.*

Sagar is an intelligent man with a strong sense of justice, and injustice; he makes clear distinctions between what is right and wrong. But in this situation, whether fair or not, he has had little power to affect or oppose decisions made about his life. By the end of 2004, his view of justice was clearly tarnished by his experience, and his optimism was lost. In an email to me he said: *Anyway, that's the life, it's always unfair and has no justice.*

The waiting process and the struggle for a normal and peaceful existence have become the basis of Sagar's life. He is accustomed to, but not immune from, a habitual pattern of anticipation, setbacks and hanging onto new threads of hope that will inevitably disappoint. My guess is that he will break down both physically and mentally when he is finally free; the threads holding him together are now wearing too thin.

When I first came into regular contact with Sagar a few years back, he had been recommended to me as someone who was reliable, intelligent and trustworthy amongst the Iraqis. He was to become a person I could rely on to distribute phone cards to the others, and I often asked him to provide accurate information on the situation in the camp. As I came to know him I found him to be reliable and honest in his dealings with me; he was indeed trustworthy and easy to deal with. It has always been hard to understand why he is still here in Nauru.

This is my first visit to Nauru since Faisal was evacuated to Australia nearly two months ago. Sagar now lives alone in the demountable shipping container positioned just outside the gate to the main camp area. Everything in this man's life is temporary, pending resolution; it has been this way for a long time. The containers of food are plastic, he has no dinner plates or ceramic mugs, and when we drink tea it is from polystyrene cups.

I remember my early visits to the camp when overly zealous Australian police suggested that my life might be endangered if I ate meals with all the asylum seekers. They even went so far as to speculate that I might be attacked with cutlery.

The suggestion was absurd. At meal time the hall was filled with security guards and the cutlery they were so concerned about was plastic. But, more than anything else, I knew that these people would always protect me from harm, not inflict it on me. It was notable that when all the other asylum seekers had departed and I came to visit only Sagar and Faisal, everyone had stopped worrying about my safety. Despite any ASIO assessments to the contrary, there were clearly no concerns about security with these two guys in Nauru.

Security assessment aside, Sagar has been assessed by Australia to be a refugee with strong claims for protection under the refugee convention. In Iraq he suffered greatly under Saddam's regime and has spent most of his life feeling unsafe and insecure. Yet, in spite of his acknowledged need for sanctuary, ASIO – the Australian 'relevant authority' – decided there *was* a security issue preventing him, and Faisal, being offered visas to come to Australia.

In August 2004 the Minister for Immigration, Amanda Vanstone, announced on the ABC *Insiders* program that the cases of the Iraqis in Nauru would be reopened – three years after they'd arrived. When I told Sagar on the phone that night, it was the first he or any of the Iraqis had heard of the decision. As was typically the case, the Minister felt no obligation to tell the people involved, before telling the Australian media. It was, nonetheless, an optimistic time when we all hoped there would be many positive outcomes amongst the group of 41 Iraqis being reviewed.

The re-interviewing began in October 2004, followed by lengthy ASIO interviews sometimes lasting for four to five hours. From what has become common knowledge about these interviews, many of the questions seemed designed to prod, poke or provoke the subjects into some sort of extreme reaction or to trigger a response that would reveal particular aversions or hidden character traits.

This practice is, at the very least, questionable when dealing with people who have come from traumatic backgrounds and who have been held in a situation widely acknowledged to have damaged their mental health. An average healthy person may not hold up well in a three-, four- or five-hour interrogation, but for a person with diagnosed mental problems, the situation is a recipe for failure. Some of those interviewed were extremely vulnerable and mentally unwell at the time.

Mohammad Faisal in particular had already self-harmed more than once by the time he was interviewed by ASIO in 2004. He was offered no psychological assistance during the initial interviews and I don't believe that he was capable of maintaining the mental focus required to survive such a lengthy interview.

Going back as far as 2002, there was evidence that some of this group of Iraqis were mentally struggling. A leaked International Organisation for Migration (IOM) report in 2002 noted that the group of Iraqis arriving from PNG (which included Mohammed Sagar) were 'a special group at risk in the AS [asylum seeker] community.' The report stated that each member of the group presented with similar symptoms, including:

Having lost all hope and faith in my future; nightmares of being captured by security forces in Iraq; about drowning ... Difficulty in getting and staying asleep...Life is over, feel like dead; dying is attractive; religion, lack of means and still feeling some responsibility toward family prevents active suicidal behaviour up to now ... Passivity, loss of short-term memory, constant ruminating or worrying ... Loss of interest in all daily activities ... Feeling abandoned and degraded: no-one cares about what is happening to me, no-one helps me; am I not a human being anymore?

Mental health reports in 2005, obtained under Freedom of Information by the *Age* newspaper in 2006, claimed that mental health problems had continued amongst asylum seekers 'for several years' and that people should be removed 'from this kind of environment and atmosphere of consistent hopelessness' as soon as possible.

Even from a security perspective, an accurate assessment does not seem likely based on interviews with people with acknowledged mental health problems. After living with uncertainty for so many years, most were not coping well at the time of the assessments. Looking back, it's surprising that more people were not rejected on the basis of their ASIO interviews.

After the interviews were finally completed, the waiting began – again. It was a tense time even though the Australian Government had been clear that quick decisions for people held under the Pacific Solution were not on their agenda. Philip Ruddock had even said in 2002 that there would be no hurry to process the people held in offshore processing centres. Mohammed Sagar wrote to me at the end of November:

I wonder whether you've heard anything about the decisions, but probably not. Doesn't matter, we are used to this. Hope to hear some good news this week. This is what we are doing for now three years, every day we say it might be tomorrow, and every week, we say it might be next week.

Finally, in December 2004, the decisions came down – all the Iraqi families with children were offered resettlement, as well as two Christian men and one who was Kurdish. Fourteen others were rejected and the cases of two men, Mohammed Sagar and Mohammad

Faisal, were still 'under consideration'. At that stage their future looked hopeful; perhaps some sort of security issue was just going to take a bit of time to work through before they were accepted to come to Australia. Things were finally looking positive.

But within weeks the obstacles started to appear. Faisal and Sagar were told that their cases were before the Attorney-General and that the finalisation of their security checks could take between six and 18 months. Neither man coped well with the news. The prospect of many more months ahead without resolution was daunting.

As the months went by without a decision, their stress intensified and their hopes disappeared. Psychiatrist Ian Hickie, who assessed the mental health of the two men in Nauru earlier this year, makes the important point that 'if a person is left in an indeterminate position that is likely to be highly detrimental to their mental health … anyone who finds themselves in a position of not knowing their status over a long period of time is at risk of developing a mental health problem'.

From a mental health perspective Faisal and Sagar's situation was disastrous. But there was nothing they could do but wait it out until a final decision came.

After an excruciating wait of more than nine extra months and regular pleas from Sagar to speed up the process, the negative security assessments were given in August 2005. The men had seen the signs of the negative decisions coming so there was no surprise, but they were both flattened.

Pouring salt into the open wound, in October it was announced that all other remaining asylum seekers would be granted visas to come to Australia – only Mohammed Sagar and Mohammad Faisal would be left behind. The blows just kept coming for these two and it is a miracle that they have survived.

I called someone in the Department of Immigration (DIMA) at the time and said, 'I can't believe you are going to leave these two guys there, it will be a nightmare.'

The cold reply was that the department will 'manage' the situation, but I suspect some were uncomfortable with the decision. Those who knew Mohammad Faisal, in particular, would have been aware that he was unlikely to cope and that he would inevitably end up in a psychological mess.

I cannot even begin to imagine what the day of departure from Nauru felt like for anyone involved, but I saw the distress of the other 25 men when they arrived in Melbourne. Their pain was still raw as they begged me never to give up trying to get their two friends out of Nauru.

I'd previously been in the camp in Nauru when people had left for a new life and it was a raw emotional experience for everyone involved. Those who are leaving are torn by survivor guilt, but are powerless to do anything but save their own lives. Those who remain are pleased that at least some get to leave, but are thrown into feelings of isolation and pain and the uncertainty of their future.

Neither Sagar nor Faisal have been given reasons for the security decision; in fact, no explanation at all has ever been made – we are all in the dark. It seems that Australia's intelligence organisation is more interested in building even higher walls around itself than around the country it is supposed to be protecting. The same would have to be said about the Attorney-General to whom ASIO is responsible. There is a certain irony in the role of Philip Ruddock; the man who instigated the Pacific Solution as Immigration Minister now maintains his harsh attitude towards these final two cases, both genuine refugees, in his role as Attorney-General.

In 2001 when Sagar, Faisal and hundreds of other men, women and children were arriving at our shores, Philip Ruddock told the world that these people were 'queue jumpers, illegals', and 'cashed up' middle-class economic migrants looking for a better life.

In reality many of the people had come from small villages where they were persecuted by warlords, while many others had suffered under the brutal ruling regimes of Afghanistan and Iraq in particular.

I remain in contact with refugees who have endured horrific torture in their lives, and others who have experienced unimaginable suffering. If the truth had been told at the time, the Howard Government's harsh response to those arriving on these boats may not have been so acceptable to many more of the Australian people. As one MP exclaimed at the time:

> *We send one FFG7 class guided-missile frigate with two Seahawk helicopters … we send two Anzac-class frigates … we send one supply ship fleet oiler … and we send three P3C Orion maritime surveillance aircraft. I remind you that that was after the event. That was after the* Tampa. *After the people were picked up and put on the* Tampa, *we sent in the navy. What did we do before that? We put the SAS on board the* Tampa *to make sure that the people did not jump overboard.*

> *We sent all sorts of other defence assets to Christmas Island to make the place safe – safe from what? That is still to be determined.*

At the end of five years, from the more than 1500 people on these boats, it seems that we were being protected from just Faisal and Sagar. But there is still no indication of the level of threat they apparently represent, or how ASIO came to their conclusion.

Everyone who has known these two guys is baffled, and so much about the assessments and the situation has *never* made sense. One wonders if the Australian Government has simply felt the need to somehow justify its rhetoric, by saying, 'See, this is why it was all so necessary.'

But if Faisal and Sagar are the people I am being protected from, then my government cannot be doing its job.

A few years ago the case of another asylum seeker in Australia clearly revealed the potential for error in ASIO's assessment process. It was only because of the doubt cast on the credibility of intelligence sources involved that ASIO eventually decided to review their original decision. The findings of the review gave an appalling insight into the processes of Australia's intelligence organisation. It was found that:

> *ASIO took no action to corroborate the allegations in the report … the reports should have been viewed with scepticism because ASIO knew that the country concerned has been assessed as having a poor human rights record, particularly in relation to the ethnic group to which the applicant belonged … ASIO failed to seek from the applicant an explanation of the adverse imputations in the reports from the overseas security service before it issued the assessment. Had it done so it is likely that he would have been able to provide satisfactory responses … where a person does not have a right to have an assessment reviewed by a court or tribunal, ASIO has as much responsibility to accord natural justice as it does when there is a right of review.*

At this stage it's impossible to know if any similar findings might apply to the cases of Faisal and Sagar. The Director-General of ASIO, Paul O'Sullivan, has said that although he did begin his own inquiry into the processes undertaken in their cases, he stopped his investigation when court proceedings began, fearing contempt of court.

Faisal and Sagar have, to date, been denied access to their assessments while maintaining, without waver, that they have no idea why they have received this adverse assessment.

While it is of course understandable that ASIO would at times need to withhold information from public view, this should surely be balanced against numerous other factors. In the federal court Judge Sunberg put forward that:

> *The primary difficulty that each of the applicants faces in bringing his claim is that he has not seen his adverse security assessment and alleges that he does not know the facts or reasoning by which the Director-General made the adverse security assessment. Without this material, it will be difficult, if not impossible, for the applicants to make out their claim that the adverse security assessments were not made in accordance with law.*

Although the court case mounted by lawyers representing Faisal and Sagar has so far had one significant win – that the men should indeed have access to the ASIO decisions – it is hard to imagine that the Australian Government will actually allow this to happen, without extensive appeals or obstructions. Nevertheless, the win is important. As one of the men's solicitors commented:

> *It's a fundamental principle of our law that if you are accused of something, you're entitled to defend yourself ... And a part of being able to defend yourself is to know what you're being accused of. None of these people know what they're alleged to have done ... And it's also in a sense an important message to the government, which is [that] your decisions are reviewable. This is not a secret state in which the government can decide things without being accountable to anybody.*

The opportunity to defend oneself should also be seen as a principle of our moral foundations as Australians. Although Australian identity is notionally built on the idea of a fair go, in practice our regimes force us to fight for levels of accountability and fairness that should already underpin our democratic way of life.

If we didn't fight, if we didn't struggle, then we would have little left to feel comfortable with in this country.

Sagar and Faisal have committed no crime and both have lived without problem in Nauru for five years. No-one has ever had any kind of security problem with either man and no-one who knows them can understand the decision. Members of the Nauruan Government have spoken out about both men, in public, and with compassion and concern for their welfare.

Surely it is reasonable to expect that any assessment of a person's potential risk should take these factors into account. Five years is a good stretch of time to monitor someone's actions, and during that time these two men have given no indication that they could be problematic now or in the future.

The enormous consequence of labelling someone a 'threat' to a country's security – without their having any possibility to defend themselves – seems lost on both ASIO and the Australian Government. Natural justice cannot be achieved under such circumstances, and the men involved are branded and ostracised from the world indefinitely. They have been tried, convicted and condemned in an ASIO office, with no right of reply.

Throughout this catastrophe, Sagar tried hard to keep himself afloat. He put his attention to his computer studies and found a place for himself at the Nauru branch of the University of the South Pacific (USP). In an email to me at the time he said:

> *I am trying to stick myself to the computer course. It might give some relief, but I still have difficulties even with doing the course ... Anyway, everything is going so difficult for me. I am not sure of whether I will be able to cope.*

For a while he did cope relatively well, his diligence and passion for study made him welcome with the Director and other staff at the university. It wasn't long before he was also working voluntarily at the USP, and was then offered a paid position in the computer lab. When I visited Nauru during this period he was always tired and preoccupied, but he was driven, almost obsessively, by a need to make up for all the years he had lost in Nauru and before.

Sagar had been 25 years old when he arrived in Nauru. On one of my visits he turned 30, but didn't even tell me until the day after his birthday. Birthdays were just reminders of more wasted years in which life had passed him by.

But while Sagar was throwing himself into his studies, Faisal was withdrawing even further from life. The more I had come to know Faisal, the more I was pained to watch him descend into even deeper despair. I felt powerless to help him, but towards the end of January, three months after his friends had left, I was so deeply worried that I wrote to the Immigration Minister:

> *I am gravely concerned for one of the men in particular, Mohammad Faisal. I do not believe that he will be able to cope indefinitely with this situation and there is a high risk that he may harm himself now or in the near future. It is my understanding that Mohammad Faisal has previously made serious attempts to harm himself whilst detained in Nauru. He also has a serious eye disorder which means that his vision is severely impaired. This only adds to his vulnerability and makes it vital that he receive adequate care and attention until his permanent situation can be resolved.*

In the letter I also discussed my concerns that the Immigration Department was no longer providing an interpreter for Faisal. His English was patchy at the best of times and when he was under stress he lost this second language completely. The argument from DIMA was that an interpreter could be provided by phone 'when needed'. But this was an irrational proposal in a country where the phones go down without warning. While these two men remained in Nauru it was Australia's responsibility to continue to provide services; taking away an interpreter was unnecessary and was certain to have a devastating effect on Faisal. They had already taken away five years of his life; he could not bear to lose anything more.

Only days after I had sent my latest letter to the Minister, Faisal made another attempt to harm himself. When Sagar called me that morning, he was in shock as he described the night they spent at the hospital after he had found Faisal in his room.

I felt sick that Faisal has been reduced to this, appalled that a human life was being denied its value. Faisal had been 21 years old when he was taken to Nauru five years before. It was the first time he had been away from his family. How would his parents feel if they knew what he was going through? I wondered if it was just as well that he had lost contact with his family at this time. Most of all I felt powerless to change what was happening to him and to Sagar.

In the months ahead lawyers worked behind the scenes on the men's cases, one describing the process as similar to trying to push something forward with a piece of string. More than six months had passed since the others had left, and all doors seemed closed. The mental health of both men was rapidly declining and I was afraid that the worst was yet to come. In another letter to the Minister, I wrote:

> *In my conversation with Mohammad [Faisal] last week he told me, as he has many times before, that he does not have a reason to live anymore and that he has no future. My private conversations with Mohammad, which I am sharing with you only because of my concern for him, are typically about his wanting to kill himself. I believe that if he is left in Nauru for much longer, without any resolution to his situation, he will simply lose his will to remain alive. All of his friends in Australia are desperately worried about him.*

Soon after, ASIO visited the men once again. The decision apparently resulted from ongoing discussions with DIMA, but I think it more likely the Australian Government was scared that someone might actually kill themselves. No-one wanted blood on their hands.

The Australian Government had shown its willingness to take people's lives to the brink on numerous occasions, but they usually baulked when a suicide seemed imminent. It is a risky and unethical game they play with human lives and one day they may take it too far.

An impending visit by agents of Australia's intelligence organisation would be daunting for any of us on the best of days, but the timing of that ASIO visit to Nauru could not have been worse for Sagar. He couldn't be blamed for suspecting a hidden agenda when it was announced – at a day's notice – that ASIO was coming for more interviews on the exact days of his exams. He had studied hard under difficult circumstances and the Australian Government was about to scuttle his efforts to help himself yet again.

I doubt, however, that the timing was designed to unsettle or deliberately provoke him; more likely it was just the usual bureaucratic indifference to an individual human life.

Both men felt a natural aversion to enduring yet more questioning and it took some counselling for them to feel calm about the process.

With their arrival imminent, it was with great fortune that ASIO itself provided light relief in what was an otherwise tense situation. This was the widely reported occasion when representatives of Australia's intelligence agency were forced to return to spend the night in Honiara, in the Solomon Islands, after failing to gain landing permission on their approach to Nauru.

It really wasn't hard to find some enjoyment in the fact that they had apparently not filled in appropriate paperwork and there was an issue involving their visas. The all-powerful ASIO was not so foreboding when seen in this light, and perhaps they were not entirely a law unto themselves.

When ASIO agents did finally arrive, the round of interviews they conducted was different from those of previous visits. For the first time the men were allowed the presence of a non-ASIO mental health professional to witness the interaction; the interviews were relatively short; and at the conclusion, both men were told that they had been co-operative.

We all felt optimistic that commonsense would now prevail and that we may be coming to the end of this nightmare.

But as the weeks went by, hope faded yet again. There was no follow-up response from ASIO, no change in the decision; there was absolutely nothing. The Australian Government did not explain ASIO's visit, nor did it provide any comment at all.

The men understandably felt manipulated into believing that their cases were being re-assessed, when they were not, and they felt betrayed by the Australian Government once again.

This was all too much for Faisal, who could bear no more. An email I received from him in August alerted me to the fact that he was in trouble. He did not want to live anymore and he called for everyone to forget him.

Reports from the mental health unit in Nauru were also clearly alarming, but the Nauruan Government was quick to act. Nauru did not have adequate medical facilities to deal with a crisis of this kind, so officials requested that Faisal be airlifted to Australia for treatment as soon as possible. Agreement from the Australian Government came through within days, and after five long years Faisal was on his way to Australia.

But it was just as well he did not know then that the months ahead would be so difficult. It was especially good he was not told that, initially, he would only be allowed out of hospital for short periods, and even then, only in the company of security guards.

In Nauru he had more freedom, but he had no future. In Australia his freedom has been more restricted, in the short term, but there is hope for his future.

Since his arrival in Australia, Faisal has managed to contact his family in Iraq. It had been two years since he'd had news, and didn't even know if they were still alive. His mother was recovering from heart surgery, his father had been injured in a recent bombing, and his brother and sisters were thankfully still alive. He does not tell them that he is still in detention, as they would worry too much and would not understand.

As the eldest son, he feels the burden of responsibility but is powerless to help them without his own freedom. He is pained to hear about their ongoing fear of persecution and violence in a country filled with bloodshed.

As I write, Faisal's situation is improving. It is now accepted that he can live in the care of people in the community when he is well enough. He is clearly of no threat to anyone, and will soon be reassessed by ASIO. This time we hope for a better outcome.

At the hospital he has won the hearts of many other patients who have taken up his cause. But although there is general optimism about his case, there is no guarantee his adverse assessment will be overturned. Until this happens, Mohammad Faisal will remain in an indefinite limbo, either in hospital or with caring Australian people in the community. His future remains uncertain.

In October 2006 the head of ASIO finally spoke about the most recent ASIO interviews conducted in Nauru. He said that these interviews had not been a review with a capital 'R' but a small 'r' review; that it had been a chance for ASIO to check the cooperation levels of the men. He said:

> *In June of this year we revisited Nauru with the intention of trying to clarify whether the conditions pertaining to when the original judgements were made persisted – in particular, in respect of Mr Sagar and whether or not the level of cooperation that he exhibited was changed or not.*

If Mr O'Sullivan's implication, in this statement made four months after the review, was that Mohammed Sagar had been uncooperative in his interview, then he should go back to check the transcripts of that interview.

I have no reason to doubt that at the conclusion of Sagar's interview he was clearly told he had been cooperative. It had, in fact, been a point of aggravation for Sagar because he maintained that he has always cooperated in all of his interviews.

When I leave Mohammed Sagar at the end of this visit I worry for his future. The normality of a regular routine at the university had kept him grounded for a while and focused his attention. But the stress has finally caught up with him and he has resigned from his position at the USP and given up his studies.

He says he could not keep going and tells me that this was the hardest thing for him to do. He is currently doing some intermittent work in the Nauruan Government offices, and they are very grateful for his assistance.

Sagar has said publicly that he has no wish to come to Australia. But, although I respect his sentiment and understand why he would feel this way, I think it is unfair to take his current feeling as the final view.

I believe it is also unethical, at the very least, for the Director-General of ASIO to be repeating Sagar's current feelings on the matter in the media. After five years, Sagar's views are undoubtedly and understandably skewed by the ongoing nightmare he has endured.

What's more, at this point no-one has offered him a visa to come to Australia, so I think all judgment should be reserved until he is in a position to make reasonable comment.

For the past year the United Nations High Commission for Refugees (UNHCR) has been searching for a resettlement country other than Australia for both men, but as yet there have been no takers. The likelihood of another country becoming involved has always been slim, even if the assessments were reversed.

Why? Because the asylum seekers taken to Nauru in recent years are clearly Australia's responsibility. Other countries have been reluctant to become involved at the best of times, and every other country has more than enough of their own asylum claims to deal with each year, without taking on Australia's.

During a speech in parliament on Thursday 3 March 1994 – seven-and-a-half years before the *Tampa* rescue and the 'children overboard' lies – Philip Ruddock, then in opposition government, stated that:

> ... *we have very important obligations in relation to refugees internationally* ... *we have obligations to fellow human beings.*

Just what the Howard Government, Ruddock's own, believes these obligations to be is difficult to discern. It certainly has not felt an obligation to resolve the situation of Mohammed Sagar, and went to the brink with the life of Mohammed Faisal.

It's November 2006 and the lives of both men remain in limbo as I write. This is surely, at the very least, a moral crime Australia has committed in denying natural justice to some of the most vulnerable people in the world.

Whatever the future holds for Faisal and Sagar there is no doubt they will both have long roads to recovery ahead of them. There can be no fairytale ending, at least not in the near future.

But despite their years of uncertainty and turmoil, beneath the pain that never goes away, it is possible to see a glimmer of the hope that sustains both men. They maintain their innocence and want nothing more than to clear their names and to live normal lives.

Neither man will walk away from this without damage; I just hope it won't be irreparable.

Postscript

It is Friday 1 December 2006 and I am in Brisbane spending time with Faisal, who has not been coping well. As I wait in line at a supermarket, a call comes through on my mobile phone – a Scandinavian country has just agreed to accept Mohammed Sagar for resettlement. I can barely reply.

The struggle has been long and intense for Sagar, and for me and others who have been involved in his advocacy. It is hard to believe that suddenly the fight is over and that he will finally begin a new life in a welcoming country. There is no indication of why this particular country (who had asked not to be named) decided to take him at this time. But they must surely have accepted that Sagar posed no security risk to their country.

I immediately try to call Sagar but the Telstra network is down in Nauru; a common annoyance. Then my phone rings; it is him, he can call out on an internet phone program. He is still trying to come to terms with the news and he knows it will take many days before he believes it is real.

Only days before, ASIO had won the right to appeal the Federal Court decision allowing the men to access their security assessments. It had been yet another blow to Sagar, whose future was looking even more uncertain. But suddenly his world is looking very different.

For me the news is bittersweet as my thoughts immediately turn to Mohammad Faisal. I know that while his case remains unresolved, the news of Sagar's resettlement will be hard for him to hear. I offered to be the one to tell him.

Faisal's first reaction is silence as he puts his head in his hands for a very long time. He is, of course, very happy for Sagar but the loneliness of being the last unresolved Nauru case from 2001 is almost too much for him to bear. He truly does not understand why he is in this situation.

In a matter of weeks Sagar will be on a plane to his new life. The first year or two will be difficult as he adjusts to an unfamiliar environment and rebuilds his life from scratch. But he does have the possibility of a future now; he will be able to make his own choices and most importantly for him, he will be free.

Faisal's future must be in Australia. He is too vulnerable to begin a new life in an unfamiliar land without support and he is Australia's responsibility. But there is still no indication of how long a resolution of his status will take. The pain of uncertainty is destroying him more each day and he will somehow need to find the strength, and so will I; for we will keep going for as long as it takes for us to gain his freedom.

Bad Bad Big Brother

Leigh Redhead

The following is a true account. Only one name has been changed: to protect the guilty.

If it wasn't for the tip-off, he would have got away with it scot-free.

The resident-manager had noticed an unusual number of attractive young women moving into the building's penthouse. They stayed for a little while, moved out and were quickly replaced. He wondered if the guy who rented the place was running an illegal brothel or perhaps dealing drugs. Either way, the high turnover was suss; something was going on up there. The manager called Crime Stoppers.

On Tuesday 2 June 2005, a couple of detectives from the Surfers Paradise CID busted into the apartment. Instead of a den of iniquity, however, they found a fairly normal three-bedroom share flat, albeit one decorated in a high '80s style with pink walls, mirrored surfaces, fake plants and glass-topped tables. Tacky crystal chandeliers hung from the ceiling and large picture windows overlooked one of the Gold Coast's ubiquitous canals.

No-one was home.

One cop searched the two bedrooms downstairs, which, judging by the accoutrements, were occupied by females. The other cop took a flight of carpeted stairs upwards and found the master suite; a large space with roof access, and a sunken spa bath smack bang in the centre of the room.

There was a switched-on computer on a desk, and when the detective looked at the screen it took him a couple of seconds to realise what he was seeing. It was his partner, searching one of the downstairs bedrooms, shot from above. That wasn't all. As his partner moved from the bedrooms to the bathrooms his progress was beamed live to the computer by other cameras apparently concealed in the ceilings and walls.

The place didn't seem to be an illegal brothel at all. The cop decided it looked more like that reality show where a bunch of good-looking young people were locked inside a house and filmed 24 hours a day. It was just like *Big Brother*.

Police arrested the leaseholder, 35-year-old Martin John Craft, later that day. They'd done a thorough search and found he'd rigged the whole apartment with hidden cameras and microphones. Devices had been hidden in the walls, ceilings and furniture. Even the laundry tub had a lens, positioned right at crotch height to capture someone undressing for the shower. Craft had gone so far as to construct false walls and drill holes for cables, so the images could be sent direct to his computer and recorded on video.

The cops found dozens of tapes with literally hundreds of hours of footage of Craft's female flatmates, past and present, going about their daily business, including undressing, showering, using the toilet, making love to their boyfriends. All filmed without their consent.

Two days later Craft appeared at the Southport Magistrates Court, charged with five counts of stalking and one of wilful damage to the property. At the time there was no law in Queensland that specifically outlawed filming people in places where they could reasonably expect their privacy to be protected. Craft was granted bail on the condition that he report to police three times a week, not contact his former flatmates or go within a kilometre of the penthouse. He was to appear in court later in the year.

With its bizarre parallels to *Big Brother*, which was then being filmed not far from Surfers Paradise, the media picked up the story and ran with it. It was all over the radio, and the *Gold Coast Bulletin* carried the headline: 'MAN CHARGED OVER BIG BROTHER CRIME: IT'S TIME TO GO – FOR MARTIN CRAFT, ANYWAY'. TV's *A Current Affair*, always enamoured with pervy stories, did a segment on the case and filmed Craft fleeing the media after his day in court, his face obscured by a magazine with, appropriately, peepholes cut out for his eyes.

All these headlines certainly caught my eye, and not just because of the salacious subject matter. You see, I knew who the guy was; I'd met him once. My little sister had been one of his flatmates.

Jean was 18 when she moved from northern New South Wales to take up a job as a pharmacy assistant in the heart of Surfers Paradise.

I tried to talk her out of going there, because the few times I'd been to Surfers I couldn't stand the place. Sure, it had a certain tacky, neon-lit charm but the pneumatic, perma-tanned blondes, and poser guys with pink shirts, gold chains and artfully tipped hair, had freaked me out. And that's not an easy thing to do. Gangs of male tourists roamed between the transplanted palm trees of Surfers, drunk and braying; desperate and disappointed that their dream of shagging a meter maid or Indy grid girl had failed to materialise. And then of course there was the screeching, vomiting, teen apocalypse that was Schoolies week.

But Jean was determined. She was young and blonde and loved sun, surf and nightclubs. Like me, she'd had an alternative upbringing, but it had made her want to rebel and she was drawn to shiny, girly things: designer clothes, trendy nightclubs, cocktails and yes, penthouse apartments. I tamped down my inner-city prejudice, decided to stop showing my age and told her to have a good time.

I caught a lift to the housewarming party with Mum. She'd met Craft when she'd helped Jean move in, and their consensus was that he was a bit weird, although neither could quite say why, exactly. Our mother, who worked as a remedial masseur, thought he might need some deep tissue work. She told me he had a stiff walk and didn't move his neck.

'He says strange things,' Jean had attempted to explain to me on the phone. 'And oh-my-god he dresses, like, totally '80s; you know – high-waisted pants with a shirt tucked in. He has these acne scars and, I mean you can't hold how he looks against him, and I'm sure he's harmless, but he creeps me out.'

I'd thought she was just being teenage-girl cruel and decided that at the housewarming party I'd have a drink with this guy; try a bit of one-on-one conversation and draw him out of his shell. I'd been an awkward teenager with bad skin and appalling fashion sense, so I thought I understood. He was probably just shy and needed someone to give him a chance.

The building was hilarious: 12 stories of pink painted brick that looked exactly like Barbie's townhouse and was called, no kidding,

Princess Plaza. Later I would wonder if he'd picked the place because it would appeal to young women, and work as a lure, but at the time Mum and I just laughed and brought along pink champagne to match the building. The flat was indeed the penthouse and would have been pretty damn slick circa 1986. It was the sort of place you could imagine Warwick Capper and Leanne Edelsten swanning about in, in their heyday. I nibbled on chips and dips and met Jean's friends, her new flatmate Rachel (another young blonde), and Martin.

He was around my age, mid-30s, of average build and about five-ten, and had short gingery hair with a slight kink in it. His complexion was pasty, in the manner of many computer aficionados, but I didn't think his skin was too bad. After a couple of pink champagnes, and certain he couldn't be all that weird, I tried chatting with him

He *was* that weird. Talking to him was like throwing words at a wall and having them hit the bricks and slide to the ground. Or maybe it wasn't a wall, maybe it was an invisible force field. And when he looked at you, it was like his gaze started about two feet behind his head, and stopped short before it got to your face. I had never met anyone quite like that before; someone so utterly impossible to engage. There was no exchange of energy on any level. On the way home I joked with Mum that he might be an alien or a replicant. He had creeped me out too.

I interviewed Jean and her flatmate Rachel in June 2006, seven months after Craft's final court appearance. We were drinking red wine in Jean's current apartment in the slick new Q1 tower: highest building on the strip, views north to Brisbane and south to Byron, and more shiny surfaces than you could poke a stick at.

I wanted to know what it was like living with a guy who could secretly videotape his flatmates. How did they both come to move in with him and what were their first impressions? Did they have any inkling as to what was going on? How did they feel when they found out what he'd been up to?

'When I first moved up to the Gold Coast I was staying with Millie and John, my Dad's parents,' Jean explained. 'It wasn't working out, and they didn't really want me there. Millie actually said to me, "You have to get out of here," and started looking in the paper for me. She circled this ad in the *Gold Coast Bulletin* that said: "penthouse apartment in Budds Beach, flatmate wanted, female preferred".

'So I rang up and the guy, Martin, said it was just him sharing with one other girl. It sounded okay, it was in my price range, and I could walk to work from there. Mum came up and took me to see the place; we met the guy and looked around.

'The apartment was kind of kitschy, but so cool. The room that was going to be my room was off the living room. It actually used to be part of the lounge room, but there was a mirrored partition you could pull across to make it into a separate area. Martin had secured it and made it into a permanent wall with a sheet of plywood and then carpet over the plywood. He said that was to make it soundproof. He'd also turned the laundry and downstairs toilet into a separate bathroom. His room and Rachel's room had an ensuite, so that meant I'd have a bathroom of my own as well.

'We went upstairs and he showed us his room and the rooftop, and said it was fine for me to go up on the roof and sunbake or whatever. One thing Mum and I noticed was that his bed had a sort of tray set up over it with computers on it, so he could see the monitor in bed.

'He saw us looking and he said, "I know it looks dodgy but don't freak out. I'm on my computer for business all night and I don't have my desk set up yet." Mum asked what he did and he said something really vague about working from home doing internet consultancy and web design.

'Downstairs we had a short interview, where I told him about my job at the pharmacy and that I really wanted the room. He said he had a few more people to see but he called me later on and said it was mine if I wanted it.

'I was stoked. I thought he was a bit awkward, sure, but I really wanted the place so I ignored it. That night Mum helped me move in. It was my first share house.'

Rachel, a couple of years older than Jean and working in a restaurant at the time, had a similar feeling when she moved in. She told me it was hard to put her finger on what it was exactly, but he made her uncomfortable so she tried to spend as little time as possible in the house. When she wasn't working she'd go out or hang out with friends.

'He was a bit weird and geeky, and he dressed badly,' Rachel said, 'but I thought I had to give him the benefit of the doubt. I thought I couldn't hold those things against him. I basically ignored my instincts, and decided I was just being paranoid.'

As Rachel wasn't home much, and Jean didn't really have any other friends in Surfers yet, she spent a lot of time in the flat alone with Martin. She tried to be friendly and nice to him, the way she was with everybody, but he continually creeped her out.

'Like when I first moved in, he said I should go and have a spa, up in his room, because he'd just cleaned it,' Jean said. 'He told me he was leaving the house to do an outcall – which I only later realised was strange because he *never* left the house – and that he'd actually filled the spa for me.

'So I had one; but I wore my bikini because for some reason I was paranoid about the thought of cameras. It was probably because *Big Brother* was on at the time and Martin was absolutely obsessed with it. He watched every show, knew all the contestants and he really, really loved it when they got in the spa!

'Then things got weirder,' Jean said. 'A couple of days later I asked if I could go up through his room to sunbake on the roof, and he said sure. After a few minutes though Martin came up too, real casual, and started vacuuming the roof!

'Who vacuums the roof? I mean, there were tiles up there. You don't vacuum tiles.

'And then,' Jean said, obviously still amazed, 'while he was vacuuming he said, "You know, you've got a pretty good body." It freaked me out and I never went on the roof again.'

I asked Rachel if she'd had similar experiences and she nodded, 'Oh yeah. The first week he said some inappropriate stuff to me but, maybe being a bit older than Jean, I was 21, I just shut him down straight away. I said, "Look mate, that's enough of that," and then I just avoided him. So he didn't try any of that shit with me.'

Jean shook her head. 'I shouldn't have been so friendly but that's just how I was with people. One night early on, Martin and I had a few drinks together; actually, we got pretty drunk on red wine and talked. I was being nice to him but everything *he* said was wrong and creepy.'

'What sort of wrong and creepy?' I asked.

'Stuff like, well, the next day he says to me, "Remember when we were talking last night and I told you I had a big penis, and you said that it turns you on?"' Jean winced at the memory.

Rachel nodded, 'Yep, that sort of wrong and creepy.'

'I was drunk,' said Jean, 'but not that drunk. There's no way I would've said it turned me on. And I told him I never said that, but he was really arrogant and laughed, "Oh, you were so drunk you just don't remember. You probably don't even remember how we gave each other massages."

'Now that was also complete crap, because the thought of him touching me would've made me sick,' Jean stated. 'He was lying and playing mind games; trying to make me believe something happened when it hadn't.'

I asked what else was strange about him, like there needed to be more, and Rachel described how he'd stay in his room for hours on end. There was no actual reason he needed to come down; he had his own bathroom, a TV, his computers, and he'd make an enormous bowl of food in the morning – like a big salad or spaghetti – and just chip away at it all day.

Unless Jean was alone in the house ...

Then he'd come downstairs.

One night, after she'd been there a couple of weeks, she'd just arrived home from the pharmacy when he appeared, all excited. He'd scored some ecstasy and wanted to take it with her. She'd had it before and he hadn't.

'But I was tired,' Jean explained, 'and told him I didn't want to; that we'd do it another day. So he started freaking out at me, "You always do this, say you're going to do something and then you never do!" He was practically stamping his foot so just to shut him up I agreed and said, "Fine, I'll take the damn pill."

'When it started to come on we were both dancing around being idiots, but then he started to move close and I started to dance away. He said, "Why are you doing that when I know you're trying to flirt with me?" I told him he was getting the wrong impression because I wasn't flirting with him.

'Then I was worried about being stuck in the house with him like that, so I suggested we go out. He didn't want to at first, but then he never, you know, went out.'

'He had no friends,' Rachel added, 'and he never left the house, except once a week when he dashed out to buy groceries, which would take him half an hour – max.'

'Anyway, that night,' Jean continued, 'he told me he was paranoid about his acne scars and didn't have anything to wear. So I untucked his shirt from his jeans, and suggested I cover the scars with make-up. And I did, and he was really pleased. He thought he looked so much better, but that could have been the E.

'We went to Mybar but there was hardly anyone there. Martin kept trying to dance with me and I was trying to dance with another guy, so Martin got really jealous and said, "It seems to me that you're embarrassed to be seen with me."

'I said, "Mate, I'm your friend, just your friend. And I want to flirt with other people. Why don't you dance with that girl over there?" He said, "I think I'm growing attracted to you." And I told him, "Well, I'm not attracted to you, so don't worry about it."

'The next day I woke up a bit freaked out by the whole thing, and Rachel was home and I confided in her and that's when we started to become friends. We bonded over red wine and started going out to places together. After a few too many nights out we decided we totally needed to detox and get healthy, so we joined a gym together and did a big supermarket shop for vegies and healthy food.

'And there we were down in the kitchen, cooking and giggling, when Martin came down and absolutely freaked out at us. He was so angry he was, like, shaking with rage. "I know what you're doing. You're being friends to wind me up. Look at you. Going shopping, cooking dinner, not inviting me. You're ganging up on me!"

'Me and Rachel, we looked at each other and Rachel said, "Calm down man. We're just cooking dinner, it's no big deal."

'But he didn't calm down and after that he seemed to be angry all the time. It was like the better friends we became, the madder he got. He stayed in his room all the time and the only time he'd come down was to have a go at us. He was either angry or creepily sleazy.'

Jean then clarified that he wasn't sleazy around Rachel, because he knew she'd tell him to piss off; he'd always wait until Jean was alone in the house.

'One time,' she said, 'I was sitting in the lounge room watching TV and Martin came into the room holding a dildo and said, "Check it out. This is me and my ex's dildo. It has an extra fast motor. Touch it." I freaked out.

'Another time he asked if I'd ever seen A-porn before. I said no, so of course he said, "You haven't seen A-porn? You gotta see A-porn!" And he raced upstairs and back down again with a tape. It was a *private* porn movie, where they filmed girls auditioning; but the girls didn't know they were being filmed. That's what he loved about it. He said, "Other porn is so fake, but this is so real. Look at their facial expressions. They have no idea they're being filmed."

'I put *that* in my statement to the police,' Jean said. She also admitted to Rachel, after the fact, that she'd always had a sixth sense that she was being watched. It turned out Rachel had the same feeling, elaborating that Martin would sometimes come up with weird stuff he shouldn't know.

Jean agreed and said that once when she and Martin were talking, she'd asked him to guess what she'd wanted to do when she was 17. He had instantly replied, 'Work on a cruise ship.'

'Now this was true,' Jean said. 'I asked how he knew and he shrugged and said, "Most girls want to do that when they're 17."

'Yeah, right; I doubted that. I still had a brochure about cruise ships tucked away in one of my drawers so I suspected he'd been through my things. I didn't know how though because Rachel and I were so creeped out by him we always locked our doors when we went out.'

Rachel said, 'He'd tell us, "You know you don't have to lock your doors." How would he know we did, if he hadn't been trying the doors?'

'It got so bad in the end,' Jean said, 'that we didn't want to be home alone with him. We would call each other up and make sure we synchronised it so we'd get home at the same time.'

Jean and Rachel said that as well as watching *Big Brother*, Martin liked to go up onto the roof and look into other people's apartments through the telescope he had up there. He'd watch them for hours. The girls used to talk about being filmed, because they felt like they were under surveillance. They even searched the house a few times, but never found anything.

They talked about moving out, but it was hard to find somewhere good in their price range. Then something happened – the final straw – and they knew they had to get out, even if they couldn't find a place they liked.

'Rachel and I were watching telly one night,' Jean said, 'and Martin came down and asked if he could use my make-up. He was always at me to do things to him: put makeup on him, streak his hair. This time I said no. "Do you know how much the stuff costs?" I asked him. "It's over 50 bucks. Buy your own."

'Well he freaked. He went totally psycho.

'He started shouting, "I thought you were my friends. You know I have an issue with my acne scars. You know I'm not so confident. I can't believe you won't let me use it!"

'Rachel stuck up for me and said, "Actually, it's her stuff. You *should* buy your own."

'And he just went off again; he went crazy, shouting and stuff, totally out of proportion to the issue. We gave each other a look – like, who the fuck have we moved in with? We were so scared and we knew then we had to get out of there as soon as we could. We started looking for places, but didn't tell him in case he freaked out again.'

That weekend Jean was out at a solarium and Rachel was home, about to go out. She assumed Martin was lurking upstairs – he always was – but when she went down to the garage to get her car she realised his was missing. They were never left alone there. She couldn't believe that he was gone, so she called Jean straight away and told her to get her butt back there – so they could search his room.

Jean said she hurried home as soon as she could, but they were shit scared it might have been a trick and that he'd come back and bust them.

'We raced up the stairs and went in,' Jean said. 'Amazingly, it wasn't locked. I guess he thought we wouldn't dare.

'The room was hideously messy and dirty, with plates encrusted with food, and an ashtray overflowing with about six months worth of butts. I kept lookout on the balcony, so nervous I was jigging up and down, while Rachel went through his wardrobe first. She called me straight over, because there was the famous high-speed dildo and this *sculpture* of a vagina. Not something you buy at a sex shop but, like, a handmade plaster of Paris thing.

'There were also hundreds of porn tapes. That's where the cops found the footage Martin had recorded; on those legit porn tapes. Obviously we didn't know that then, but there would be about five minutes of porn and then his stuff would start up.'

Jean and Rachel then went through Martin's drawers, where they found some amphetamine tablets and an unemployment benefit form. It turned out their flatmate wasn't working at all, although they were in for a bigger shock when they came across the lease to the apartment.

Jean, still angry, said, 'We discovered the whole apartment only cost $320 a week. He was charging Rachel $140 and me $120, which meant he was only paying 60 bucks for the big room with the spa!'

They also found some stuff he'd printed off the internet, including instructions on how to pick locks. They tried to turn on his computer, but couldn't crack the password and then found a voice-activated tape recorder in the drawer.

'Rachel pressed play,' Jean said. 'It was music at first, and we were going to turn it off when we heard voices – *our* voices. He'd been recording our conversations. That's when Rachel said, "Babe, we have got to get out of here, now."'

Rachel recalled, 'I got Mum and my brother Scotty around the next day, for protection for when I told Martin I was leaving, and that Jean was too. He just went nuts, freaked out and almost got into a fight with Scotty. We got my stuff out straight away, and then went and picked Jean up from work and took her back to get her stuff.'

Jean took over the story again. 'Martin had taken my stereo and my CDs hostage and he wouldn't give them back. He stood over me, trying to intimidate me. He was staying stuff like, "So you're gonna move out on me too, and move in with that conniving bitch Rachel? Well good luck, she'll fuck you over too."

'He wasn't going to hand over the CD player until Rachel's mum threatened to call the police.'

Jean and Rachel stayed with Rachel's mum for a while, and eventually shared another flat together. They occasionally wondered if Martin might go completely off his head and turn into a serial killer – an exaggeration maybe, but as far as they were concerned they'd had a lucky escape. But their two months 'with a psycho flatmate in the pink penthouse' became little more than a dinner-party story – until a year later, when Jean was at work one day.

'The pharmacist, who'd been listening to the radio, called out to me, "You hear about that guy in a penthouse at Budds Beach who just got arrested for having secret cameras in girls' bathrooms and bedrooms? Didn't you used to live in a penthouse in Budds Beach?"

'I felt faint. Straight away I knew, my God, that's him. I rang the radio station and then the police but they wouldn't give me any information. I started crying uncontrollably and someone had to drive me home. I rang Rachel at work and told her. She knew it had to be him too.'

Rachel said, 'After I hung up the phone, my legs went out from under me. I collapsed and only just dragged myself up in time to make it to the toilet and throw up. I literally vomited when I found out.

'I rang the police and told them I thought I'd lived with the guy they'd arrested and a cop rang back and asked me if I had any tattoos. He said we had to come in and look through hours of videotape, taken from cameras hidden in the bathrooms and bedrooms, to see if we could identify ourselves.

'I felt sick all weekend. I couldn't eat. I thought of all the things that might have been on camera: me undressing, going to the toilet, putting in a tampon. And it wasn't just him who'd seen it, but all the cops as well.'

Jean continued, 'We were so freaked out, so scared, that we had to get pissed before we went into the police station, just to be able to deal with it. We recognised the apartment, the bedrooms and the bathrooms but, amazingly, we didn't see ourselves on the tapes. We don't know if he hadn't been recording then, or if he'd recorded us and gone over it with new footage. But we saw the other girls. He'd even put a camera in the laundry basin around waist height. You saw one shot where it didn't quite pick up her crotch, and in the next one it did. He'd been down there to adjust it.

'The cops hated him, thought he was arrogant. Apparently after we left the penthouse he changed his MO. He wouldn't wait for the girls to get creeped out and leave like we did, he'd kick them out himself. He'd get his footage of them, make up some excuse and kick them out so he had new ones to film. That's why he got busted; there were so many girls coming and going. The cops charged him with stalking; it was the only thing they could charge him with. We hoped he'd get a jail term. We wanted the bastard put away.'

The committal proceedings, held to determine if the case against Martin Craft should go to trial before a jury, took place on 8 November 2005 at Southport Magistrates Court. The proceedings didn't last long. The police prosecutor, Constable Jobberns, submitted witness statements for the magistrate to read: Jean's, Rachel's, the other girls who'd been filmed, and those of the investigating officers.

The defence lawyer, Moloney, also submitted something. He wanted the magistrate to have a look at a decision handed down in the District Court of Queensland where a judge had given a pre-trial ruling in a case that was, Maloney said, almost identical to Police v Craft.

The magistrate, Ron Kilner, went off to examine the documents. When he returned, Constable Jobberns said she believed it was inappropriate for the court to hear submissions from the defence at that time, before all the evidence was available for the court to look at.

The bench inquired as to what this other evidence was, and the constable told him it was videos. The magistrate then asked if the complainants were aware they were being videoed and the prosecution replied that there were inferences in their statements. The other girls seemed to have had the same feeling that Jean and Rachel had.

'They were aware they were being watched in some way,' Jobberns said.

'There were a couple of statements where they said they were frightened that they might be,' the magistrate countered.

'Yes, but they were that paranoid to go searching for cameras, anything, that could alleviate their fears.'

'But they didn't find anything. They didn't find anything, did they?'

'... They had an element of awareness.' Jobberns quoted from various statements: '"I felt like I was being watched ... I looked around a few times for a camera, I was that paranoid ... When I was home alone I would feel uneasy in my room, like someone was watching me."'

'On what objective basis did they have this awareness?' the magistrate asked.

'Call it women's intuition, Your Honour,' Jobberns replied.

The law defines stalking as a form of harassment; behaviour designed to intimidate or torment another person by such activities as following, watching, threatening or intimidating. For the behaviour to be an offence under the law it must reasonably 'cause you to fear violence to yourself, your property or to someone else or their property; cause you serious mental, psychological or emotional harm; prevent or hinder your actions; or cause you to act in a way you wouldn't in normal circumstances'.

The defence barrister pointed out that under this law, if the person who is being stalked is not aware of the stalking, then there is no apprehension or fear, and stalking can't be proven.

Magistrate Kilner told Jobberns that in a court of law women's intuition did not provide an objective basis for reaching the conclusion that the flatmates were aware of the surveillance.

Nobody was denying that Craft had videotaped the women without their consent, and the defence even mentioned how ironic it was that on that very day, new laws were being introduced into state parliament that would cover that exact offence.

Nobody denied that the secret filming was morally reprehensible either, but the magistrate reminded everybody that his was not a court of morals; rather, a court of law.

The stalking case was thrown out.

Craft pleaded guilty to wilful damage to the apartment, and was fined $1000. No conviction was recorded. If the new laws banning intimate, covert filming had been in effect, he would have faced up to two years behind bars.

The media were waiting for him when he left the courthouse. A reporter asked if he wished to apologise to the women he'd filmed; he did not. He ran away and jumped a fence to escape the cameras. He didn't seem to like it when they were pointed at him.

Jean and Rachel were understandably disappointed with the outcome.

'I still can't believe he got away with it,' Jean told me. 'We *knew* we were being filmed; all the girls did. We just couldn't find the cameras, they were too well hidden. As for no apprehension and fear – we were terrified of him in the end. I had a nightmare after I moved out. I dreamed that he tried to kill me; that he was in my room and he sliced my throat.'

Rachel did too. 'I dreamt we were back at that place, up in the roof, watching out for him, only this time he suddenly came in and went psycho.

'I knew he was a geek, but at first I really thought he was harmless. I didn't think he'd turn out to be a pervert. I've since read that that's how most of them start out, as peeping toms. What I've learned from this is to listen to my instincts, even though the law doesn't recognise them at all.

'If you think someone's dodgy then they probably are. If someone's creeping you out, don't be all nice and sweet and give them the benefit of the doubt – just get the hell out!'

An Awful Truth

Heather Osland: A Symbol of All that's Wrong with the Law.

Kathryn Deans

When does fear become intolerable? At what point does somebody say, 'Enough'?

> *Imagine you're asleep. It's a deep sleep because you're exhausted, worn out by another day in hell. Suddenly, somebody seizes a handful of your hair. You're jerked out of bed and dragged across the floor, dazed and terrified. He's talking, telling you what a useless bitch you are, and you realise you've done something wrong again, even though you'll probably never know what it is. Sprawled on the floor, trying to protect your face from his feet and fists, you hope it's going to be over quickly this time. But it never is. Deep down you know it's never going to end ...*

When do the scattered hours of wondering if you're going to get through another day become constant, or the dread that this time he's going to go too far become unbearable?

When *is* enough, enough?

Heather Marjorie Osland found the answer to that question on the evening of Wednesday 31 July 1991 when, in concert with her elder son David, she ended 13 long years of imprisonment. Convinced that he was saving his mother's life, David found a piece of metal pipe in the shed and walked into the bedroom.

Heather went with him, determined to help. Mother and son had no doubt that if Frank woke up, he would kill them both.

A few years later Heather Osland was tried and convicted in a Bendigo court of killing her abusive husband Frank. At the time she said, 'There was just so much fear. You've no idea. Every day there's so much fear you just can't think.'

So what leads a woman to take such an extreme way out? In Heather's case the last straw was bed knuckles.

Frank would regularly set tasks for Heather to do. In 1991 he was working on an old brass bed that he was putting together more or less piece by piece. On the day before he died, the task he set Heather was bed knuckles. She was to go out to an old antique store and get hold of some, so he could continue work on the restoration.

Unfortunately, the store didn't have any. Heather knew that her failure to obtain the knuckles would mean trouble. At the very least Frank would yell at her, but it was far more likely he would give her a beating.

It's hard to describe the atmosphere in the house in Moran Street in the days leading up to Frank's death. There was an escalating sense of tension, partly due to the presence of 24-year-old David in the house. In the week leading up to the 31st, Frank had ordered his stepson to go, threatening to 'chuck him out' like he'd done with Heather's youngest daughter Erica.

Throwing David out of the house would be the least of it though; Frank had been threatening a great deal more than that. He'd started saying that if David didn't get out, he'd kill him. But David stayed, worried that something terrible would happen to his mother if he didn't. And, despite Frank's threats, Heather had wanted her son to stay because she was terrified of being left alone with her husband.

It's difficult to explain, to those who have never experienced it, the feelings of somebody who lives in a brutal domestic war zone. There's a persistent sense that something unpleasant is always on the brink of happening.

The atmosphere was always strained in the Osland household as Frank had rules that had to be obeyed. Heather wasn't allowed to talk to her children, nor they to her. She and the children had to be home before him – and if they didn't make it he'd lock them out of the house, no matter what the weather – and Frank had to be served his meal first. Heather wasn't allowed to shower before him, go to sleep before him or have friends over.

Each day, before he went to work, Frank would outline what he expected Heather to do that day, and God help her if she didn't do what was expected.

On that last Tuesday, Heather's task was the bed knuckles and, after failing to obtain them, she and David were in such a fog of despair that they drove around aimlessly. They headed into the bush, parked the car and simply ... sat. They knew that there would be trouble that night and were consumed with a sense of desperation.

That helplessness led them out of the car and into the scrub where they decided to dig a hole. In many ways it was a symbolic act; there was no thought then that they might put Frank Osland in it. They simply decided to dig a hole.

Wednesday 31 July 1991

You could always tell the kind of mood Frank Osland was in as soon as he got out of the car when his mates dropped him off after work. Perversely, if he didn't look all that happy then there was a good chance he wouldn't be hitting anybody that night. But if he was smiling, or worse, laughing, then things were probably going to get ugly.

Heather spent years looking out the window, waiting for her husband to arrive home so she could look for the signs; anticipating what his behaviour would be. Each day as he headed up the driveway she'd pull back, careful not to be seen, and she'd listen to the sound of his boots, first on the concrete and then coming across the veranda. And all the while her chest would close over as she tried to suppress the age-old instinct that tells a human when they're in danger – flight or fight. Problem was, with Frank neither was an option.

Frank Osland was laughing when he arrived home that Wednesday evening. Heather's heart dropped at the sight, and with good reason. Much later, Heather and David told the police what happened when Frank walked in the door that night.

Heather had been to the hairdresser that day, and that was all it took to trigger an immediate, violent explosion. Frank entered their home, took one look at his wife and started ranting, furious that she'd gone and changed her hairstyle. When he was finished yelling about

Heather's hair he started on about David, demanding to know if her useless son had left yet.

David was in his room. He knew that the sight of him would trigger another unpleasant outburst and he didn't want to do anything that would aggravate Frank further.

But Heather told her husband that David was still there, so Frank took it – whatever it was – out on her. He slammed her back against the wall and hit her around the face.

Heather would later tell the police that she couldn't remember any of the things Frank had been yelling at her; that she could see his mouth moving but couldn't 'hear his words'. This a fairly common response, to repeated abuse, of women who live with a violent partner.

Frank was furious and began choking her, all the while screaming at her, telling her what a useless bitch she was and how he was going to kill her son.

When David heard Frank's bellowing he rushed out, tackled Frank and tried to pull him off his mother. Incensed, Frank turned and punched David in the face, dropping him to the floor.

As shocking as most people would find this scene, it was all too common in the Osland household. Frank was a violent man who believed in controlling his wife absolutely. He treated her as he would treat an animal: with ruthless mastery. As it is with many abusers, his control of Heather wasn't just physical, but psychological and sexual as well, and all designed to debase and degrade her on a daily basis.

Desperate to quieten her husband down and avoid further outbursts, Heather crushed up some of her sedatives and mixed them into the curry she'd made for his dinner. At that stage she only wanted him to settle down; for his anger to just...go away.

Frank only ate half his meal, claiming that she'd made it for David, not him. He pushed the plate, sending it crashing onto the floor, and stormed out of the house and down to the shed. He didn't stay out there long; the sedatives took effect and he was back inside within 15 minutes, swaying on his feet. He headed for the bedroom, kicked the door open and fell into bed.

Heather and David had been terrified, but now they were dead scared. It seemed inevitable that when he woke up Frank would question *why* he'd felt so groggy. They knew they were in serious trouble this time and doubted Frank would let it go with just a simple beating. For such a dire transgression, he might very well do what he'd been threatening to do for years: he might just kill them.

What to do? It was Heather who finally decided that enough was enough. She'd put up with her husband's brutality for 13 years and she couldn't face it any longer. That night, she was going to end it once and for all; she was going to kill him.

So mother and son discussed how they were going to go about it. Heather decided their best chance was to hit Frank while he was asleep. David told her that she wasn't strong enough to do it herself; that he'd have to be the one.

The young man didn't doubt for a minute that his mother was right about what would happen in the morning when Frank woke up and realised that his sleep had been too abrupt to be natural. David had witnessed the escalating violence in his stepfather, had felt the tension that hung over the house like a sickness while his mother had slipped like a shadow through it all, scared for her life. Kill or be killed; there didn't seem to be much choice in the matter.

For some time they argued about what to use, pacing through the rooms, whispering in case they made too much noise and woke Frank up. David decided to go and look in the shed; he came back with a length of pipe. It took several tries before he could work up the nerve to hit Frank, but finally he did it, with his mother beside him.

Heather told the police when they arrested her that it wasn't David's fault; he was only trying to save them both. Despite everything that had happened to them, it's hard to imagine the kind of courage needed to do what young David Albion did that night. But what followed was almost as traumatic.

Between the two of them, they managed to manoeuvre Frank into the car. It was still sheer terror that was driving Heather; she was shaking so hard she could barely help David carry the body. Frank was a big man, 1.79 metres tall and well over 80 kilos, much bigger than she was.

They took Frank to the hole they'd dug in the bush, placed him in it and covered him with dirt. Heather later said that the whole time they were doing that, she expected Frank to wake up and then it really would be all over, because they'd be the ones going in the hole.

When they were done, they went home. Then Heather remembered Frank's car so they drove it towards Melbourne and left it at a truck stop, certain, or hoping, that somebody would come along and steal it.

At that stage Heather had no particular story in mind for where Frank was. She thought, perhaps, she could just say he'd gone, that he'd taken off somewhere. There had been no plan; everything had been done in jolting, panicky steps. And despite the fact that Heather had seen her husband go into that hole, she was convinced he'd be back at any minute, and the fear made it hard for her to stop shaking. David was only marginally better and when they both finally went to bed that night it was in a state of dazed exhaustion.

The Battered Wife and the Abusive Husband

People who have never lived within an abusive relationship have a difficult time understanding why a woman stays with a man who abuses, degrades and ill-uses them. To them, the obvious question is: why doesn't the woman simply leave? The thing is that the real question is: why *couldn't* she leave? Or even better: why does she stay?

Why do the victims of abuse feel that they have to stay with their abusers?

Battered Woman Syndrome came into prominence in the 1980s when it was introduced in court as a mitigating defence in murder trials. Studies of women, who'd been the victims of abusive relationships where the husband had inflicted extraordinary control over them, revealed that most of them shared similar traits. The women had low self-esteem, were frequently depressed, and they usually hid their abuse from the world. It was discovered they were, are, ashamed of the abuse because they're convinced they are to blame for the way they are treated.

Battered women constantly relive their experiences, which traps them in a state of heightened awareness but can make their thinking cloudy and unfocused. Many believe that if they leave, their abuser will come after them and hurt their children or family.

There have been parallels drawn between BWS and Stockholm Syndrome. The latter is a condition where people who are kidnapped often end up sympathising with their captors. The abused partner in a marriage is akin to a kidnap victim, held hostage in their own home with threats or acts of violence, but where any small kindness can convince them that their abuser will change, that things will get better and life will improve.

Victims of BWS have an elevated sense of danger because they basically live their lives according to someone else's moods. They have to be endlessly vigilant for signs and signals that will hint at their partner's state of mind; for the indicators that will allow them to modify their own behaviour accordingly.

If their abuser is angry or annoyed, they become placating, or they go quiet, hoping not to attract attention or, at least, to allow their partner's anger to be diverted elsewhere. Sometimes, however, it is this very passivity that enrages their abuser.

Prior to taking up with Frank Osland, Heather was a bright, positive personality who ran her own business and had a wide group of friends. After entering into the relationship with Frank, however, her behaviour began to change. She developed a poor self-image and started suffering from profound bouts of depression, for which she took antidepressants.

Frank disliked her attracting the interest of other men. He regularly told her that she was so ugly that no man would look at her, or he would burst into a jealous rage and accuse her of behaving like a slut.

Heather's friendships dropped off because Frank disliked her having friends in the house. If they did visit, they rarely came back because he made them so uncomfortable.

Abusive, controlling men usually remove the other important relationships in their victims' lives. They want their wife, or partner or girlfriend, to be entirely dependent on them, without any kind of support or, most importantly, any avenue of escape. By alienating friends and family, their victims have no choice but to rely on them alone.

To a certain extent, Frank Osland did the same to all four of Heather's children. They were forbidden to have friends around, and were not allowed to go to other children's houses after school. Without those opportunities, normal childhood bonds couldn't really be formed and the kids were pretty much alone.

> *She had to catch the kettle before it boiled. It wasn't allowed to whistle. If Frank heard it whistling he'd come into the kitchen, fists balled, telling her that she'd done it again; that he didn't like the water that hot, she knew he didn't like the water that hot; what the hell was she, stupid or something? And then he'd hit her because he had to teach her, he had to punish her, because she should understand the way he wanted things in his own house.*

There is a recognised 'pattern of abuse' in relationships that involve violently dominant men and passive women. The first is the tension-building stage where negative feelings start to pile up within the abusers. During this stage, such men subject their victims to minor physical or verbal abuse. The violence then becomes progressively more severe until it escalates into an acute battering incident. It's at this stage that women are most likely to be badly hurt or killed.

Just like steam from a pressure valve, the abusers' stress is released by any intense outburst and their tension levels are relieved. Often much calmer afterwards, they may even show contrition for their behaviour, and will usually apologise. These men nearly always promise to change, even though they believe their wife or partner, their victim, is at fault; that they were driven to such violent lengths.

Frank Osland was a model of the abusive husband. He needed to be in control. From the day Heather and her four children moved in with him, he laid down the law – his own personal and rigid rules and regulations. Initially Heather had laughed; she'd thought he was joking. But it didn't take long at all before she realised that he was deadly serious.

In Frank Osland's house, he was God. He told his wife that he owned the very air she breathed and, like most victims of Battered Woman Syndrome, she came to believe him. He controlled her life, her actions, and her responses to almost every aspect of living.

The most extraordinary thing was that Heather Osland found the courage to break free.

The most disturbing thing was that the courts found her guilty of murder, and sentenced her to 14 years in jail. In effect, she swapped one prison for another.

Dr Kenneth Byrne, a clinical and forensic psychologist, gave evidence about Battered Woman Syndrome during Heather's trial. He testified that, having spoken to Heather and reviewed the evidence, he was convinced she had been living within a battering relationship.

Unfortunately, supporting evidence regarding Frank's violent history was ruled to be inadmissible. Why this was so, is inexplicable. Nothing else could explain the events that took place that evening in 1991 more clearly than the individual instances of Frank's cruelty to his family. Considering her situation, and the fact that Heather fitted so well into the category of a battered wife, there was a very strong case for diminished responsibility.

Part of the problem at the time of the trial, however, was that Heather was suffering from post-traumatic stress disorder. She couldn't verbalise all the terrible things that she'd been through, either to the police or in court. Her mind had been so damaged by her years with Frank that it took a long time for memories to shake free to the point where she could talk about them. Heather, quite simply, tried to block out the horror. There was no doubt it was a survival mechanism, but in many ways Heather became her own worst enemy. She was unable to defend herself, becoming confused and bewildered when questions were put to her. Considering what she had suffered through, you would think this was perfectly understandable.

Unfortunately, that's not how a jury saw it.

Frank Osland

Frank Osland lay undisturbed in that hole for three and a half years. It says a lot about a man that nobody, not even his mother, was interested enough to come looking for him. In the large country town of Bendigo, he'd made few friends and had been fired from five jobs in the area. Not only did he have an uncertain, violent temper but he was apparently dishonest and inclined to steal stock from his employers.

His last job was at a quarry in Axedale about 20 minutes' drive from town. Frank had been unable to get a job in Bendigo as he'd developed too much of a reputation as a troublemaker. Nobody was willing to take on a man who was probably going to cause them grief, and sooner rather than later.

As is often the case with such men, Frank blamed Heather for his inability to hold down a job.

Born in 1948, Frank's real surname, until he changed it himself, had been Bratuza. His mother Maria had come to Australia from Gratz in Austria and had spent time interned in a camp in New South Wales. Even when he was young, Frank had been a violent child, lashing out at people physically. If he'd ever undergone a psychological evaluation, there seems little doubt that he would have been diagnosed as psychotic.

The men he'd worked with in the mining town of Karratha in Western Australia had treated him with wary caution. He was considered 'extreme' and prone to bouts of uncontrolled aggression.

One fellow worker, Lindsay McDermott, recalled how Frank had gone to a session of tae kwon do. While they were going through the warm-up, Frank lost control completely and kicked McDermott in the nose, breaking the tip of it. There was no reason for him to lash out; he simply lost it.

McDermott also remembers a woman Frank lived with before Heather moved in. He said Margaret and her daughter Katrina were occasionally seen dragging a tea-chest with their possessions down the road, trying to get away while Frank was at work. He always found them and brought them back. Another acquaintance remembers seeing Frank and Margaret together shortly before she disappeared; he was holding a gun to her head.

Nobody is quite sure what happened to Margaret or her daughter; it's possible – because the alternative is too awful – that she planned her last escape more carefully and finally managed to get away.

> *Sometimes Frank would drag her out of the house naked, and take her down to the shed. He'd slam her against the wall and tell her that he was going to use his staple gun to nail her up. 'Who'd miss you? Nobody gives a shit if you're alive or dead.' She'd be crying, terrified, imagining the staples piercing her skin, imagining being left to hang there …*

Years later the sound of one of the guards using a staple gun in prison sent Heather into such a state of panic that it took two guards and a prisoner to calm her struggles. It wasn't until that moment that she remembered the staple gun, the shed, and Frank's threats to leave her hanging.

Frank's cruelty to animals was a clear indication that he demonstrated psychopathic behaviour, with uncontrollable episodes of rage or, upon occasion, a coldness that must have been chilling.

There was, for example, the case of Frank's young Staffordshire terrier. Frank insisted that Heather and the children not touch the dog, ever. It was supposed to be 'a one-man dog' and he didn't want anybody but himself handling him. The dog used to sleep on the floor on Frank's side of the bed but during the night it would slip over to sleep next to Heather, sensing a more sympathetic nature. The children, too, had a hard time not patting him as the dog actively sought out affection.

So, one day, Frank took his rifle and shot the dog in front of Heather's youngest two children, Paul and Erica. He told the shocked pair that if the dog wasn't going to be a one-man animal, then it wasn't going to be anything at all.

On another occasion Frank brought home Luke, a young German shepherd, as a guard dog. He tied the dog to the clothes line on a short leash so the animal could barely move and told Heather not to give it any food or water. The dog was half savage from dehydration and hunger but Heather, unable to bear the poor creature's suffering, would come home early from work and give Luke water. Frank lost his temper with the dog so badly once that he beat it with a piece of four-by-two wood.

As soon as the man of the house left, Heather took Luke to the vet, although getting him into the car proved difficult as the poor dog couldn't stand up or walk. When she finally got to the clinic, she couldn't get him out of the car, and when the vet and the nurse approached Luke, he snapped at them, half-crazed with pain. They finally managed to sedate him but Frank had beaten the dog so badly that his hip was smashed, as were all the bones in its rear leg and the ribs on one side of the body. The vet had no choice but to put Luke down.

His behaviour towards the creatures in his care indicates the kind of personality Frank Osland was; but his cruelty and violent tendencies weren't limited to animals. If Heather or the children made him angry, he liked nothing better than to get out his rifle and threaten to shoot them all. The children would discuss which of them would die first.

On a visit to Melbourne he became enraged when the driver in front of him was too slow off the mark, and Frank missed the lights. He exploded out of his car, stormed up to the luckless motorist in front and began kicking the driver's door panel in. The man behind the wheel was, luckily for him, too terrified to get out.

Frank also objected to people walking down the footpath in front of his house. He claimed that their dogs were 'shitting all over the place' and he took to hurling abuse or, on several occasions, bricks at the offenders. The locals learned to cross the street to pass on by. There were dozens of other instances of antisocial and aggressive behaviour from Frank, and cruelty to animals and strangers alike. But he saved the worst for his family, the people he was supposed to care about.

> *The bath water was never allowed to be too deep. If she ran too much water he would hold her head beneath it, half drowning her, keeping her under until unconsciousness threatened. When she ran a bath of her own, she would always kneel in the water because sometimes, if he was in a foul mood, he would come at her and it was easier to keep her head above water if she wasn't sitting down.*

Heather hasn't had a bath in years and it's doubtful she ever will again. She still has nightmares about water closing over her head and being unable to breathe.

Although it is difficult to say with any certainty without a doctor's evaluation, it seems quite likely that Frank Osland was suffering something along the lines of dissocial personality disorder. This is usually characterised by an inability to care about the feelings of others; an inability to tolerate any kind of frustration; outbursts of violence, usually brought about by the inability to deal with the frustration; and a tendency to blame others for anything that goes wrong in their lives.

Unfortunately these types of people, most of whom are male, don't come with a warning sign stapled to their foreheads. They often appear to be charming or, at the very least, pleasant and normal.

In the years that Heather had known Frank before they got together – he'd been a workmate of her then-husband Alan in Karratha so she'd seen him on a semi-regular basis – she'd always thought of him as a nice guy, a hard worker with a good sense of humour. One of the reasons she decided to take a chance and enter into a relationship with Frank was that she thought he'd be a great role model for her two boys.

She wasn't the first woman – and won't be the last – to make such a mistake with 'a man just like Frank'. Unfortunately people who suffer from the kind of psychological disorder he had don't have any trouble *establishing* relationships; it's what comes afterwards, when the facade they present to the world is allowed to drop away behind closed doors, that their true natures are revealed. And by that time, it is often too late to get out, because if there's one thing men like that are very good at, it's dividing and conquering.

Women don't generally expect to have relationships that are going to damage or scar them. Most of the time they act in good faith, just as Heather did when she agreed to move in with Frank Osland.

But it's interesting to note that, after Frank's body was found, very few people came forward to mourn him. He was considered to be a loose cannon; a man who could lash out at a moment's notice, who caused trouble on the job, who could display outbursts of violence if things didn't go his way.

Back in Karratha, Lindsay McDermott had called him an angel at work and a demon at home. But despite the fact that he could be an excellent tradesman, he was treated with caution by those who worked with him. McDermott was surprised when he heard on the news that Frank Osland had been killed. He'd always expected that it would be Heather whose body would turn up one day.

February 1995

Traumatised by the killing of his stepfather, David made a drunken confession to his younger brother Paul one night when they were in the garden. It was three-and-a half years after the fact. Paul was astonished. That his brother, a gentle quiet-natured man, had done such a thing – could have done it – was incredible. Sure, they'd all wanted Frank out of their lives, and God knows they'd all been despairing enough to wish him dead, but Paul had never thought it would happen. He knew David must have been desperate to have taken such a step. Unfortunately for David and Heather, Paul wasn't the best confidant. Unwisely, Paul himself spoke of it and Frank's fate soon came to the ears of the police.

Bendigo is a country town where gossip is a way of life, and there had been a great deal of speculation about just where Frank Osland had taken off to. Not that anyone cared, but he had mentioned moving to Queensland so people wondered if that's where he'd ended up. They figured he'd either gone north or somebody had finally done something about him; after all, ugly endings were often the fate of violent, unpleasant men. One thing seems clear: nobody asked too many questions.

But with whispers of Frank's possible murder becoming more insistent, it seemed maybe there was a more sinister connotation to the man's sudden disappearance. The police applied for and obtained permission to tap Heather's phone, and they also took her younger son Paul in for questioning.

The police offered Paul $10,000 if he'd tell them everything he knew about the disappearance of his stepfather. In effect they wanted him to dob on his own mother and brother. Paul didn't take the money but he *was* in a bad way. He was a drug addict and unstable because of it, and, after hours of questioning, he admitted that David had told him that he, along with his mother, had killed Frank.

That was enough for the police. They arrived at the Moran Street house in force to arrest a shocked and horrified Heather Osland. They went through the place with hurricane force, pulling up carpets and turning the place inside out in their search for evidence.

For nearly four years Heather had been living the quiet life she had always craved. She had a bevy of pets that she was devoted to, spent a lot of time in the garden, socialised with friends, and worked hard at her job.

There was only one thing that hadn't changed and that was her fear of Frank Osland. It didn't matter that she knew he was dead, that he'd never be coming back again, because a part of her mind could not accept it. Not a day went by when she didn't listen for the sound of his boots coming across the veranda. His hold on her was still so strong that the rules he had instilled in her over the years continued to dominate her. She never let the kettle fully boil, she hadn't been able to take a bath, food was still cooked exactly the way Frank had liked it …

His grip on her – and the fear that had been such a central part of her life – had lessened a little; but he was still controlling her, even from the grave. And then the police came.

She was taken from her house to the police station where officers began their long interrogation. Initially Heather remained silent, but when they began discussing the part David had played in his stepfather's death she spoke up. She told them that it was all her idea, that David had only been trying to save her. If anybody was to be punished for what happened to Frank Osland, then let it be her.

The flood gates having opened, Heather cooperated fully. She took them to Frank's grave. She told them what had happened that night and she did her best to tell them why. Reliving the events was terrible but she was desperate to convince the police that David had only acted to protect her.

After Frank's death, David had returned to the Western Australia mining town of Karratha, but it wasn't long after Heather's interrogation that the police arrested him and brought him back to Victoria.

As Heather had very little money, legal aid was organised for her, with her house as collateral. (To this day she owes an enormous debt to Legal Aid that she hasn't a hope of repaying). When she was released on bail, however, she arranged legal representation for her son as he had nobody to defend him.

Heather's bail supervisor, Christa Mamot, worked hard gathering evidence and information for the trial. Felicity Hampel, now a judge with the County Court, but at the time a Senior Counsel, was Heather's barrister. From the outset they, and David's counsel Aaron Schwartz, decided that Heather and David must try for a self-defence plea. It was, after all, the truth and their best chance of avoiding a guilty verdict.

Everybody considered that Heather fell squarely beneath the banner of Battered Woman Syndrome and they sought expert testimony on her behalf. That whole period was a confusing blur for

Heather as she met with her legal council and they went over the details of her life. The post-traumatic stress she suffered meant she couldn't enunciate everything that had happened to her – not then anyway. Heather's children, however, were more than happy to tell what life had been like living with Frank Osland.

At Heather and David's trial, presided over by Justice Hedigan in Bendigo, the prosecution claimed that mother and son had planned and executed a 'coolly premeditated murder' – ostensibly for financial gain. Those rumours, before his 'disappearance', of Frank going off to Queensland were the basis of that theory. He would have, the prosecution claimed, taken half of everything that he and Heather owned.

While there appeared to be no solid evidence that Frank was actually planning to go anywhere, there's no question that Heather would have, in fact, been glad to see the back of him. As she had bought houses prior to her relationship with Frank, and as it was she who was in steady employment, the idea that Heather killed Frank for financial gain was preposterous. There's no doubt she could have survived on her own.

The main thrust to support the prosecution, however, was that of premeditation. That hole that Heather and David had dug together in the bush came back to haunt them, along with the sedatives she'd put in his meal. The police seemed unable to conceive that the pair hadn't planned Frank's death in advance.

Mind you, there is the notion that the police were, to a certain extent, also culpable for what happened to Frank Osland. It could be argued that their failure to give assistance to Heather and her children was a failure in their duty of care. The local police knew about Frank; they had been called out to the Osland household when Heather had been looking for help. While police records showed that only one visit had been recorded, Justice Hedigan acknowledged that there were many other instances when the police hadn't bothered to record the call or the visits, and that this was due to 'incompetence, laziness or exclusion'.

Is it ironic, or just plain tragic, that not only does it appear that they let Heather down in their duty to protect her from a violent husband, but they then prosecuted her for taking matters into her own hands?

And if the police failed Heather, then so too did her doctor. This man treated her for constant bouts of chronic urinary tract infections from 1982 to 1991. Frank brutalised Heather in the bedroom, raping her anally and vaginally. His attacks were so savage that Heather had to be treated for extensive tearing on more than one occasion. Her doctor admitted that he suspected that something wasn't quite right at home and even made note of possible 'marital problems' in Heather's file; but he didn't report the incidents. He did treat Heather for depression, prescribing medication after she suffered a nervous breakdown, so there was ample evidence that something really *wasn't* right in Heather's household.

The AMA is currently reviewing doctors' obligations to their patients and is working to ensure that some kind of reporting is put into place if abuse is suspected. While these reforms show that deficiencies are being highlighted, it all comes a little too late for women like Heather Osland, whose fate might have been very different if she and her family had received the support of the community.

Despite the expert testimony as to the state of Heather, her marriage and life in the Osland household, the prosecution convinced the jury that neither the hole that the two accused had dug, nor the sedatives they used, indicated an act of self-defence.

(Since Heather's trial, the laws concerning what constitutes self-defence have undergone a revamp, with new legislation coming into place to allow a much broader interpretation of the meaning.)

The trial lasted 22 days, in September and October 1996, and the jury deliberated for four days. On Wednesday 2 October, they found Heather Osland guilty of the murder of Frank Osland, and on Monday 11 November 1996 she was sentenced to 14 years' jail, with a minimum of nine-and-a-half.

Ironically, again, while Heather was convicted of murder, the jury could not reach a decision about David. A retrial was ordered for the young man who had actually delivered the blow that killed his stepfather. It took place in December 1996 and that time the jury had no qualms about agreeing on David's motivation. They came back with a verdict of not guilty due to self-defence.

It still seems absurd that the woman, being protected by her son, and who didn't wield the instrument of Frank Osland's death, should be convicted of his murder.

It's a 'legal' discrepancy that has frustrated and enraged Heather's supporters for years.

The Appeal

The inconsistency of the verdicts between the two cases formed the basis of an appeal to the High Court in Canberra in 1998. Dr Jocelynne Scutt, a leading feminist lawyer, agreed to take on Heather's appeal. She contended that David's verdict, delivered after his mother's, should have thrown Heather's conviction into question. After all, how could one of the two people accused of murdering Frank Osland be innocent by reason of self-defence while the other, the one that didn't actually do the killing, be guilty?

Dr Scutt contended that Heather's sentence should be quashed, and a retrial should be held.

The Release Heather Osland Support Group worked tirelessly to bring the injustice of the case to the attention of the state government by drafting letters and generating as much publicity as possible. They also wanted to bring Heather's situation onto the radar of the general public, to tell as many ordinary people as possible.

On 23 and 24 April 1998 Dr Scutt argued her case in front of five High Court judges. She argued the inconsistency of the verdicts, and the misdirection of the trial judge to properly instruct the jury. Justice Hedigan, Dr Scutt maintained, was clearly not in favour of Heather's plea of self-defence and provocation. He seemed to think that her appeal rested on Battered Woman Syndrome, which it didn't. BWS was a supporting factor in the plea of self-defence, but that was all. Dr Scutt said that his summing up also mentioned Heather's 'lies' and her 'motive' for killing Frank. As a jury tends to listen to the trial judge, perhaps it wasn't so surprising that they brought back a guilty verdict.

While Dr Scutt convinced two of the High Court judges, she had no luck with the other three, resulting in a 3–2 decision. Heather's appeal for a retrial was denied. It was a real blow to a woman who was already into the second year of a possible 14-year sentence.

Prison Years

Heather had been sent to the minimum security facility, Tarrengower Correctional Prison for Women, in Malden. She knew, better than anyone, just how much her family was suffering from her incarceration. Her four children had already been through so much, and having a mother in prison for murder was hardly going to help any of them deal with the past.

No matter how well run a correctional facility might be, prison is not a nice place to spend time. For a quiet, frightened woman like Heather Osland, it was yet another trauma for her to endure. The members of a prison population are obviously there for a reason. They all had their own stories and had probably broken the law; but many women in prison, like Heather, also had relative degrees of guilt.

Heather shared her space with other women who had committed a variety of offences, often drug related. It was hard to get used to the rules and regulations, the regimented days, the lonely nights. After every visit from solicitors, family or friends the wardens made her strip down to her skin. It was a routine indignity that all inmates had to endure; part of a penal system that was trying to control the supply of drugs into the place. For Heather, an intensely private woman, it was deeply disturbing.

Her philosophy became 'one day at a time' – an attitude it was necessary to adopt, if she was going to survive. She focused on each small thing she had to look forward to, such as visits from the family or her growing league of supporters; and letters of support and treasured pictures of her grandchildren. She made her children's children knitted dolls and bears. They were intricate and beautiful creations – the only thing she *could* do for them behind bars.

Determined to do something for herself, Heather completed TAFE courses in horticulture and IT. She was a model prisoner but that's hardly surprising; nobody who ever met Heather Osland could think of her as anything but a caring, compassionate woman.

After serving nine and a half years – her minimum sentence – Heather was granted parole and released from Tarrengower. On Friday 22 July 2005 she was greeted by her children, her supporters and the media.

You'd think that would be the end of the story and that Heather could settle back into society. Unfortunately, life isn't always like that …

Frank's Legacy

Frank Osland claimed he owned the very air that Heather breathed. He told her that she'd never get away from him. A bullet, he'd tell her, travels further than a restraining order.

He took a bright, positive, buoyant personality and made her scared of her own shadow, terrified for her children's safety and her own. He sexually assaulted several of her children and left all four with psychological scarring that will be with them for the rest of their lives.

He damaged the bonds that should – and did – exist between Heather and her daughters. Paul and Erica (who'd been nine and seven when the family moved in with Frank in 1977) both have a history of drug abuse that they have battled for years. Her eldest child Sharon (12 in 1977) has determined that she will live her life without her mother, a decision that has hurt Heather deeply.

The tragedy is that even though the man who inflicted so much damage is out of their life, he haunts them still. Heather's children were each awarded compensation for the pain they suffered, but the truth is, no amount of money can make the past go away.

As for Heather ...

As a convicted criminal, she's not entitled to any kind of financial restitution. She is on parole and is forced to abide by the conditions of that parole until she's 65 years old. She cannot sell her house – the one that she shared with Frank – because the money would have to go to Legal Aid, and she'd have nothing with which to start over. It's difficult also to find a job because of her history.

All Heather Osland wants is to have a decent life. Her dream is to be reunited with her four children, under the one roof; to be a family again. But the past won't let her go and she has to live with the legacy of her abusive marriage. Her 13 years of hell with Frank was followed by nearly a decade of incarceration. She was punished again for finally deciding that enough was enough, that she would no longer live in the shadow of death.

The awful truth is, there was no justice for Heather Osland in Victoria. The very things that should have helped her – the police and the legal system – collaborated against her, leaving her faith in the law in tatters.

Such is the strength of her personality, however, that she will survive, and she now reaches out to others who are suffering the same nightmare she once had to endure, as an advocate for the silent pleas of abused women everywhere.

One way or another, Heather Osland will continue to fight.

Due Process

Robin Bowles

Bernard Munro's daughter Birgit, de facto wife of Dr Neil Boyce, died suddenly on Tuesday 31 March 1992. Birgit's father has never been able to satisfy his need to find out why she died. Establishing the cause of her death haunts and obsesses him, and has cost him and others dearly. Six years after he lost his daughter, his wife Brigitte died – of a broken heart.

For years this retired computer analyst pursued his quest as it snaked its way through intrigue and innuendo, trying to decipher the complicated languages of the medical and legal fraternities, taking the battle from the Coroner's Court in Melbourne to the Supreme Court, and all the while sliding surely from relative prosperity to near penury.

Many became tired of his persistence; some wanted his questions silenced for good. After the death of his wife, Bernard Munro seemed to give up. To those who did ask what had stopped him in his tracks after five years' relentless pursuit, he always gave the same answer: 'I couldn't afford to go on.'

In early 2000, however, Bernard received a letter on state Attorney-General's letterhead, in answer to a request some of his supporters had made on his behalf in July 1999. They had asked for help and financial reimbursement for the personal money Bernard had spent, on what some saw as the state's responsibility of trying to establish the cause of his daughter's death.

The letter, signed by the Attorney-General himself, read, 'Having closely examined all of the relevant considerations, I have determined that it is appropriate to grant you an ex-gratia payment of $25,000 on the basis set out on the enclosed deed of settlement regarding this matter. I would be pleased if you would return the executed deed to me at your convenience so that I may arrange for payment to be made.'

Ex-gratia payments from governments to ordinary citizens are very rare. So what was the reason behind this unusual offer?

I first heard about Birgit's unresolved death over Christmas drinks with a friend at the end of 1996. I learnt of the grief and confusion her family and friends had, and still have, about the conflicting expert opinions regarding the case. They were dissatisfied with the Coroner's finding and wanted the case reopened.

When someone dies in action in a war, or goes missing without a trace, or dies without an understandable cause of death, then there is no peaceful closure in the minds and hearts of those who mourn. There is also a sense of them reaching from the grave until there is resolution. That is how Birgit's friends and family felt.

In the middle of 1997 my friend urged me to contact Bernard Munro. She told me that people were becoming concerned that Bernard was very depressed because he'd come so far and was still no closer to achieving his goal. She said he had interviewed dozens of people and collected a huge amount of technical material, but he was just one grieving old man against the entire weight of the legal system. My friend thought, as many people do, that a story in some public arena might influence the course of justice. This rarely happens, but I agreed to talk to him anyway.

Bernard Munro told me he would like this story to be told, but an appeal from Dr Boyce, against a Supreme Court order that he had obtained to reopen the inquest into his daughter's death, was pending. Bernard couldn't discuss the case right then, but said he'd be very happy to tell me everything afterwards.

I told I would get back to him. I was becoming interested in his single-minded journey through the corridors of power. I was keen to discover if the light at the end of the tunnel he was traversing would actually illuminate the cause of justice.

Bernard's story is one of pain and loss. It demonstrates the pressures that can be exerted on someone who is vulnerable, through loss and obsession, and highlights the failure of the due process of the law – because an old man ran out of money.

Bernard Munro's story goes like this.

The day before she died, 36-year-old Birgit Munro dropped by her parents' home to show off her new car. A healthy, highly qualified nursing sister, Birgit was her usual happy self. After leaving her parents, she attended her regular Monday German lesson at 5.30pm – her teacher noticed nothing amiss – then Birgit went home to her partner of 10 years, Dr Neil Boyce. Both Birgit and Boyce, a renal specialist, worked at Monash Medical Centre.

That Monday night, as was usual, while Birgit attended her German class Boyce prepared the evening meal, which they ate in front of the TV. 'That was our sloth night,' Boyce later told police.

Birgit had been suffering from intermittent diarrhoea during the preceding week, which was apparently very unusual for her.

'She was as fit as a trout,' Boyce said later. 'She used to regard a cold every two or three years as a complete affront.'

After a couple of bites of her meal that night, however, Birgit collapsed on the floor, ashen. Boyce was stricken. He tried to get a pulse but, in his panic, at first he couldn't. Birgit revived, looked at him and said, 'You silly prick, of course I've got a pulse; you just can't feel it.'

He helped her to the bathroom and insisted she should go to hospital. Birgit, like many nurses, was not keen on hospitals or becoming a patient, and especially didn't want to arrive in an ambulance.

Boyce agreed to phone a neighbour, medical colleague Professor Steve Holdsworth, to drive her to the Mercy Hospital where Boyce was well known. After calling Holdsworth, Boyce then phoned Dr Cade, another colleague for whom he did occasional locums. Cade practised at the Mercy and Boyce asked him to get a bed ready for Birgit and facilitate her admission.

This request was not unusual. As an ex-nurse myself, I know the medical fraternity always looks after its own.

When they arrived Dr Cade, true to his promise, admitted Birgit himself. 'I was in the Specialist Care Unit when she arrived and attended her immediately,' he said. 'She said she had been well, apart from a urinary tract infection (self-treated), until she developed a profuse watery diarrhoea on Monday 23 March.'

Birgit was well enough at that time to give Cade her own history.

Cade commenced immediate intravenous treatment for shock, extreme nausea and infection, but she continued to dry retch in spite of anti-emetics being given intravenously. Cade ordered many samples to be taken for culture and close nursing observation.

Birgit's parents were notified but, due to the lateness of the hour, Boyce suggested that he stay with Birgit and they should come the following day.

At 7.30 the next morning, Cade called in consultant physician cardiologist, Dr William Heath, who reviewed Birgit's condition and agreed with Cade's provisional diagnosis of 'enteritis with generalised septicaemia and toxic manifestations'. He referred her to a neurologist because of her drowsy state and, in consultation with Dr Cade, ordered more antibiotics and other treatment.

Boyce phoned Birgit's sister, Barbara, who lived in Tasmania, to inform her of Birgit's sudden collapse. Barbara obtained the first available flight to reach her sister's bedside, having understood, from the phone conversation she'd had with Boyce, that her sister's condition was critical.

Birgit's mother, Brigitte, takes up the story. 'On Tuesday 31 March, Neil rang around 6am. Neil said to come in, it was urgent. I arrived about 7am. Birgit looked awful with big black circles around her eyes.

'Neil was there and a couple of nurses. Dr Tomlinson, a neurologist, had just arrived to examine Birgit. He said Birgit responded well and there was no brain damage resulting from the coma she'd gone into earlier in the morning.

'Birgit seemed to have improved at lunchtime. I recall her saying how nice it was to have us all there. Later on, they connected her to a monitor. She was very weak, but her eyes were clear. I recall Birgit was breathing very heavily. Her veins looked like ropes on the side of her neck.

'I said, "Please connect her to a machine so she doesn't have to labour so hard. Her heart could get damaged." The nursing sister said her heart was fine and her lungs were working normally.'

This 'laboured breathing' is known as acidotic breathing, a body's means of trying to expel the build-up of acid, or carbon dioxide, in the system. The lungs strain to improve the gaseous exchange of oxygen, to counteract the high levels of carbon dioxide in the bloodstream.

At one stage, late in the afternoon, Birgit whispered to her sister and mother, 'Thank you for looking after me.' They both felt, later on, that she knew she was dying and was saying goodbye.

The family members went home to eat at about 6pm and returned around 8pm. Boyce then left to eat, returning at about 10pm. Around 8.30pm, Birgit's condition had deteriorated. Dr Cade visited and an oxygen mask was put on Birgit.

Her mother recounted later, 'At about 10.25, Neil said to us, "Birgit will settle down for the night, why don't you go and get some sleep."

'I didn't want to go,' she said. 'Birgit had her eyes closed, but she nodded; she understood.'

As they were leaving the hospital, however, they heard an alarm and rushed back upstairs – knowing instinctively it was Birgit. They saw Boyce in Birgit's room with the nurse, desperately trying to revive her, but they – Brigitte, Bernard and Barbara – were not allowed in. A nun came and asked them if they wanted to pray with her.

'I wasn't in a condition to do anything,' Brigitte said. 'Barbara and I just cried. Some time later, the door opened and Neil said, "She's gone."

'They eventually let us into the room. A sister came with us and Neil. We just had time to kiss Birgit and then the sister moved us out. I said, "Can't I go in and kiss her once more?" and after I kissed Birgit again she moved me out. I was just quietly crying.'

Night sister Susan Lonergan, who'd taken the handover from the afternoon staff, describes Birgit's last minutes. 'I noticed a change in Birgit's rhythm on the central monitor [in the sisters' station]. I did a 12 lead ECG on Birgit. There were gross changes.'

Thinking Birgit looked moribund, Sister Lonergan commenced emergency procedures. She said later that when the resuscitation staff arrived, Boyce 'left straight away. Once he left the room, he was punching the wall and shouting'.

Shortly afterwards, it was decided to discontinue resuscitation.

'I informed Neil, who was extremely distressed,' Sister Lonergan said. 'I recall [Birgit's] mother being able to comfort the other family members as well as Neil. She told me what a perfect couple they were.'

Following Birgit's death, Doctors Cade and Heath maintained their provisional diagnosis of toxic enterocolitis (a severe form of bowel inflammation caused by a toxin in the body). However, neither felt confident enough to sign a death certificate stating that cause of death. Dr Cade later said in a statement to the police, 'I cannot say what caused Birgit Munro's death and would not presume to do so.'

The next day, Wednesday 1 April, Birgit's mother phoned family friend, and State Ombudsman, Norman Geschke. Norman's son Phillip had been married to Birgit before she began living with Dr Boyce. Phillip and Birgit's divorce, some months before that, had been amicable, and the parents had remained good friends. Through her sobs, Brigitte told Geschke of Birgit's sudden death.

Geschke was devastated – and then suspicious. His son, Phillip, had told him that Boyce's first wife, Josephine, had also died suddenly, 10 years before.

Unknown to Birgit's parents, Geschke phoned another friend, State Coroner Hal Hallenstein, and suggested a full autopsy be done on Birgit's remains. During this phone call Geschke raised a number of issues, which caused the Coroner to commence an inquiry into the circumstances surrounding Birgit's death – and that of Josephine Boyce in 1982.

The file on Josephine Boyce's death was delivered for review to Dr David Ranson, the forensic pathologist who would be performing the autopsy on Birgit. The report on Josephine, by veteran pathologist Dr John Hicks, was short and to the point: 'The cause of death was asphyxia following aspiration of vomitus in pregnancy.' No further investigations were considered necessary, the death was described as 'natural causes' and Josephine was cremated soon afterwards.

The autopsy on Birgit was performed by Dr Ranson at the Victorian Institute of Forensic Medicine, in the Coronial Services Centre Melbourne, on Friday 3 April. It was attended by Dr Cade and several other curious doctors. Ranson found very little wrong with Birgit's previously healthy body, apart from 'a mottled red-yellow appearance' on the heart muscle and a similar slight mottling of her liver. Her trachea (windpipe) was slightly red, but there was no sign of inflammation, ulceration or necrosis of any part of her gastro-intestinal tract. In particular, there was no nidus (localised area) from which a severe toxic bacterial infection could have sprung.

Ranson reasoned the damage to her heart tissue could have been caused by the vigorous attempts to resuscitate her over at least 20 minutes, or even from lack of oxygen to the heart while her body was experiencing acidosis; but he noted them, just the same.

Dr Ranson took many samples of tissue and fluids for further testing. He finalised his report by saying, 'The cause of death is unascertainable.'

Bernard and Brigitte Munro questioned why this highly qualified pathologist was unable to identify the cause of death.

Neil Boyce was reportedly almost inconsolable after Birgit's death and turned to a number of friends for support. One of these, Dr Jennifer Bartlett, he'd known since medical school.

Dr Bartlett later said, in evidence, 'After Birgit died, Neil was an emotional mess. He had trouble functioning and leant on me, Steve Holdsworth and others for support. I was very worried about him and made sure I spoke to him every day. He came for meals and at times, just to sit.'

Boyce had renewed his friendship with Dr Bartlett during the months preceding Birgit's death, because they had been working closely together organising the removal of Prince Henry's Hospital to a new site in Clayton. Bartlett was the medical administrator and Boyce was secretary of the Division of Medicine. Due to his workload during the day, from time to time he called in to Jennifer Bartlett's home in Murrumbeena on his way home to South Melbourne from Prince Henry's or Clayton.

Bartlett left work each day at around 4.45pm to collect her nine-year-old twins from their after-school carer. She said, for this reason, several people used to call in to talk to her at home, because as a separated sole parent, she had to be there with the children.

Bartlett told the inquest later that Boyce 'started dropping in every couple of weeks during 1991, to discuss work-related matters'.

When asked if they discussed any other matters, such as her forthcoming divorce, she replied, 'Not extensively, but we talked about matters other than work.' She said she did not know if Birgit was aware of these frequent visits.

Two days after Birgit died, Jennifer Bartlett asked Boyce's best friend, Professor Steve Holdsworth, if she could be of any assistance. She recounted that on Thursday 2 April 'Steven Holdsworth asked me to resolve any outstanding matters with Nursing Administration with regard to Birgit's death. I agreed to do that'.

The manager of Personnel Services at Monash Medical Centre, Kevin Crisp, later told police: 'On 2 April 1992 the sum of $23,722.56 was paid into the account of Ms Birgit Munro … [which] was a joint account with her de facto, Neil Boyce … who works at the hospital … Due to an administrative error, the money was paid into her account whereas it should have been held pending advice from the executors of the estate.'

According to Kevin Crisp, the sum was made up of Birgit's entitlements on 'cessation of employment'. She was, at the time, earning in round figures $36,000 p.a. (an equivalent in today's figures to $46,000).

On the following day, 3 April – the day of Birgit's autopsy – Dr Bartlett's application for divorce was heard and granted. Neil Boyce arranged for 100 red roses to be delivered to Jenny Bartlett's home 'to celebrate'.

Bernard Munro began investigating the true cause of his daughter's death. He explored every avenue, including contacting the deputy Health Services commissioner, Ms Vivienne McCutcheon. He expressed surprise that Birgit had been taken to a 'small' hospital where Boyce was well known, but where there were no emergency facilities. He asked why she hadn't been taken to a large teaching hospital with an Intensive Care Unit.

He told Ms McCutcheon that nursing records about Birgit's last night, which he had obtained, had not been written at the time, but some time later. He thought this was most irregular. As an ex-nurse, I found this surprising too.

The nursing notes state that the Night Report for 31 March 1992 was actually written on 2 April 1992. A note at the end says, 'The above notes are retrospective as reports were not written at the time.' But the notes follow on from the afternoon shift notes, and, as Birgit died at around 11.30pm, I was surprised the Night Report notes were not written up before the night shift went off duty at around 7am.

Bernard also told Deputy Commissioner McCutcheon about a conversation he'd had with Dr Cade, soon after Birgit's death, confirming that Dr Cade suggested the case be investigated by police. Cade had told him, 'There are drugs, substances or poisons, which can be – which can cause death and leave no trace at all.'

Bernard told McCutcheon, 'It made me think, well, what's going on here? What are they trying to tell me? This is a doctor who treated my daughter and he tells me to get it investigated.'

Ms McCutcheon did investigate Birgit's family's concerns and told Bernard that Birgit had received the best possible treatment in the Critical Care ward of the Mercy from eminently qualified nursing and medical specialists. Everything that could have been done, was done.

Bernard Munro said he did not have a criticism of the care Birgit received. But he kept repeating, 'I just want to know the *cause* of her death.'

Acting on what he believed to be the advice of Dr Cade, Bernard took his concerns to Sergeant King at the Victorian Coroner's Court. The court has a small police presence, rotated from time to time, to assist the Coroner in inquiries requiring police investigations. Bernard gave King the lists that he and his wife Brigitte had compiled; lists that detailed every small remembered irregularity regarding their daughter's final months, and her relationships at home and at work.

The mist of suspicion and innuendo began to swirl around Dr Neil Boyce, particularly in view of the fact that the Coroner had called for the file on the death of Josephine Boyce.

Neil Boyce ignored the undercurrent of whispers and the much-altered attitude of his former in-laws, who were now lukewarm towards him. Bernard, as executor of Birgit's estate, refused to finalise matters, as the 'cause of death' remained unknown.

Throughout the months following Birgit's death, Boyce threw himself into his work and spent a lot of time with Jennifer Bartlett.

Bartlett takes up the story again, as she told it at the inquest. 'At the end of June 1992, I accompanied him to Sydney for a two-day business trip. Our relationship until that time had been platonic. Our relationship evolved. We discussed at length what was best for all concerned, particularly my children, and finally agreed to get married.

'During the last week in August we went to a conference in Budapest for a week. On our return, we told my children we were getting married. During the 10-day period between returning from Budapest and getting married, Neil stayed overnight at Murrumbeena on occasions. Neil and I were married on 11 September 1992.'

It was not quite six months since Birgit Munro's death.

In July 1993 members of the Homicide Squad were assigned to investigate the circumstances surrounding the deaths of Josephine Boyce and Birgit Munro. On 1 July they asked Neil Boyce to attend an interview of 992 questions. Before the interview, Boyce was cautioned and offered the services of a lawyer, which he declined; he had already consulted the lawyer who acted for Monash Medical

Centre. Boyce obviously didn't think the Homicide interview, which lasted from 10.13am to 1.06pm, would take long, as he hadn't cancelled his afternoon appointments.

The detectives interviewed many others too. They traced the police and ambulance officers who attended Josephine Boyce's death, as well her obstetrician, her friends and workmates. They also interviewed Birgit's workmates, the people who cared for Birgit in her dying hours, her relatives and friends, and anyone else with any relevant recollection of her.

The full extent of the Homicide Squad's inquiries was made evident at the inquest held into the death of Birgit Munro in September 1994 before Acting State Coroner Iain West.

The bulk of the four-day hearing was made up of minutely detailed evidence from medical specialists. Doctors Cade, Heath and Tomlinson – visiting consultants at the Mercy Hospital – were in the witness box for hours. In principle, these highly qualified specialists stuck to their provisional diagnosis.

In addition, forensic evidence was heard from Forensic Medicine Institute pathologist Dr Ranson, and from Dr Byron Collins, an independent pathologist, who was engaged by the Munro family.

Dr Ranson's evidence described the outcome of his autopsy. Obviously he'd had some misgivings due to the 'unascertainable' cause of death, and had conferred with a number of cardiac and pathological specialists about the tissue and other samples he'd taken.

He said, 'I showed them to a number of people, Professor Stephen Cordner [Head of the Institute] and many of the other staff pathologists. Most people agreed that the changes in the heart were unusual ... but have not been able to give me any unequivocal impression as to what these changes indicate.'

Ranson was asked about his reaction to a report from Dr Byron Collins. In his report, Dr Collins said, 'Quite certainly a cause of death has not been established ... The medical diagnosis proposed by Dr Cade of toxic shock consequent on an attack of an acute and fulminating attack of enterocolitis cannot be substantiated, despite extensive microbiological examinations on both ante- and post-mortem samples ... There is a wide range of drugs/poisons that may cause gastrointestinal symptoms, of which two notable substances, ricin and thallium, have been used in homicidal poisonings ... I am of the firm opinion that the most likely cause of death of Birgit Munro has, at this stage, not been identified. In reality, it may never be ascertained. However, it could not be concluded that the investigations thus far have been exhaustive.'

Ranson said he had no issue with this report and reiterated that, on the information he had, there was simply no way he could identify the cause of death. Further discussion ensued about thallium and ricin. Ranson said tests on Birgit for these substances had not been done, but could be done for thallium on samples still in his possession. Testing for ricin was not so easy.

'Whether these agents would cause that entire constellation [of symptoms] in that particular fashion I really don't know.' Ranson went on to say that, generally, deaths from ricin poisoning are pretty rare, and the known symptoms of ricin poisoning did not exactly reflect the set of symptoms exhibited by Birgit.

Ranson agreed further testing might uncover a cause of death and that until then, as a matter of logic, one couldn't discount the possibility of other factors being involved in Birgit's death. He said, 'The same applies to all deaths, not just Birgit Munro. The avenues for possible investigation are almost never closed.'

Dr Cade said in his evidence, 'At the time I thought she died of an acute toxic enterocolitis and I documented that and I still believe that. [But] a definitive diagnosis requires … the cause of the condition to be established. We didn't achieve that. No organisms were grown and in the absence of a proven aetiology, a *definitive* diagnosis of an entero toxic E. coli can't be made. But [this diagnosis] without specifying cause, I think, can be made.'

Another very important question was canvassed with Cade, to allay some of the rumours that had been flying around since Birgit's death. Cade said he had known Neil Boyce professionally over a period of 10 years and that he was aware of the nature of Boyce's work.

He was asked, 'If it were to be suggested that [Boyce] was involved in growing cultures and that in this way he would be able to get hold of some poisons or some bacteria that would enable him to cause some damage with it through his work in the medical field, what would you say to that, from your knowledge of what his work is or was?'

Cade said, 'I think I would say that to the best of my knowledge germs in the laboratory would be absolute anathema to the work that he does … if you're culturing tissues you wouldn't want any germs around … I'd be hard pressed to think of any area where germs would be less desirable. It would be incompatible.'

Cade said that from the time of Birgit's admission to hospital, he was in no doubt that a toxic infection was present and that its severity was 'overwhelming'. He described her condition as a common manifestation of an uncommon illness.

Dr Heath agreed, although he had been a little equivocal at the time of Birgit's death about the actual cause. It was put to him, 'To your knowledge, no-one at the Mercy Hospital was prepared to sign a death certificate.'

He acknowledged, 'No. I advised that the death certificate should not be signed.'

'Was that because as far as you were concerned, the cause of Birgit Munro's death was not established as a consequence of what was known at the time?'

Dr Heath replied, 'Yes. There was some uncertainty about the cause of death.' He said that he thought a toxin had caused Birgit's death, but 'there was no way the toxin can be isolated' and it could not be determined if it was organic or chemical. After detailing Birgit's many symptoms, Dr Heath dismissed the possibilities of both ricin and thallium and explained his reasons.

He said he'd initially been unable to provide a diagnosis because he felt 'if it's not enterocolitis, I don't know what it is ... I haven't heard one word that is contrary to the diagnosis of enteritis and toxaemia'.

He continued, 'I saw the patient. I'm aware of the history. I was aware of the findings. I'm aware of the pathological changes and in addition, I've had a copy of the autopsy report. I put it all together. I can see no reason to alter the original diagnosis.'

The Coroner had heard evidence from four highly qualified experts in their fields. One of these was his own senior pathologist; another, an impartial consulting pathologist; and the other two had been on the spot, treating Birgit through the short course of her mystifying illness. The only thing they all seemed in agreement about was that they couldn't agree.

The time interval factor meant Birgit had not survived long enough to metabolise a poison, if there'd been one. Equally, the course of her illness was so swift that a naturally occurring toxin hadn't been confirmed either. The non-appearance of any bugs in the cultures done ante- and post-mortem could be attributed to the huge doses of antibiotics Birgit was given almost as soon as she was admitted to hospital. The effect of the antibiotics could have prevented cultures from growing.

The heart changes were considered abnormal by nearly everyone. It seemed it could be 'more of this' rather than 'more of that', but there was no corroborative evidence for any hypothesis. After a long day discussing the various options, the 'best guess' diagnosis seemed to be the best on offer to the Coroner, at that stage.

The next morning, there was a change of direction. Dr Kenneth Waldron, obstetrician and gynaecologist, gave evidence about Josephine Boyce. He said, 'I first met Josephine Boyce on 18 November 1982, when she attended for her first visit at eight weeks pregnant.'

Waldron's notes indicated 'at the time of me seeing [her, she] was having a normal pregnancy'. He said Josephine was referred by Dr Neil Boyce, whose letter made no mention of severe vomiting or even morning sickness; only endometriosis. Waldron told the court that 'endometriosis doesn't cause nausea or vomiting'.

He continued, saying that Jo had attended for her scheduled ultrasound – one week before she died – with no mention of any problems at that time either.

Dr Waldron was asked, 'In the course of a record of interview with the police, Dr Boyce indicated that his wife … had dreadful morning sickness and soldiered on. He said it was severe enough to take her to see an obstetrician and that on numerous occasions she was vomiting … all day and often for much of the night. She had very great difficulty holding fluids down and he said [her morning sickness] was far and beyond normal and it was of great concern. [He] couldn't recall the obstetrician who saw her, but the obstetrician tried a number of therapies, including the prescription of Vitamin B6 and also changing her patterns of meals. He said the problems had occurred "up until her death". Do you have any recollection, independent of your notes, of anything of that nature being mentioned to you by the wife?'

Dr Waldron's response was, 'No.'

Later, Waldron was asked by Mr Kirkham, the Munros' lawyer, 'In the record of interview, Dr Boyce categorised the illness from which his wife suffered as *hypromesus gravidarum* [severe and excessive vomiting] … At no stage was there any indication, either from Dr Boyce or from Mrs Boyce, that she was suffering at any stage … up to the time of her death, from that illness?'

Waldron relied, 'No. That is correct.'

Dr Boyce's lawyer, Mr Stanley, wanted to establish a few things with Dr Waldron too. He asked if 'that condition … is a more serious or more severe situation than normal morning sickness?'

Waldron explained, 'Yes, we generally reserve the term *hypromesus gravidarum* for a severe form which frequently requires admission to hospital.'

Mr Stanley asked Dr Waldron, 'Would it surprise you if Mrs Boyce had been of the view that morning sickness was part and parcel of being pregnant?'

Waldron replied, 'Yes, it *would* surprise me.' He went on to say, later in his evidence, that he was not in the practice, either in 1982 or since, of prescribing Vitamin B6 for excessive vomiting in pregnancy.

Bernard Munro had said in his statement to investigators, 'During the time Neil and Birgit were together they always appeared very happy and there were never any outward signs that there was any trouble in the relationship.'

He told of the concerns he'd developed following Birgit's death. He had been worried because 'Dr Cade and another doctor' (Ranson) had expressed what appeared to be concerns to him. Bernard had attempted to follow up some of his own concerns while awaiting the inquest.

He had discovered, for example, that 'Neil was seeing Jennifer Bartlett while Birgit was still alive', and that 'Neil had sent Jennifer 100 roses when her divorce came through'.

Bernard had originally thought Boyce had sent the roses to Jennifer Bartlett while Birgit was still alive, and this rankled him to the point of anger. However, during the inquest he agreed, with Mr Stanley, Boyce's lawyer, 'that in fact, any flowers that were sent were sent after your daughter's death'.

Bernard replied, 'Three days after.'

'And on the day of the …'

'Autopsy,' Bernard said.

'The day that Dr Bartlett in fact …'

'Got her divorce.'

Stanley continued, 'You are aware that prior to your daughter's death that she, Dr Bartlett and Dr Boyce all worked together at the same hospital? They were colleagues.'

'Yes.'

Mr Kirkham, Bernard's lawyer, asked his client why he'd begun making his own investigations into Birgit's death. Bernard explained that a number of medical and other experts had advised him that if they were in his position they'd be asking questions, but that 'it was this office [the Coroner] which referred it to Homicide, not me'.

'Since then,' asked Kirkham, 'you have been concerned to do what you can do to try and find out the cause of death of your daughter?'

'Absolutely, yes.'

'And that is all your concern is?' Kirkham asked.

'I want to find out the cause of death.'

At this point, Mr Stanley rose to his feet again. 'Mr Munro, you heard the evidence of Dr Cade and Dr Heath yesterday as to the cause of death. Have you understood it, as best a layman can?'

'Yes,' Bernard stated.

'Do you now know the cause of death?'

'No,' Bernard rejoined. 'They don't know it either.'

Unruffled, Stanley continued, 'You contacted Mr Geschke within a very short time of your daughter's death?'

'I did not. My wife rang him and told him our daughter died. Our daughter had been married to their son.'

Bernard went on to say he'd been unaware that Geschke had approached the Coroner and that the autopsy was a surprise for him. 'I was not asked. I really thought that the parents should be asked. It was a complete surprise. If it was [arranged] by someone else, it was without my knowledge. I think it was because no death certificate was signed.'

Bernard said he'd had no idea of Geschke's involvement in the autopsy request until about two months before the inquest, when he'd received the summons for the inquest and the details of the statements.

Responding to questioning about her thoughts on the cause of death – questions prefaced with 'being as fair and honest as you can, having been at the hospital, having heard all the doctor's evidence' – Barbara Munro said that she accepted there was no conclusive evidence to the cause of her sister's death.

'I don't believe I have a satisfactory answer to what Birgit died of. Two out of four experts know and the other two don't know. I'm not convinced.'

She said that during Boyce's first visit to Hobart with Birgit in March 1983, they appeared to be physically close during the few days they stayed at her home. When asked about the sleeping arrangements during that period, Barbara replied, 'They slept together downstairs in a room.'

She was asked, 'Did she tell you what was the nature of her relationship with Dr Boyce during that first quarter of 1983?'

'I believe she was comforting him,' Barbara replied.

Picking up a thick pile of paper, the lawyer said, 'I'd like to read you one small portion of the transcript of the record of interview that Dr Boyce had with the Homicide police in this matter. "Question: When did you actually commence the relationship with her? Answer: If by commencing a relationship you mean when did we start a sexual relationship, it would have been six or seven months after Jo's death."

'Now,' the lawyer asked Barbara, 'did you understand that Jo died [28] December 1982?'

'Yes.'

'As to your observations of Dr Boyce and your sister at Hobart in March 1983, what do you say?'

'I cannot say that I saw any sexual relationship, but they were an intimate couple.'

'During the period they stayed at your home, they slept together?'

'Yes.'

Birgit Munro had a best friend called Lyn, who also gave evidence to the Coroner, Iain West. She said, 'I remember she [Birgit] was working at Prince Henry's and that a doctor there was showing her friendship … that he had come to see her … She said that they were sleeping together … I think she was happy with the relationship, but she wasn't … comfortable with the fact that she was having a relationship with someone who was married.'

Lyn gave evidence that Birgit had told her that Neil Boyce said he 'liked both Josephine and Birgit and that he was unhappy about Josephine falling pregnant … It wasn't something he'd planned'.

She went on, 'I know Birgit used to receive letters from Neil when he was away with his wife. I remember this because I saw a couple of them and Birgit used to say she needed a dictionary to read them.' She said she also knew that Boyce used to take flowers to Birgit's house … 'particularly freesias, which were her favourite'.

Mr Stanley challenged her on her evidence about Birgit's relationship with his client. 'What you're suggesting is there was not just a friendship; you're suggesting there was more than that. You're suggesting that there was a sexual relationship between your friend, Birgit Munro – that she was committing adultery, not only with a man who was married, but whose wife was pregnant?'

'That's correct.'

'Do you see that as the behaviour of someone who's moral and straight as you believed Birgit to be?' Stanley asked.

Lyn responded, 'Well, I'm sure she's not the only moral person who would have had an affair. I'm sure there are many people who have had affairs.'

When homicide Detective Sergeant Linehan was called, he gave a short summary of his investigations and produced in evidence a three-hour video and a typed transcript of the interview he had conducted with Dr Boyce.

Linehan agreed with Mr Kirkham that in April 1992 Norman Geschke, the Victorian State Ombudsman, had contacted Mr Hallenstein, the State Coroner. Geschke told him he was Birgit's former father-in-law and expressed concerns about her death. The detective said the file was then sent to Homicide by the Coroner, and it was as a consequence of Mr Geschke's unilateral action that the brief had been compiled.

Linehan told the Coroner, in the usual dispassionate police intonation, 'Inquiries [about Josephine Boyce] have revealed that, on the day of her death, Neil Boyce came home to comfort her as she had complained of being ill. [Boyce had told police he'd left his hospital rounds just after lunch to go home as his wife had contacted him and asked him to come home.] Neil Boyce left the house, for approximately five minutes, apparently to get some medication for her and upon his return found his wife dead on the bed. Efforts to revive her were fruitless. The ambulance officer said the situation looked straightforward when he'd arrived around 4pm. He did notice some 'coffee grounds'–type vomit.'

The pathologist, Dr Hicks, found that 'Josephine Boyce had died by choking on her own vomit'.

Linehan told the Coroner 'it was understandable' that the Munro family had questions and concerns regarding Birgit's death; and agreed that 'there were circumstances which justified making inquiries relative to the involvement of Dr Boyce'.

Linehan was asked, 'I take it the investigations that you made were extensive and far ranging?'

'Yes, they were.'

'As a result of those investigations, nothing at all was revealed or exposed to implicate Dr Boyce, either directly or indirectly, in the death of Birgit Munro, was there?'

'That is correct.'

On legal advice, Dr Neil Boyce declined to give evidence at the inquest into Birgit Munro's death, on the grounds that it might incriminate him.

The Coroner delivered his finding on 2 September 1994. 'While Dr Ranson and Dr Collins stated there was no positive feature at pathology consistent with the diagnosis, they conceded their findings were non-specific and they didn't find anything inconsistent with it … I am satisfied, on the balance of probability, that the cause of death was acute toxic enterocolitis, causing damage to the heart and ultimately, to its failure.'

He also said that Josephine Boyce's death had been treated as a natural causes death, but the perceived similarities between her death and Birgit's had caused Birgit's family to initiate inquiries and provide material they thought was relevant. 'A loving family would do no less,' he added.

Mr West concluded that, on all the evidence available to him, 'nothing has been revealed that either directly or indirectly implicates Dr Boyce in the death of the deceased … I am further satisfied, on the evidence before the inquest, that the death of Josephine Boyce has no material bearing on the facts in issue in this inquest. Whilst the family cannot be criticised for pursuing the answers to which they are entitled, it is disturbing that the reputation of Dr Boyce has been so publicly questioned, as a corollary of them doing so. And I further find that there is no evidence before the inquest that supports a finding of any person contributing to the cause of death'.

The Munro family were confused and disappointed because they thought the Coroner had not equally weighted the evidence of the four experts. They believed if he had done so the finding may have been left open, and this would have allowed investigations to continue. The Munros felt that while the finding might be satisfactory legally, medically it was not.

Bernard visited the Homicide office and spoke to Chief Inspector Rod Collins, who told him that without an open finding, their hands were tied, leaving them 'unable to follow up certain matters'.

Bernard Munro sought advice about how to get the Coroner to reconsider. Under Victorian law, there is no course of direct appeal against a Coroner's finding. But there is a provision in the Coroner's Act that states, 'Any person may apply to the Supreme Court for an order that some or all of the findings are void.'

The Supreme Court has the power to order the Coroner to re-open an inquest or hold a new one – but the process is not for the poor, or faint-hearted.

There are four grounds upon which to base an appeal. Bernard Munro appealed on the grounds that 'the coroner erred in law ... as his finding was against the weight of the evidence'.

Bernard's wait in the court list began, and his costs mounted daily. His appeal was a matter of public record for any court clerk, or indeed anyone who had any interest in the case.

The case was assembled through Bernard's own exhaustive chasing of anyone who'd listen or talk to him. With help from staff at the Supreme Court, he collated the resulting material into an acceptable format.

Meanwhile, the financial commitment to his quest was already biting. Bills from the inquest and the process since had begun to mount. Driven by his need to get to the bottom of his daughter's death, Bernard collected letters, medical opinions and supporters for his appeal during the long years leading up to his day in court.

One of the most important new pieces of information to emerge was an opinion from Dr Peter Habersberger, a leading cardiologist, who expressed strong reservations regarding the finding.

'From my experience of almost 30 years of medicine I do not believe that there is sufficient evidence which can be obtained from the clinical features, or the pathological findings at autopsy, to support the Coroner's diagnosis.'

Habersberger outlined all his concerns, in his comments about the case, and concluded by saying, 'Just because the clinical diagnosis was enterocolitis, it does not necessarily mean that the patient died from this condition.'

The main cause of his concern was the sudden and deadly alteration to Birgit's ECG readout, which he says occurred around 7pm on the evening she died. Dr Habersberger's opinion is, 'Birgit did not die from an infection, she died from a heart problem. Her ECG indicates to me that an extremely toxic agent caused sudden, widespread heart damage leading to death.'

Habersberger showed Birgit's ECG to colleagues around Melbourne. All agreed with his assessment. He reviewed international medical literature regarding poisoning with various agents, and he found similar cases with identical electrocardiographic patterns. These people had all died from a deadly, identifiable poison, used in hospital laboratories, but not freely available.

Habersberger says Birgit could not have died from a heart attack either. Her autopsy showed no evidence of this; even though her heart muscle appeared damaged, the type of damage was inconsistent with a heart attack.

Other experts wrote to the Institute of Forensic Medicine, stating they believed Birgit had died from poisoning. Some named poisons, others didn't; but they all seemed to agree that the Coroner's finding was not necessarily an unreasonable legal attitude – but medically, they'd expect there to be some corroborative evidence.

Bernard Munro's barrister placed his material and their witnesses before Mr Justice Smith in November 1996, almost five years after Birgit died. By this time Bernard had spent close to $63,000. The strain on his wife and family was almost unbearable, but he felt he had to go on, for Birgit's sake.

The Coroner was represented as 'the Defendant', but he did not actively defend the case. The officers of the Coroner's Court rightly believe their responsibility is to offer every opportunity to discover the cause of any death, and, if it is shown they may have erred, in most cases they are willing to re-examine the facts.

At the commencement of the two-day hearing, Bernard's barrister was asked by Mr Justice Smith whether any other party should be joined to the proceedings. The barrister responded by submitting that a person's right must have been affected by the finding, in order to appeal. As the Coroner had not made a finding affecting any other person's rights and thus, who may have an interest in this appeal, no other person need appear.

Mr Justice Smith said words to the effect that 'the worst that can happen, should the appeal be successful, is that there could be another inquest'.

Unfortunately, wise as he may be, the learned judge was mistaken. Worse could happen – and the subsequent financial and personal costs of this ruling were largely borne by Bernard Munro.

On 7 February 1997, Mr Justice Smith granted Bernard's appeal, and ordered that the inquest be re-opened. 'In all the circumstances I consider it desirable and important that the matter be revisited and finalised ... by either ordering the holding of a new inquest or directing the reopening of the inquest by the Coroner ... The plaintiff did not press for a new inquest ... There was no reason to think that the Coroner would not proceed appropriately if the matter is returned to him. To direct a new inquest would cause considerable inconvenience, expense and trauma ... Accordingly I propose to do no more than order the inquest be re-opened [for] the Coroner to receive further evidence from persons who had already given evidence before him and to reconsider the various subsidiary findings relevant to his findings, that I propose to declare void.'

Bernard Munro's elation was short-lived. Almost immediately, Neil Boyce's solicitors lodged an appeal against Mr Justice Smith's judgment. A strongly worded affidavit from Boyce's solicitor stated that neither he nor Boyce had been advised of Munro's appeal; that Boyce was not given the opportunity to be present or represented; that if he'd known, he would have been an opposing party to have the matter properly contested and argued; and that the first Boyce knew about the entire process was on seeing the news stories that appeared following Mr Justice Smith's judgment. The affidavit asserted that 'a plain reading of those articles [which were attached] indicates that [Munro] continues to assert that [Boyce] has some responsibility for the death of the deceased and is continuing what [Boyce] believes to be a campaign of false allegation and innuendo against him'.

The legal grounds for their appeal were 'that the learned judge erred in law in failing to accord natural justice to the appellant'. Three other grounds were listed. They also asked for their costs to be awarded against Munro.

In the months leading up to the appeal hearing, Bernard's solicitor received various communications from Boyce's lawyers, offering to drop their action and not seek costs if he'd drop his crusade. Bernard refused. He couldn't imagine why anyone would not want the answer he wanted – the cause of his daughter's death.

Late in 1997, lawyers made submissions for several days before three Appeal Court judges. They argued about the definition of 'finding', the meaning of 'any person' in Section 59 of the Coroner's Act, and whether or not Boyce should have been advised of Bernard Munro's appeal.

They talked about 'natural justice' and discussed the potential damaging affect on Boyce's reputation if the inquest was re-opened. To support their arguments they referred, often, to several kilos of bound booklets of photocopied material – entitled 'List of Authorities' and 'Book of Materials' – which listed precedents and summarised 'the case so far'.

All the while Bernard watched, dismayed. The Supreme Court action had already cost him $25,000. He'd now spent about half his superannuation.

The Appeal Court judges handed down amended orders. They set aside the Supreme Court order and ordered that the appellant (Boyce) be added as a defendant to the proceeding (the appeal to the Supreme Court) and that there be a new trial of the proceeding. Bernard Munro was ordered to pay Boyce's costs.

The Crown Solicitor, representing the Coroner, informed the State Coroner of the above as follows. 'Boyce sought his costs on the basis that Munro [appealed] by stealth and this warranted a punitive costs order.' He reported that costs were granted on a party/party basis, and that, 'As Mr Munro may have possibly exhausted his savings, it is possible that he may discontinue the proceeding brought by the originating motion.'

After five-and-a-half years, Bernard Munro felt that he'd not only lost, he was beaten. If he wanted to pursue the matter further, he'd have to go back to the Supreme Court and start all over again. The prospect was overwhelming; nevertheless, he stubbornly applied to have his original application placed back in the court list to obtain a new trial date. He'd come too far to give up.

Shortly afterwards, however, an account arrived from Boyce's solicitors for a staggering, but neatly itemised, $42,562.38. Bernard's own costs for the Appeal Court were around $21,000. Just being heard in such exalted surroundings is very expensive.

He and his ailing wife faced the prospect of life in penurious circumstances. His cash reserves were gone. He couldn't pay this bill, never mind the cost of a new Supreme Court trial, without selling his only asset – his home.

Within days his lawyer received another phone call from Boyce's lawyers. Bernard went in to his solicitor's office and they did some paperwork.

Christmas that year was awful. Then on Monday 5 January 1998 his wife Brigitte died. Suddenly, Bernard Munro appeared to drop the whole campaign.

His friends and most of his relatives assumed he'd just had enough.

But they were wrong. It ate away at him. He felt very angry that as a private citizen he'd had to spend so much time and money doing what he saw as the job of the state – to ascertain the cause of his daughter's death. His friend, Norman Geschke, and his strong supporter, Dr Peter Habersberger, agreed. Habersberger thought he had important new evidence that should be presented to the Coroner.

In July 1999, after trying a number of other avenues, the two men attended an appointment with the Crown Solicitor to seek his support for re-opening the inquest, and to ask for some financial compensation for Bernard. They were heard sympathetically, but were told the Attorney-General, Jan Wade, was retiring following the approaching election. However, they were assured she would 'fully brief' her successor to follow up their concerns. They've heard nothing since.

I called Bernard Munro back about six months later, when he responded quite differently from our previous conversation. He couldn't discuss the case; 'not allowed to' were the words he used, I think.

During a trip to Tasmania, I interviewed Birgit's sister Barbara, who told me her father had signed some agreement not to discuss the case.

'Why would he do that?' I asked.

'Can't say,' she replied.

I became curious. I interviewed a lot of people and learnt a lot of secrets. I verified nearly all of them. My file grew very thick. I didn't learn for sure what lay behind Bernard Munro's silence, but I began to suspect.

I phoned Bernard again and said, 'If you won't talk to me, would you authorise your lawyer to answer some questions?' He agreed. His lawyer was very occupied, but he said he'd be pleased to get the three big boxes of Munro material out of his office and returned to his client. I could pick them up whenever I liked.

A lawyer's material is usually beautifully organised. It's a necessity, considering how much paperwork they need at a moment's notice in court. My notes were all my scraps and scribbles; but here was the whole story laid out in bound books, complete with yellow tabs and lawyerly marginal notations. In one of the boxes I found a document that stopped my scrabbling and sat me down.

Dated April 1998, it was a copy of a Notice of Discontinuance for Bernard Munro's Supreme Court action. This was pretty soon after he'd received the big bill from Boyce's lawyers. Could there be any connection?

I tried to question Bernard's lawyer about why his client had pulled out, but he told me Bernard was bound by a confidentiality agreement and could not and should not discuss with me the reasons for his sudden and uncharacteristic withdrawal. I assured him Bernard hadn't, which was why I was ringing him. He said he couldn't say anything about Bernard's reasons either, even though Bernard had authorised him to.

He did, however, explain one aspect of the stalled case. He said that Boyce had won his appeal to protect his good name – the 'natural justice' bit; but the Appeal Court had sent the case back to the Supreme Court for further argument of Bernard's original application – to get the case reopened.

But, for Bernard at least, there was a risk. There was no reason to believe a different judge would automatically agree to re-open the inquest, especially if Boyce was in court putting his arguments against this. But, as Bernard was the appellant for the Supreme Court appeal, it was his responsibility to keep the ball rolling. If he dropped the ball, the game was over.

And, I added silently, because everyone thought he'd run out of money, they weren't that surprised he'd stopped playing. Pressing on and implementing the Court of Appeal's orders depended on his bank balance, and many people knew it. Even the Crown Solicitor had referred to his dwindling funds.

If, let's assume, Bernard was saved from having to pay $42,562.38 and withdrew his application, the courts would close the books.

I went to the Coroner's Court to check the file. Since the Appeal Court orders were made on Wednesday 2 December 1998, and Bernard hadn't made his application to withdraw until April 1999, it was likely the Appeal Court orders would be attached to Birgit Munro's file. Sure enough, there they were.

There was also another letter from the Crown Solicitor. This one, dated 4 May 1998, said, 'The solicitors for Boyce have now advised me that this matter between their client and Mr Munro has been resolved on confidential terms and the proceeding is to be discontinued. It is, however, agreed that this discontinuance is conditional upon the Coroner not seeking his costs of the proceedings from Mr Munro.'

He calculated the total amount to be around $21,000. He informed the Coroner that no orders for the Crown Solicitor's costs had been made and ended his letter saying, 'As there is now an opportunity to dispose of a matter that had the potential to result in a further inquest having to be conducted I recommend that for the record you consent to discontinuance of the proceeding on the basis that you will bear your own costs. The proceeding can then be struck out.'

Struck out. That had certainly happened to Bernard. Partly by his own hand, you might argue, if he signed an agreement with Neil Boyce. But who wouldn't, put in his position? Like love, the course of justice is not smooth; in fact, it can get pretty overpowering and financially ruinous.

And this 'secret agreement' was not so confidential after all. What's the old saying? 'Two men can keep a secret, providing one of them is dead.' You'd have to be blind Freddie not to be able to work out the conditions. There was the Notice of Discontinuance all right, signed by Bernard in April 1998, bringing his daughter's file up to date and off the books.

Some time later, I challenged Bernard Munro about why he'd dropped the case. He deflected my question by saying, 'I don't want to talk about that. I've received another letter today, which really upsets me.' He passed me the letter from the Attorney-General, which had arrived just before I did. It was an answer to him regarding the visit made by Geschke and Habersberger in July 1999. It said that the Attorney-General had considered their submissions and was prepared to offer Bernard $25,000 if he signed a confidentiality agreement with the Attorney-General's department, which was enclosed. They also requested that he continue to abide by his agreement with Boyce.

I could hardly believe my eyes. An offer from the Attorney-General of $25,000? This was getting personal now. This was *taxpayers'* money we were talking about. And how did *Boyce* get into *this* agreement? If the settlement with Boyce was so confidential, how come the Attorney-General's office now knew about it too?

'You're not going to sign this, are you Bernard?' I said. 'Look, this is a political document; it's not even part of the due process of the law. It's designed to shut you up forever because you're a nuisance and they know you're likely to accept. As the Crown Solicitor put it, it's "an opportunity to dispose of a matter that had the potential to result in a further inquest having to be conducted". You're 75, and if you refuse or ask for more they'll gamble on your dying before they make another offer.' I left him thinking about it.

I don't know if Bernard signed the Attorney-General's offer or not; if he did, he wouldn't be allowed to tell me. But it seems everybody in the legal loop knew he signed Boyce's offer, even though Bernard couldn't tell anyone. But it's in writing – on the public record.

No doubt the ex-gratia payment documents will be available under Freedom of Information eventually too. And if they aren't they should be – it's our money, after all.

I think both offers are immoral and have hindered the due process of the law. The government has committed about $46,000 for legal fees and an ex-gratia payment since Bernard Munro's Supreme Court appeal. It seems a similar amount has been incurred by Boyce.

Bernard Munro was offered a lot of money to keep quiet, but he was sick of secrets. All he ever wanted was for the cause of his daughter's death to be re-examined.

There's a direction from the Appeal Court saying the appeal against the Coroner's finding should be heard. Because some parties to this proceeding have more money than others, that direction has been derailed. The question was, and still is, what *was* the cause of Birgit Munro's death?

Postscript

On Saturday 20 August 2004 Bernard Munro took an anonymous call at his home. A male voice said, 'I'm ringing regarding the death of your daughter Birgit some 12 years ago. You were all barking up the wrong tree. Someone should look at the medical experiments being done at Monash around the time of Birgit's death.'

Bernard said he didn't know anything of the nature of the work of the Monash laboratory, but that if the caller had any information he should go to the Coroner or the police.

The caller replied, 'This is a medical matter and if the appropriate authority would investigate the use of ricin in the laboratory they would get valuable assistance from the Monash staff.'

'Who am I talking to?' asked Bernard.

'Just bring the information to the attention of the right people,' the caller replied and hung up.

Bernard was bewildered and wished he'd asked more questions. He contacted both Norm Geschke and Dr Peter Habersberger. Geschke rang the Coroner, who was unable to discuss the matter in case an investigation could be compromised. (As no investigation was taking place, this is difficult to understand.)

Dr Habersberger did initiate some inquiries at Monash, but got nowhere.

Bernard Munro died in December 2005. He went to his grave not knowing the true cause of death of his beloved daughter Birgit.

And Justice for All

Kerry Greenwood

No-one knows what really fuels writing. No writer I have ever met or heard of can really tell where the stories come from. The Great Well of Tales, perhaps, into which we dip our subconscious bucket.

There are exceptions. Writers attempting to denounce an injustice, reform an unjust law, solve an old mystery or redress an improper conviction know where the impetus comes from. It comes from Jonathan Swift's 'savage indignation'; it comes from Charles Dickens' 'wounded humanity'; it comes from a strong desire to see justice done.

In this essay I shall discuss some of the successes of authors who tried to redress such wrongs. This is not an all-inclusive list. I chose the cases that I felt best addressed my own categories. These are:

1. Freeing a prisoner wrongly convicted, or at least clearing the person's name
2. Solving a long-standing mystery
3. Reforming a legal system that is manifestly unjust, inefficient and downright wicked

Conan Doyle and Oscar Slater

Doctor Sir Arthur Conan Doyle, an essentially modest man, quickly grew tired of his ubermensch detective, Sherlock Holmes. He finally resorted to fictional assassination in order to rid himself of 'this insufferable incubus', as he called his creation in an exasperated moment. The reading public, however, would not pay proper attention to Doyle's historical novels or his spiritualist research and insisted on Holmes, so the author resurrected the Baker Street sleuth and plodded on with yet more tiring demonstrations of Holmes' brilliance.

The idea of Sherlock Holmes as the man who could right all wrongs is still strong. I have been shown the letters that people still write to Sherlock Holmes – to Holmes that is; not Conan Doyle. Perhaps we need him now more than ever to redress wrongs.

Early last century, when Miss Marion Gilchrist was found dead in her Glasgow apartment and Oscar Slater was convicted of her murder, the most impressive miscarriage of justice of the century was going to need a Sherlock Holmesian effort to sort out. It is hard for this writer to understand how anyone could have assumed that Oscar Slater was the murderer; but at least then Conan Doyle was still around to help. The facts of the case are as follows.

Miss Gilchrist, an elderly lady of 83 with a fondness for jewellery, was found in her upper-floor apartment, beaten to death 'by more than 60 blows'. It was December 1908.

On the day of the murder Miss Gilchrist had sent her attendant, Helen Lambie, out to buy a paper. When Miss Lambie came back, the ground-floor tenant Arthur Adams said he had heard groaning and thumps from the flat above. When Lambie and Adams entered the apartment a man ran past them and down the stairs 'like lightning'. The man fell over Helen Barrowman, a 14-year-old girl, in the street outside.

The maid then found Miss Gilchrist dead, but only one piece of her jewellery, a crescent-shaped diamond brooch, missing. A local informer told the Glasgow police that Oscar Slater, a 37-year-old German Jewish ponce, had been trying to sell such a brooch in a Glasgow pub.

And that, ladies and gentlemen, is the case against Oscar Slater.

No matter that the description of the murderer, by the three people who *actually* saw him, was of a slim, young, fair and clean-shaven man, in either a fawn cloak or a dark overcoat and a round hat.

No matter that Slater was short, thickset, moustachioed and dark.

No matter, indeed, that Slater was in that pub trying to sell 'his brooch' three weeks *before* the murder.

In fact, the man had been in Glasgow only six weeks, staying near the Gilchrist residence, and then boarded an ocean liner for New York.

But Oscar Slater was their man and the Glasgow police bent all their efforts into catching him.

Now, Slater was not a good citizen (he was an illegal gambling den operator) and he was probably not a very nice man, but the law is not supposed to be concerned with such things. (If it was, my other job as duty solicitor would be impossible.)

Oscar Slater was extradited from America to stand trial for the murder of Marion Gilchrist; was convicted on the 'evidence' of Lambie, Adams and Barrowman; found guilty of murder; and sentenced to hang. The main reason, it seems, was because he was a German Jewish man who lived off the earnings of a prostitute.

In moments a petition for clemency had 20,000 shocked signatures, and Slater was reprieved; he was sentenced to life imprisonment instead. There was no Scottish Court of Criminal Appeal in 1909. So Slater appealed to Conan Doyle – in effect, to Sherlock Holmes himself.

Doyle, a Scot, was outraged so he began to research the case. He interviewed witnesses, policemen, ladies of negotiable virtue and pub owners; and, while he did not approve of Slater's lifestyle, he became easily convinced of his innocence. He wrote a book called *The Case of Oscar Slater*, which was published in 1912 and caused widespread interest, but the authorities refused to move.

Then a courageous Glasgow policeman, Detective Lieutenant John Trench, went public with his opinion that all the witnesses had been bribed and browbeaten. This merely meant he suffered the curse of most whistleblowers: he was dismissed from the force in disgrace.

Oscar Slater, meanwhile, remained in jail. In 1925, Slater managed to smuggle out a despairing letter to Conan Doyle, who took fresh action. He located Helen Lambie – safely out of British jurisdiction in Pittsburgh, Pennsylvania – and she admitted that she'd been threatened and bribed to give false testimony.

Public interest was raised again in 1927 with the publication of a journalist William Park's book, *The Truth About Oscar Slater*. A friend of John Trench, Park's re-examination of the case not only questioned the veracity of the eyewitness statements, but much of the evidence as well. When those witnesses began coming forward to recant their statements and testimonies – by either correcting how the police had (mis)used their information or admitting to being bullied into their testimony – the court had little choice but to deal properly with Slater.

On 14 November 1927, Oscar Slater was released from prison; not pardoned, but released after serving nearly 19 years for a crime he did not commit.

Slater then appealed to the newly constituted (1926) Court of Criminal Appeal and, with Conan Doyle watching on, accepted compensation of £6000. Slater then retired and married.

No-one was ever identified as the Gilchrist murderer, and modern commentators suggest that a gang of burglars were interrupted by the old lady as they were riffling through her jewellery, which she sometimes bought in dubious circumstances.

Slater died in 1948, at the age of 75, still protesting that the court had never declared him innocent, which they never had; and which is partly why he didn't even send Doyle a thank you for helping to secure his release. Poor Oscar Slater, to the end, tried to believe in British justice.

Doctor Sir Arthur Conan Doyle believed in justice, too; and he had made a difference in the real world although, oddly enough, we can thank Sherlock Holmes for Oscar Slater's freedom.

Estelle Blackburn and John Button

It has been observed that while Sydney has gang murders, Melbourne has family murders and Adelaide has really strange murders, Perth is fairly quiet on the murder front, going in mainly for the standard domestic or spousal murders with a reasonable number of incidents that happen when there are visiting sailors and unlimited alcohol.

But in 1963 Perth had its very own home-grown serial killer, every bit as frightful and indiscriminate as Peter Kurten, the Monster of Düsseldorf. Like Kurten, he killed women and men and children. Like Kurten, he was almost impossible to predict and thus to catch. And like Kurten, his crimes were attributed to other people.

This killer's name was Eric Edgar Cooke and he was the Monster of Nedlands. A childhood of appalling brutality and an accident-prone adolescence had left him hare-lipped, deformed and hating everything alive that was happier than he was; and almost everything was. He began as a burglar, a vandal and a fire-raiser, and then moved on to killing people. He married but was a cruel husband to the woman who bore his six children, two of them subnormal. He never forgave the world for what it had done to him.

When finally caught in an ingenious police trap and asked why he had shot, run over, clubbed, raped and mutilated, he replied simply, 'I wanted to hurt someone.'

In that, he succeeded. In a way, he even hurt Perth. People who lived through Cooke's reign of terror never left a back door unlocked again.

Eric Edgar Cooke was responsible for hit-and-run murders, shooting murders, rapes, over 200 burglaries and consequent grievous assaults on sleeping women. He damaged or affected the lives of nearly everyone with whom he came in contact, and many he never even so much as bumped into. Cooke's brutal crime spree completely ruined the life of one young Perth man, even though the two never met.

It was February 1963 and 19-year-old John Button was, unfortunately, in the wrong place at the wrong time. While Cooke was cruising the streets of Perth for victims, Button was having a fight with his 17-year-old girlfriend Rosemary Anderson. She got out of his car and announced that she was going to walk home. Button, offended, let her walk away into the dark. Then he recovered his wits and turned the car to follow her.

In the interim, Rosemary Anderson had met Eric Edgar Cooke, and he had run her over and killed her. By the time Button arrived on the scene, Rosemary was dead; and by the time the police arrived, he was distraught.

Unhinged by grief and feeling utterly responsible, Button initially agreed with an ingenious police theory that the girl had been shocked by his sexual advance and had stalked off, whereon he had driven after her, full of male pride, and hit her with his car.

John Button was not going to tell a policeman that he was already engaged in an intimate relationship with the young woman, if it meant besmirching her good name, even though it explained why her underwear was in his car. There was no other evidence against John Button.

No-one knew about Cooke at the time, but there was still nothing to connect Button to the death. The dents in his car did not match the body, there was no contact evidence, and he retracted his confession as soon as he regained his balance. Despite this, John Button was convicted of manslaughter and sentenced to 10 years' hard labour.

Meanwhile, the trap was closing about Edgar Eric Cooke. On 3 September 1963 he was duly caught, and cheerfully began confessing to all of his crimes. This, as can be imagined, took time. It wasn't until the 12th that he confessed to murdering Rosemary

Anderson. It's a good confession, with supporting details and hardly a single mistake.

You would think that this would have led to the release of John Button, but you would be wrong. For a start, Cooke was playing with his interlocutors. He retracted confessions, invented new ones, and boasted a lot. Then, when it seemed that he might be reprieved from the gallows in order to examine some unsolved crimes, he quickly repudiated all of them, unwilling to be delayed on his way to the scaffold. He refused all petitions for mercy. But he did sign an affidavit of confession for John Button's appeal. He confessed again to the Chief Justice at that appeal.

This did not help. He was not believed, and John Button's appeal was refused.

Before becoming that last man hanged in Western Australia, Cooke confessed again to his wife and others that he had committed two killings for which other men had been convicted. One was the hit-and-run murder of Rosemary Anderson, for which Button was serving time; the other was the brutal axe murder of 22-year-old chocolate heiress Jillian Brewer in her Cottesloe flat, for which Darryl Beamish, a deaf mute, was serving life after his death sentence was commuted.

Eric Edgar Cooke was hanged on 26 October 1964, and with him went any chance of further testimony.

Button's application for special leave to appeal to the High Court had been refused on the grounds that no special circumstances had been disclosed. John Button's last legal avenue had been blocked off. He spent five years in jail before he was released.

John Button became a committed Christian and now says that it was all God's will, but from the day of his release he spent the next 40 years of his life struggling to clear his name.

It wasn't until the 1990s, and the crusading efforts of Perth journalist Estelle Blackburn to unearth real evidence in the case, that John Button ever really had a chance of clearing himself. Blackburn spent six years and her life savings researching the injustices done to both John Button and Darryl Beamish. Amongst other things she discovered that Cooke had specifically confessed to five other hit-and-run murder attempts involving seven girls, and managed to track some of them down.

Estelle Blackburn's book *Broken Lives*, published in 1999, relentlessly outlines exactly how John Button got enmeshed in the gears of the Western Australian judicial system, and even collects a bundle of letters in which is it is demonstrated that the one thing that Officialdom never says is 'sorry'.

Without Estelle's meticulous work, the parents of Rosemary Anderson might still believe that John Button murdered their daughter. As a result of the fresh evidence in Estelle's book, the morning after her appearance with John Button on the ABC's *Australian Story*, a WA judge rang her, agreeing that an injustice had been done, and suggested a couple of lawyers – Tom Percy QC and Jon Davies – who might be willing to take on the case pro bono.

The WA State Attorney-General agreed to reopen the two separate cases of convicted killers John Button and Darryl Beamish. One of Estelle's fellow journalists Bret Christian managed to track down, via the internet, an American pedestrian crash test expert, Rusty Haight. The Texan travelled to Australia, financed by the editor of a Perth suburban newspaper, and carried out tests on the types of vehicles driven at the time by Button and Cooke. In his opinion, and finally agreed on by the court, it was obvious that Cooke's Holden had been responsible for Rosemary Anderson's death, and she had not been hit by John Button's Simca.

There were 12 other witnesses for the defence, including six survivors of Eric Cooke's hit-and-run murder attempts, and Cooke's widow, Sally, who repeated her husband's gallows confession.

In 2001 Estelle Blackburn won the prestigious Walkley Award for Most Outstanding Contribution to Journalism, but the award and even her book had only been by-products; proving John Button was not a murderer had always been her goal. He was the definitive example of someone who was in the wrong place at the most wrong time possible.

On 25 February 2002, the WA Appeals Court made legal history by declaring a miscarriage of justice and clearing John Button of all charges – nearly 40 years after his arrest. Button's innocence was finally restored not through the due diligence of the law itself, nor even because the real perpetrator confessed to the crime several times including just before his execution, but because of the painstaking research and sheer determination of one woman. Estelle Blackburn interviewed more than 200 people, including original witnesses and many others not questioned at the time, and her tenacity and professional courage even uncovered examples of alleged police and other official blunders in the cases against John Button.

Kevin Morgan and Gun Alley

As a researcher of the 1920s for my own fictional detective series, the Gun Alley Murder naturally came to my attention. It happened near the Eastern Market in Melbourne, where I set *Raisins and Almonds*, one of my Phryne Fisher books. Phryne cannot solve the case, even in fiction, partly because it happened in 1921, which was seven years too early for her, but mostly because Kevin Morgan has already done it – solved it, that is.

On New Year's Eve 1921 the body of a 12-year-old schoolgirl, Alma Tirtschke, was found in Gun Alley, near the Eastern Market. She had been raped and asphyxiated and the body had been left splayed, and shockingly half-naked, in a filthy lane. Alma lived with her grandmother in Jolimont and had been sent into the city to pick up some smallgoods. She had collected her parcel from the butchers and then vanished. Her family sat up all night waiting for her to come home, and she never did.

The police got nowhere with a very contaminated crime scene and a lack of suspects; the papers complained and offered rewards; the Commissioner pressed for a result. And then suddenly a lot of very unreliable people said that Colin Ross, ex-proprietor of the Australian Wine Shop, was the murderer.

Admittedly the Wine Shop was a squalid and dubious locale, and shots had been fired there on occasion. The fortune teller in the Eastern Arcade complained that her female clients did not like walking past it; it was a dive.

But on the day that Alma had died, Colin Ross was moving out; his lease was up. His goods were loaded onto a cart to be taken to Footscray, where he lived with his mother. Not, one would think, a day for murdering a chance-met child.

Nevertheless the police arrested Ross. Throughout a coroner's court and then a trial, Ross stuck to his story: he had seen the girl in the street that afternoon, and that was all.

Unfortunately a number of people came forward to say that he had been seen with the girl, and indeed had 'confessed' to murdering her. The only physical evidence was some hairs on a blanket, which were said by an 'expert' to be the same as the dead girl's. The defence counsel for Colin Ross, known as 'not a good cross-examiner', failed to make capital out of the contradictions in the stories, and could not, by practise, question the antecedents and police records of the prosecution witnesses, because that would have opened his client to the same treatment. Ross was convicted by the jury and sentenced to death.

His junior counsel, TC (Thomas) Brennan, was outraged and appealed to the Supreme Court. About the case, he said '... they (the jury) were invited to hang a man on contradictory confessions, in which he is alleged, by thoroughly disreputable witnesses, to have made, which on his oath he denied having made, for the making of which no reason could be assigned, and which were so seriously in conflict to suggest that they were never made'.

Unfortunately his rhetoric was of no avail. The Full Court of the Supreme Court refused the appeal. On application for leave to appeal to the High Court, the High Court refused to re-examine the evidence given at the original trial. Leave to appeal to the Privy Council was not attempted because the client was, by this time, beyond its jurisdiction. He was dead.

Colin Campbell Ross protested his innocence to the end; then he was horribly dead. His hanging was bungled and he strangled slowly, choking to death over 20 interminable minutes.

Still outraged, TC Brennan wrote a book about the case, citing the inadequacy of the judge's summation, the barefaced contradictions by the witnesses for the Crown, and the fact that evidence crucial to establishing the innocence of Ross was not permitted. He offered no other suspects, however.

The matter remained a mystery until the intervention in the 1990s by researcher Kevin Morgan, who, having become intrigued by the murder, found an envelope in the Public Record Office Victoria (PROV) that contained the hair samples presented as evidence in the case. He managed to get permission to have them tested. The three samples were from the blanket in Ross's house, from his friend with blonde hair, and from the dead girl. Microscopic examination by the Australian Federal Police confirmed that they were all different. The hairs on the blanket were not those of the murdered 12-year-old.

So who did kill Alma Tirtschke? In *Gun Alley: Murder, Lies and Failure of Justice*, Kevin Morgan's 2005 book of his investigation, he offered persuasive evidence, given by Alma's younger sister Viola, of a paedophile uncle whom they had always avoided. Alma was a child, barely pubescent, not a budding young woman as might attract one who is normally sexed.

Morgan explains how public hysteria, media criticism of police and politicians, and the testimony of unreliable witnesses conspired to assure that Colin Ross was hanged for the heinous crime. Yet more than 80 years later – even though many involved in the case have since died – Morgan was able to establish that Colin Ross could account for all his movements on that day Alma died; not only for the time the girl went missing, but for later that night when her body was dumped in the now-notorious Gun Alley.

His book took 11 years of research, whereon Kevin Morgan then organised a 31-page 'petition for mercy' – arguing the flawed forensic results and the false witness statements. It was signed by the relatives of both Alma Tirtschke and Colin Ross; of the murdered girl and her 'convicted' killer.

The State Attorney-General then wrote to the Chief Justice asking for her opinion on whether, in light of the fresh evidence, there had been a miscarriage of justice, and if so, for her to consider the plea for mercy.

In October 2006 the State Government began the legal proceedings for Victoria's first posthumous pardon. Strangely, even if Ross is granted a pardon, his murder conviction will stand. For it to be overturned, the Court of Appeal would have to order a retrial, which is not possible in his case.

But if Colin Ross is still able to take an interest in things of the earth, he must be relieved that now, the truth is known, and his statement of innocence is accepted. Apparently he wrote to his family, just before he was hanged in the Old Melbourne Gaol, saying: 'Dear ones, do not fret too much for me. The day is coming when my innocence will be proved.'

Stephanie Bennett and the Gatton Murders

On Boxing Day eve 1898 the Murphy siblings set out to go to a dance in the small Queensland town of Gatton. They were Michael Murphy, aged 29, his sister Norah, 27, and their younger sister Ellen, 18. The dance in Gatton was cancelled so the three headed home, but were fatally delayed.

The next day their pony trap was found in a paddock. The horse had been shot and the three Murphys were dead. Michael had been shot, after being sexually assaulted. His sisters had been pack-raped and then bludgeoned to death with a tree branch. It was the most horrible crime that Gatton could imagine.

Unfortunately, the investigation of this outrage was entrusted to Captain Frederick Urquhart, a man who was enthusiastic and organised but who had no talent at all for understanding human nature. It was also unfortunate that by the time anyone thought of employing black trackers, whose skill was legendary, the crime scene had been too thoroughly contaminated. Practically the entire population of Gatton had walked into Moran's paddock to view the scene of the crime. The trackers were unable to tell the police anything helpful.

Urquhart decided, on no evidence at all, that the crime had been perpetrated by one man. One man had held up the trap, diverted it into the paddock, caused Michael to tie his sisters' hands, and committed all the outrages on them by himself. He was a man of legendary capacity too, it would seem, since the sisters' clothes were drenched in semen.

Having jumped to conclusions, Urquhart was loath to suspect any persons in the area, so went looking for a tramp. And times being what they were in 1898, there were plenty of these.

No-one could say that the captain did not try; but he ignored information brought to him by his underlings, failed to follow up anonymous letters, and generally made as total a hash of the investigation as possible. After two months he gave up and told his superiors that the crime could not be solved.

Over the years many people have considered the Gatton murders, assigning varying degrees of blame to the 'mysterious man by the fence' and others. Some have even decided that a scream of 'father', heard by a shepherd's wife, meant that Patrick Murphy had murdered his own children. This has always been unlikely. Fathers certainly do murder their children sometimes, but they do not rape them all beforehand.

It took an ingenious, fresh mind to investigate the character of the victims, something that any detective of the present day would do as a matter of course.

Stephanie Bennett in *The Gatton Murders* produced the most convincing exposition of this crime. She wondered why, for example, an 'In Memoriam' notice was found at the crime scene. She also followed up two other recent deaths in the district: Catherine Ryan, aged 19, who died in a Brisbane hospital in 1897 of what could have been a septic abortion; and Edith May Cook, likewise dead in 1896 of similar causes.

Abortion was illegal then. Doctors of the time have described how women were brought to their hospitals after botched terminations, already dying of a perforated uterus, a fulminating infection, or a tetanus-like disease, and how horribly they died.

Both of these dead young women, Catherine Ryan and Edith Cook, had been close to the murdered 29-year-old Michael Murphy.

Bennett's book, published in 2004 and subtitled 'A true story of lust, revenge and vile retribution', traces Michael Murphy's contacts and reveals that he was not the virtuous young man everyone thought him to be. She explains the murders thus: Michael, having been responsible for the pregnancy and death by abortion of two young women, was taking up with another – Delia Barlow, the 17-year-old wife of the publican.

Bennett posits that brothers and cousins of the dead women decided to teach Michael and his snooty sisters a lesson. They gathered a pack of young men together and sabotaged the dance at Gatton so they could reliably depend on the Murphys being on a particular road at a particular time. Then they decoyed the siblings into the paddock, where the 'punishment' the brothers had decreed got out of hand.

As a duty solicitor I know how groups of young men can find themselves in the middle of a dreadful crime without quite knowing how it happened, unable afterwards to explain why they had done, in company, what they would never have done by themselves. They behave like a pack of feral dogs.

Thus the Murphys were outraged and murdered, not merely humiliated and brought down a peg or two. The wild boys were left with blood on their hands. Then, of course, the Irish closed ranks, no-one knew anything, and the mysterious never-found tramp was the only possibility.

Of all possible explanations, Stephanie Bennett has produced the most meticulously researched and the most convincing for the Gatton murders.

Peter Rees and Juanita Nielsen

In the early 1970s Juanita Nielsen, heiress to the Mark Foys retail fortune, was running a paper called *Sydney Now* and living in a renovated terrace house in Victoria Street, Sydney. In a hangover from the '60s when the old was to be despised and the new embraced, a builder called Frank Theeman wanted to tear the Kings Cross terrace row down to build a 20-storey tower block – with parking.

Juanita took exception to this and formed the Victoria Street Residents Group. The developer spoke to an old mate of his, Jim Anderson, who had some very unpleasant employees, who he subsequently set loose on Victoria Street.

Juanita appealed to the Builders Labourers' Federation (BLF) and their gentle and charming leader, Jack Mundey, who put a 'green ban' on Victoria Street in 1972. The green bans saved a lot of the city that Sydney now values highly, including Glebe, the Rocks, Woolloomooloo and Darlinghurst. We folkies used to sing a little song, 'Swallow your drivel and shovel your gravel/Green bans, now and forever,/Take your bulldozers away!'

The stage was set for the Siege of Victoria Street, where a gang of thugs rampaged through the houses, breaking down doors and smashing fittings, while the well-bribed local police watched. In 1973 Arthur King, head of the residents' action group, was kidnapped by two unidentified men who put him in the boot of their car and drove him to a motel on the south coast. He was held for three days before being released under threat of death. King quit the action group and moved out of Kings Cross. It was never proved that the men had been hired by Theeman.

Other residents were regularly harassed by men employed by Theeman, as he attempted to have them evicted from their houses. The men were led by Frederick Krahe, a former detective with the New South Wales Police who'd been sacked amidst allegations of organising bank robberies and murdering Sydney crime figures. Residents would squat in each other's houses so that no house was left unattended. Most of the tenants were forced out or eventually ran away, but Juanita wasn't beaten. Not yet.

When the corrupt Jolly Green Giant, Norm Gallagher, was enabled to take over the BLF and withdrew the Green Ban, Juanita talked to the Federated Engine Drivers and Firemen's Association and got them to black the site. She still refused to move despite threats. The tone of her denunciations became more fulminating. This was a woman who would stop at nothing to defeat the modernisation of Victoria Street. Clearly, she had to go.

On 4 July 1975 Juanita Nielsen, wearing a tangerine leather coat, went to the Carousel Club in Kings Cross for what turned out to be her last newspaper job. Owned by Abe Saffron – aka Mr Sin or Boss of the Cross (and allegedly one of the major players in Australian organised crime in the latter half of the 20th century) – the Carousel Club was managed by James Anderson (who happened to owe developer Frank Theeman a lot of money), and run by a known gangster, Eddie Trigg.

The tangerine coat should have made her hard to miss, but only one person ever said that they saw her again, and that person was probably lying. Juanita went into the Carousel that day to meet Eddie Trigg and his wannabe-gangster sidekick Shane Martin-Simmonds; she never walked out again.

Despite a remarkable amount of effort from two of the few straight policemen that New South Wales employed at that time, little progress was made with finding Juanita, dead or alive, although everyone involved was pretty sure that she was dead. The location of her body, however, eluded them, as did a straight narrative about what happened to her.

Eddie Trigg and Shane Martin-Simmonds were jailed for 'conspiracy to abduct' Juanita, but no-one has ever found her body. A later inquest returned an open finding, and when the National Crime Authority had a chance to investigate the matter, they blew it in an ultimately futile attempt to snare Abe Saffron for tax evasion.

It was left to an indefatigable Sydney journalist, Peter Rees, to track down and re-interview Loretta, the transsexual receptionist of the Carousel Club, and Marilyn, Trigg's lover of the time.

Rees pursued his investigation of Juanita's disappearance for over 25 years, forcing a federal parliamentary inquiry and a secret reopening of the case under the personal orders of the former NSW Police Commissioner, Peter Ryan.

In his book *Killing Juanita* (2004) Loretta and Marilyn say the same thing: Juanita Nielsen was shot in the little room under the stairs, and her body disposed of in some final way. She might have been cut to pieces and fed through the kitchen disposal unit, the mince being taken out in the boat and used for ground bait; or she might repose in the concrete foundations of the Glebe Point Bridge.

Whatever ultimately happened to her remains, it's almost comforting to find that she was not abducted and tortured – just executed. The long mystery of Juanita's death, if not her final resting place, has been solved.

And the 20-storey tower that Theeman wanted to build in the Cross was reduced to an undistinguished low-rise development, which slides down Victoria Street and entirely fails to match the heritage houses.

Doubtless it, too, will go the way of the Melbourne's hideous Gas & Fuel building, now that public taste has improved so profoundly.

Juanita Nielsen might well be there when someone wields the first pickaxe.

Charles Dickens and the Court of Chancery

A nice young man once wrote to Charles Dickens and asked him whether he was a radical or a conservative. Dickens replied by saying that he followed no political party, for 'the instant a man became a politician he became a liar'. But he added that he aimed to reform specific abuses: public hangings, the Poor Law Amendment Act of 1834, the debtor's prison; and the Court of Chancery.

It is notable that, in a life that ended when he was only 58, Charles Dickens did manage to do all of these things – through his fiction; through the stories he told. He forced real-world changes in the Poor Law in all his books, ending with *Our Mutual Friend*. He got public hangings abolished with one anguished, outraged description in a newspaper essay, of the crowd at a hanging; *Little Dorrit* took care of the debtor's prison; and *Bleak House* (1853) tilted at the Court of Chancery and wounded it to death.

He was not alone of course. What Dickens did was give a human face to the abuses that right-minded people had been complaining about for years. The Court of Chancery was his biggest target, but people had been protesting its existence for at least 50 years before Dickens wrote *Bleak House*.

It has been said (by George Bernard Shaw) that it was not that Dickens knew what the Victorians wanted; it was that *he* wanted what the Victorians wanted. He wanted a just and merciful state, and he meant to get it. In this instance, Victorian society fell obediently to heel behind his rampaging virtue.

Almost the worst thing that could happen to you as a landed person in the 19th century was to have something left to you in a will, which was then challenged by a litigant to the Court of Chancery.

Contemporary law notes advise the practitioner to admonish the recipient to surrender the property rather than get involved in *that* court.

Unlike the other courts, it was not staffed by salaried judges. The Chancery judges were on a commission of the amounts that passed through the court. They were paid out of the fees, as were a horde of leftover medieval and regency clerks, who did not have to attend the court or do anything whatsoever for their share of the plunder.

Real Property law had not been reformed into any consistent codex; it had accreted like a coral reef and was almost as unnavigable. And it was to the advantage of the court itself to keep cases running until the fortunes of all concerned were completely exhausted, along with the estate itself.

Jeremy Bentham called it 'a labyrinth without a clew'. Various attempts at reform had been made, but they simply whittled away at the edge of the abuses, rather than tackling the main problem, which was the court itself.

'The one great principle of English law is to make business for itself,' Dickens wrote, in *Bleak House*. 'There is no other principle distinctly, certainly and consistently maintained through all its narrow turnings. Viewed in this light it becomes a coherent scheme and not the monstrous maze the laity are apt to think it.' Ouch!

In the novel Chancery ruins and corrupts everyone it touches: poor mad Miss Flite; fierce Mr Gridley; all of the lost Jarndyces; Mr Snagsby, the law stationer; and even Richard Carstone, a ward of the court, who is gradually seduced by the pie-in-the-sky prospect of wealth and dies miserably. Dickens describes very accurately how a case in Chancery was extended, for fees, long after the original applicants had given up and died of despair.

> *The lawyers have twisted it into such a state of bedevilment that the original merits of the case have long disappeared from the face of the earth. It is about a will and trusts under a will – or it was once. It's about nothing but costs now. We are always appearing, and disappearing, and swearing, and interrogating, and filing, and cross-filing, and arguing, and motioning, and sealing, and referring, and reporting, and revolving about the Lord Chancellor and his satellites and equitably waltzing ourselves off to dusty death, about costs. That's the great question. All the rest, by some extraordinary means, has melted away.*

Dickens very carefully refutes the arguments against reform: cost, difficulty, and the abolition of the livelihood of respectable practitioners with 'three daughters and an aged parent in the Vale of Taunton'.

(When I was a law student and the new Family Law Act was brought in, the same argument arose: what would happen to all those divorce lawyers if no-fault divorce came in? Well, I did not notice any ex-divorce lawyers begging on the street after the act was law. The legal profession adjusts quite well to changes; it just doesn't like them.)

In 1875, stung into action by Dickens' scorn and by the number of people who had read the book and felt they ought to protest to a politician, British Parliament finally abolished the Court of Chancery. It sacked all the judges, closed the building and merged the remaining business with the Court of Equity, which had salaried judges and reasons to speed things along.

Thereafter it was not a recipe for instant ruin to challenge an unfair will, as costs were paid out of the estate. The reform had been done by many, but the driving, emotional edge was *Bleak House*, and its importance must not be underestimated. It is a great pity that Charles Dickens never saw it. He had died five years earlier in 1870.

The pen is mightier than the sword – and easier to write with.

Champions of the Innocent

by PD Martin

Imagine what it would be like to be wrongly accused of a crime. It's the stuff of nightmares, of books, of movies – right? How much harder then to envisage being wrongfully convicted of that crime you didn't commit?

But you're Australian, and Australia is an advanced civilised country with a strong legal system, so surely, if you were unlucky enough to be wrongly accused, a jury would realise the truth and acquit. Not necessarily.

So, you're in jail faced with years of 'doing time' – now imagine the loneliness and sense of injustice; it would be overwhelming, wouldn't it? And yet, it could still be worse. You could be in prison with limited resources to fight your wrongful conviction.

You'd really need a champion; someone to fight for you, to take up your cause.

Enter the Innocence Project, a group of people dedicated to freeing the other victims of the criminal justice system – the wrongly convicted.

Most Australians, indeed most people living in developed countries where democracy reigns, believe in their justice system. So, how many people currently serving time in Australia's prisons are innocent of the crimes for which they're convicted?

A Snapshot of Some of Australia's Wrongfully Convicted

Leonard Fraser was on trial for the murder of Natasha Ryan in 2003 when she showed up alive and well.

The Mickleberg brothers spent 15 years in jail between them for robbery; it was later proved that the evidence was fabricated.

Frank Button of Queensland spent a year in prison before DNA evidence excluded him at appeal stage.

John Button of Western Australia spent five years in jail for the manslaughter of his girlfriend (after a false confession) and then nearly four decades trying to clear his name.

Kelvin Condren, an indigenous Australian, confessed to murder and was imprisoned for seven years before it was discovered that he couldn't have committed the murder because he was in police custody at the time.

Lindy and Michael Chamberlain were wrongfully convicted, on expert scientific evidence, of the murder of their daughter, Azaria. On 2 February 1982 they were committed to trial following a coronial inquiry, and later that year they were found guilty; a verdict that was upheld in a 1983 appeal. Their 1984 High Court appeal was also unsuccessful. In 1986 when the remains of Azaria's jacket were found at the base of Ayers Rock, a Royal Commission was held. Lindy Chamberlain was released from prison on 7 February 1986. (Michael Chamberlain had already served his time.)

Andrew Mallard spent 12 years in jail for a murder he didn't commit. He was a victim of his own mentally vulnerable state and dubious police processes.

The more cynical among us may say none. Others may say that perhaps there are 10 people, but maybe 15 or 20 is more realistic. Certainly these numbers seem plausible; logical even. But the reality is far more shocking than the best-imagined whodunit.

In the USA, DNA exonerations have exposed a disturbing number of wrongful convictions. Men in jail for crimes such as murder and rape have been exonerated based on DNA tests conducted after the fact – sometimes years into their prison sentences. DNA can be damning evidence; but it can also set people free. To date in America,

182 people have been exonerated post-conviction through DNA evidence. But these people had already, between them, spent approximately 2500 years in prison.

While it's impossible to put an exact figure on wrongful conviction – let's face it, usually only the convicted person truly knows if he or she is innocent – estimates of wrongful conviction in the US range from 0.5 per cent to five per cent. Given America's population, even the lower estimate means there are thousands of innocent people currently serving time in American prisons.

Estimates for Australia, and other parts of the world, generally sit around one per cent. This figure sounds fairly high, but maybe not shockingly so – until you realise that one per cent of our 'prison population' means that there are around 200 people wrongfully incarcerated in Australia. Then the figure becomes jaw-dropping stuff.

While it would be nice to think that Australia's criminal justice system is perfect, it simply is not. How can it be, when human involvement inherently leads to human error? Police officers can't be right all the time; scientists can't be right all the time; juries can't get it right all the time, nor can judges.

So – not counting any cases where the word cover-up could be bandied around – 'simple' human error means that every year a number of our convicted criminals are, in fact, innocent of the crimes for which they've been charged, prosecuted and convicted.

The first Innocence Project was founded in the USA in 1992 to combat wrongful conviction and help the innocent fight for their freedom, or simply clear their names after their release. (In many cases the person will end up serving their full sentence while trying to prove their innocence.) Established in New York by Barry C Scheck and Peter J Neufeld, the Innocence Project has been responsible for freeing more than 140 people in the US, including 14 people who'd been sentenced to death.

There are now about 30 Innocence Projects in the US, across all states. The original Innocence Project in New York works on 200 cases at any given time, but has around 4000 requests under active consideration. To date, exoneration has occurred in approximately 40 per cent of the cases that the New York Project investigated to conclusion.

The Griffith University Innocence Project – Australia's first – was established in 2001 by Lynne Weathered, from Griffith University, and Gold Coast lawyers Chris Nyst and Jason Murakami. Their Project takes on 'cases where initial investigations support an inmate's assertions that they have been wrongfully convicted and where innocence may be established through the use of DNA technology or other fresh evidence'.

The Griffith University Innocence Project adopted, with some alterations, the US model. While it works independently of the New York original, the Griffith Project is part of the Innocence Network, an international organisation made up of over 30 groups in the US, Canada and Australia who work on behalf of the wrongfully convicted.

The Innocence Network shares knowledge and its experiences. Lynne Weathered says, 'Wrongful conviction is now recognised as an international problem. As such, longer-term or larger issues can involve international collaboration. When it comes to understanding causation, correction and prevention of wrongful conviction, we can all learn from each other.'

There are now three projects in Australia – the Griffith University Innocence Project, the University of Melbourne Innocence Project and the Perth-based Western Australian Innocence Project. (The project at the University of Technology Sydney is not currently operational.)

Innocence Projects are generally university-based and largely resourced by students – an important aspect of their modus operandi, given the amount of time required to investigate claims of innocence.

The Griffith University Project is staffed by lawyers, students and academics, all working together towards freeing innocent people. The students work for course credits, the lawyers work pro bono, and the academics volunteer their time and work on the Project as part of their university roles.

Students, working in teams of two to five, go through trial transcripts then attempt to find new evidence, relevant information, new witnesses, and so on. Investigation is the main role – the Project doesn't, itself, legally represent the wrongfully convicted, although students are advised by specialist criminal lawyers once a week.

In most cases, an innocence project is the only avenue open for re-investigation of an applicant's case, once they've progressed through the court system.

'Innocence Projects are not themselves the answer to wrongful conviction … They do, however, offer a practical way to help a limited number of wrongfully convicted persons,' said Weathered.

The Griffith University Innocence Project has roughly 100 current cases and has received over 300 requests for assistance since its establishment in 2001. The Project is typically involved in the more serious cases, such as rape and murder, although they do receive a variety of applications.

'We are interested in cases where biological testing of evidence would be probative of innocence. For example, we would not take on a rape case where the issue is *consent*, because DNA is not probative in such an instance,' Weathered explains.

All applications undergo a four-stage process at the Griffith Project:

1. Initial screening: determining whether the case generally falls within the ambit of the Project
2. Initial investigation: A further review of the case based on documentary evidence
3. Full investigation: To find possible new evidence of innocence
4. Referral to a pro-bono lawyer: to act as the solicitor for the applicant where the case is to be considered for an appeal or pardon petition

Weathered says that proving someone's innocence is generally a lengthy process. 'Years of investigation prior to exoneration is typical of innocence work around the world.'

This process is magnified by the fact that the applicants have usually exhausted all their appeal rights in the legal system, and do not have a lot of options available to fight their conviction. Despite the best efforts of the Innocence Project, the reality is grim for the wrongly convicted. Often, during the Project's four-stage process, many of the cases will be rejected.

'Rejection may not necessarily reflect the guilt or innocence of a person, but the availability, or lack thereof, of new evidence of innocence,' Weathered says. 'Indicators are that in the majority of cases, the innocence of people will remain invisible. Evidence will not be kept which could have been subjected to DNA innocence testing. Evidence will not come to light which could show innocence. Some convictions will remain simply because nothing significantly new can overturn them.'

Because of this, working with an Innocence Project is frustrating work. Often the students, academics and lawyers will believe the applicant is innocent – but they just can't prove it, or can't find enough new evidence that would force a re-trial or pardon. So what keeps them going?

For Lynne Weathered it's her sense of justice. 'I feel a deep sense that this is the work I am supposed to be doing, and it appeals to the ideals of justice that I hold. The voices of the wrongly convicted are often lost in the catch-cry that "everyone in prison says they are innocent". They are so easy to dismiss, and already so disempowered. Time and time again I have seen that it is only through the most enduring efforts of family or friends, in conjunction with lawyers or Innocence Projects, that the innocence of these people comes to light – eventuating in their release from prison.'

To remind herself – or perhaps to remind others – of the importance of the work they're doing, the importance of freeing the innocent, Lynne Weathered has a Martin Luther King Jnr quote on her door: 'Our lives begin to end the day we become silent about things that matter.'

And no matter who you are, an innocent person sitting in jail *does* matter.

So, how does wrongful conviction occur? Weathered has identified 10 major factors that contribute to wrongful conviction:

1. Faulty eyewitness identification
2. Incorrect informer evidence
3. Overzealous or improper police investigation or prosecution
4. Tunnel vision
5. Bad defence lawyers
6. Incorrect scientific evidence
7. Plea bargaining
8. False confessions
9. Media attention
10. Race

Faulty eyewitness identification is a fact of life. How often have you seen someone in the street you thought you knew, only to discover it wasn't really them at all? Our memories are fallible, particularly when you add an element like stress. One famous case in the US exemplifies the very real possibility of a faulty eyewitness ID.

In 1984 Jennifer Thompson was raped for hours in her own home. During that time she studied her attacker carefully, determined to make sure – if she survived – that he paid for his crime. She did survive and she later identified Ronald Cotton as her attacker. He was arrested, convicted of the rape, and given two life sentences. There was no doubt in Jennifer Thompson's mind that her attacker was behind bars, and she had some sense of closure on this horrific event in her life.

Of course, Ronald Cotton claimed from the get-go that he was innocent – just like everyone who goes to jail, right? But police began re-investigating the Thompson case when convicted rapist Bobby Poole started bragging to his fellow prison inmates that *he'd* raped Jennifer and got away with it.

In 1995, 11 years after the attack, police asked Jennifer Thompson to give a blood sample for DNA purposes. To her absolute shock, DNA evidence cleared Cotton and confirmed that her real attacker was Bobby Poole.

How was this possible? During the attack Thompson spent several hours with her rapist, centimetres away from his face for the whole time, yet she got the ID wrong. It certainly makes you question cases where someone is convicted by the ID of a passer-by, someone who sees an accused person for a few moments and often from metres away.

Lynne Weathered says that faulty eyewitness IDs could be significantly reduced if we introduced double-blind sequential line-ups. In a double-blind sequential line-up, the police officer conducting the line-up doesn't know who the suspect is, *and* the photographs are shown to the witness(es) sequentially, rather than having them all presented at once (on one board).

Many of the factors that contribute to wrongful conviction are difficult to address, due to the costs involved or time constraints etc, but eyewitness ID isn't one of them.

What Happened to Ronald Cotton?

Ronald Cotton was released from jail and Jennifer Thompson, plagued with guilt, requested a meeting with him. She needed to see and apologise to the man who'd spent 11 years in prison because she'd incorrectly identified him. Surprisingly, it was not an angry meeting and now the pair tours America educating others about the inherent problems of eyewitness identifications.

Informer evidence is another area that can lead to unreliable information and wrongful conviction. Informants are often rewarded in some way for the information they give, and that can be powerful motivation for anything from embellishment to flat-out lies. There are quite a number of cases around the world where informer evidence was later disproved. There have even been some in which the informer was the perpetrator, but had set someone else up to look guilty.

Police or prosecution responsibility in a wrongful conviction can be accidental or deliberate. The part they can play ranges from the extreme – corruption or evidence fabrication; to the more moderate – overzealousness and **tunnel vision**. But whether extreme or moderate, the affect can be disastrous if the wrong person ends up in jail.

Andrew Mallard's case in Western Australia is a good example of the role the police and prosecution played in a wrongful conviction. Police were certain Mallard was their man (tunnel vision) and aggressively questioned him for long periods of time, despite his mental state, and were allegedly violent during the interview. When the case went to court the police and/or the prosecution withheld evidence from Mallard and his lawyers, and the handwritten notes of the interviewing officers were submitted as evidence, as part of a supposed confession.

A bad defence lawyer can obviously be devastating for anyone who goes before the courts, but is particularly disastrous for a wrongfully accused person. In the US there have been cases where the defence lawyer has been drunk or asleep during a trial. In Australia the legal standards are hopefully higher, but there are many cases of inexperienced legal aid lawyers taking major cases to trial. These lawyers are not negligent, simply inexperienced.

Incorrect scientific evidence always raises controversy in cases of wrongful conviction. While most sciences are seen as absolute, the reality is that experts can and do get it wrong. In addition, while science is sometimes seen as completely objective and foolproof, scientific evidence is open to interpretation. One name says it all for Australia in this area – Lindy Chamberlain. The Chamberlain case is our most famous example of wrongful conviction. Both Lindy and Michael Chamberlain were convicted on scientific evidence that was later found to be incorrect. Remember the blood (rust) in the car and handprint on Baby Azaria's jumpsuit?

Plea bargaining can cause a raft of problems in terms of valid convictions, because innocent people will plead guilty to a lesser charge for a number of reasons: to deal with the matter quickly; to get released immediately (for example if they've already served some time while awaiting their trial); in the hope of a much lower penalty; or if they're advised by their lawyer that the evidence will be too difficult to refute at trial.

While we'd all like to say we'd fight any invalid charge, and fight for our innocence on principle, several months in jail could turn even the most righteous of us.

A false confession might seem like the most stupid reason for being wrongly convicted – it's hard to imagine why someone would confess to a crime they did not commit – but it does happen. In fact, many DNA exonerations in the US have 'reversed' false confessions. But how or why does it happen?

False confessions often occur during particularly aggressive police questioning, where the suspect feels they have no choice but to agree with the interrogators; they literally get to the point of: 'I'll say anything, sign anything, just to get you off my back.'

One well-known Australian case was that of John Button, who found his girlfriend badly injured by the side of the road. She later died. During his long police interview, Button confessed to murder. Even though he recanted, he was charged and then convicted of manslaughter. Despite a known serial killer later confessing to the crime, Button served his full sentence and then spent decades trying to clear his name. He now spearheads the Western Australian Innocence Project.

Lynne Weathered says: 'For John Button, who is one of the gentlest people I have had the privilege to meet, it appears that [his confession was the result of] the extreme emotional state he was in, having earlier discovered his girlfriend by the side of the road, in conjunction with a lengthy and traumatic police interview. John stated eventually he just agreed to let the police write down whatever they wanted in order to remove himself from the interrogation, and that he signed the confession in the belief that no-one could be charged and convicted for something that they had not done'.

It seems that sometimes a belief and trust in our criminal justice system can get you into trouble.

A high-profile false confession in America involved the rape of a Central Park jogger. In this case, five teenage boys all confessed to the crime and were convicted. Many years later, a notorious serial rapist in New York came forward to confess to the crime, and DNA tests confirmed he was the perpetrator.

So, while false confessions can be hard for most of us to acknowledge and understand, the facts point to them as a consistent factor in wrongful conviction.

Media attention can also lead to problems in our criminal justice system. Despite safeguards put in place, can a jury truly be unbiased if the case they're sitting on received significant media attention at the time of the crime? Again, the Chamberlains are a great example of this. By the time Lindy and Michael Chamberlain had their day in court, years had passed since Azaria's death; but could there really be anyone in Australia who had escaped the media frenzy and the whole 'a dingo took my baby' case? Could anyone have truly claimed objectivity and impartiality?

Race is the last, but by no means the least, contributing factor in wrongful conviction. We have a very high representation of indigenous Australians in our prisons, and it's anyone's guess how many are innocent but faced with cultural and communication issues.

If Kelvin Condren is any indication, then he's also the tip of the iceberg. Condren confessed to murder and was imprisoned for seven years. It was later discovered he couldn't have committed the murder, because he was actually in police custody at the time! So much for the concept of a thorough investigation. Condren was convicted in 1984 and exonerated in 1990.

These 10 factors contribute to the number of people who wind up convicted of crimes they did not commit. But why does it take so long to clear their names? Why do so many people have to spend years and years in prison before being released?

The answer is simple – it's the structure of our legal system. Our criminal justice system may like the 'innocent until proven guilty' concept, but it does not make it easy for someone convicted of a crime to bring their case back to the attention of the courts.

While there are some variances between the states and territories in Australia, in most cases the process is the same: the accused person will stand trial in the corresponding state/territory criminal court; if convicted they will then generally have one month in which to lodge an appeal; if the appeal is unsuccessful, they can then apply to have their case heard by the High Court of Australia.

So any one person can have up to three chances to be found not guilty. This may sound fair enough (three strikes and you're out) but there are at least five major hurdles, or problems, with this 'fair' system.

Firstly, with only one month to lodge an appeal, it's unlikely new evidence that clears the convicted person will turn up in time.

Secondly, even if new evidence *is* discovered, for an appeal to be granted on the basis of 'fresh evidence' it must be proven that the evidence could not have been uncovered with due diligence at the time of the original trial.

Thirdly, if the case does get to the High Court, the High Court won't consider cases with new or fresh evidence. Next, appeals are not automatic – an appeal lawyer will put forward an application that must cover *why* the appeal should be heard, but this application can be rejected. In fact, only five per cent of applications to the High Court are granted.

To top it all off, even if your appeal is granted, Australian courts have generally shown reluctance to overturn a jury verdict.

Once someone has exhausted their appeal process, if they've been wrongfully convicted they really only have three options: a pardon from the governor of their state, a Royal Commission, or escaping from prison! While of course the third option is not recommended, there are difficulties with the two legitimate options.

A State Governor's decision whether or not to grant a pardon, or order a re-trial, is purely discretionary, and there's no transparency in the process – no understanding of why the governor made a particular decision, and no explanation required. Plus, there may also be a political agenda that comes into play.

A Royal Commission is unlikely to happen unless the case is extremely high profile. For example, it was a Royal Commission that eventually cleared the Chamberlains, and another that freed Charles Edward Spatt, who was wrongfully convicted of murder in South Australia. But Royal Commissions cost time and money and are certainly not the normal course of action. It's definitely not something a wrongfully convicted person can even hope for, let alone rely on.

So, while our justice system is good at fixing legal and technical errors that occur during the trial and appeal process, it doesn't cope very well with claims of factual innocence.

To address these problems in the legal system, in addition to case work, Innocence Projects are usually heavily involved in lobbying for legal reform. Lynne Weathered says that law-reform activities have become a major part of the Griffith University Innocence Project's work. 'What has been demonstrated during our years of operation is the urgent need for law reform to enable convicted but innocent people the opportunity to prove their innocence.

'The Innocence Project's unique experience with obstacles facing the wrongly convicted, particularly in Queensland, has highlighted that wrongful conviction applicants have no right to have biological evidence or crime scene samples preserved; no right to information regarding crime scene evidence retained in their case; no right to access DNA evidence; and no right to have DNA innocence testing performed.'

So what does this mean for people claiming to be innocent? Weathered can cite a perfect example.

Frank Button of Queensland (not to be confused with John Button of Western Australia) is considered to be Australia's only DNA exoneration. Button was convicted of rape and spent almost a year in prison before additional DNA testing was undertaken prior to his appeal.

'This later testing,' Weathered explains, 'included a bed sheet that had not originally been tested, and excluded Button as a contributor to the seminal stains on it. In addition, further testing of the complainant's swabs resulted in the conclusion that the same male was the donor of the sperm on the bed sheet and the swab, effectively exonerating Button.'

In the case of Frank Button, while he was wrongfully imprisoned and did serve time, at least he was able to clear his name at a relatively early stage, at Queensland's Criminal Appeal Court. But what would have happened if the bed sheet wasn't tested?

Weathered believes Button probably would have remained wrongly convicted and would have had to serve out his whole sentence. 'Under the current Queensland policy on preservation of evidence, the biological evidence relating to his trial and appeal would most likely have been destroyed, or the bed sheet returned to the family of the victim. If he was fortunate enough to have it, or samples from it, preserved, he would not have the right to know that such evidence was still available. Nor would he have the right to have a DNA test performed on the evidence. As such, it is likely that Button would have been left in prison, not only wrongly convicted but also prevented from establishing his innocence.'

Frank Button's case, in fact every case of wrongful conviction in Australia, highlights the need for legal reform in Australia. Think about the prison times of just the high-profile wrongfully convicted in Australia: Andrew Mallard served 12 years in jail, Frank Button one year, John Button five years, Lindy Chamberlain four years.

So what should be done to make the system fairer and more robust? Obviously we don't want to free the guilty, but we don't want the innocent sitting behind bars either. According to Weathered, just 'acknowledging that wrongful conviction occurs is the first step in addressing its correction'.

Change is more likely when more Australians become aware that miscarriages of justice happen in cases that are much less 'sensational' than the Chamberlains, and that they're a lot more common than reported in the media.

Innocence Projects will, of course, play a large part in effecting change through their lobbying efforts. The Griffith University Project, for example, has made submissions to Queensland's Attorney-General, and hosted a DNA forum in 2006 that posed the question, 'Should a convicted person have the right to a DNA innocence test?' These activities not only help raise awareness and bring key issues before the legislators, but thrust them into the public arena as well.

Lynne Weathered is passionate about 'better processes'. In fact, her current academic area of research is looking at how the ideal system would work.

'Wrongful conviction must now be acknowledged as an unenviable but inevitable part of any criminal justice system,' she says. 'And, as such, I believe reforms designed to correct wrongful convictions must and will be incorporated into Australia's criminal justice system.'

Of course, change can take time, but Weathered believes there are some immediate things that could and should happen while we look at larger reforms. 'Access to DNA innocence testing is one way forward. This change would at least immediately open up some options for wrongful conviction applicants, and those, such as lawyers or Innocence Projects in this country, who work on their behalf. Australia's failure to provide appropriate avenues to potentially prove innocence through DNA testing cannot equate to justice in a modern society that must, at the very least, recognise the possibility of wrongful conviction.'

New South Wales did actually set up a system for this; however, it was later suspended. The Innocence Panel was established in October 2001 to facilitate DNA testing for NSW applicants who had been convicted of serious crimes (such as murder, manslaughter and serious sexual assault) but who claimed innocence. A 2003 review of the panel indicated that it will operate again at some time in the future, possibly under the State Attorney-General's Department. In addition, the Bar Association of New South Wales has recently made a submission to Parliament for the re-establishment of a DNA Reference Panel for DNA innocence testing.

For post-conviction DNA testing to work, the evidence needs to be preserved – and again, this is something that law enforcement could start doing immediately. An individual's future rests on evidence being available for examination down the track, and this is especially pertinent given that science is continually developing. Even the use of DNA is relatively new, so what will scientists come up with next? What will they discover in the coming decade?

Currently in Australia, there is no system or requirement to preserve evidence and it's often discarded or returned to victims. It's a similar situation in the US where the crime-scene evidence has gone in 75 per cent of the cases reviewed by the New York Innocence Project. The preservation of evidence is essential for the wrongfully convicted.

Weathered says that work has and is being done in this area, with the Australian Law Reform Commission noting the importance of preservation and access to evidence, and recommending legislative reform that will require all crime-scene samples to be permanently preserved to facilitate DNA innocence testing. The Victorian Parliament Law Reform Committee held an inquiry into forensic sampling and DNA databases, and as part of that inquiry considered preservation of, and access to, DNA samples for purposes of both criminal investigations and potential exoneration.

As for legal reforms, Weathered also suggests looking overseas – particularly at England, Canada and the USA. For example in England, in 1997, the Criminal Cases Review Commission (CCRC) was established. This body was set up to investigate suspected miscarriages of justice in England, Wales and Northern Ireland. In one 'sample' of 200 cases that the CCRC referred back to the appeal courts, 64 per cent of the convictions were quashed.

In Canada, the Criminal Convictions Review Group investigates claims of wrongful convictions. This body was set up in 2002 to deal with these claims as part of Canada's legislative reform.

And in the US, the New York Innocence Project successfully lobbied for convicted people to have access to DNA innocence testing, with legislation introduced in 2001. In more recent developments, the *Justice for All Act 2004* is federal legislation that provides for the enhancement of DNA collection and analysis, and provides authorities with funding to improve the representation of capital-offence defendants. Part of this Act is the *Innocence Protection Act 2004*, which addresses post-conviction DNA testing for federal cases, increases compensation in federal cases of wrongful conviction, and established $US25 million in grants over a five-year period for post-conviction DNA testing legislation.

Of course, being wrongfully convicted is about more than just crime-scene evidence and legislation. More than anything else, it's about the people. Lynne Weathered says, 'I have had the privilege to meet several men and women who have been exonerated. I have heard their heart-wrenching stories first hand. It is their stories that propel my passion for this work. The grace and forgiveness of many of these people is one of the most remarkable things to bear witness to.'

Being wrongfully convicted would be a traumatic event, so it stands to reason there must be psychological repercussions. Early studies on this subject have indicated that the wrongfully convicted can suffer from personality changes and severe post-traumatic stress disorder. A recent study by the US-based Life After Exoneration Program found that the exonerees surveyed had 'considerable difficulty rebuilding their lives', with half living with their families, only one-third financially independent, one-third having lost custody of their children, and more a quarter suffering from post-traumatic stress disorder.

There's also a residual, often constant, stigma even after exoneration. Frank Button, despite DNA exoneration, still feels people see him as guilty. And, on top of the psychological effects, there's also the lost time – which can often be years or even decades. Wrongly convicted American Eric Sarsfield once said: 'What 10 years of your life would you want gone? One to 10, 10 to 20, 20 to 30?'

The impact on the person's family should also be considered, because they go through the trauma with the wrongfully convicted person. They're tortured by the knowledge that their loved one is innocent and in jail; or perhaps even worse, they question their loved one's innocence, which puts an enormous strain on the relationship.

The victim and/or victim's family also suffers. When someone is convicted of a crime, there's a sense of justice, of relief. But if it's discovered or suspected that the wrong person is in prison, this sense of closure might be shattered, hijacked or may never come. Certainly, if the real perpetrator is still wandering the streets then justice has not been served.

People who work with an Innocence Project see much of this first hand. Lynne Weathered says, 'When working in law, there is the need for objectivity; but at the same time, I do care and do not pretend otherwise. The human factor makes this work all the more frustrating and more emotionally exhausting – but also all the more important.'

Working with the wrongfully convicted must be both rewarding and disheartening, and balancing the two extremes must be hard. When asked how she copes, Weathered says: 'Balance is an interesting concept and one which I don't think I do very well. The frustration is intense. But I try to focus on the small steps forward that we make. All that we can do is our best, and that's what we're doing.

'If the reforms we hope for eventuate, then this will be a major step forward. If we can help one person who has been wrongly convicted, it is worth all the effort. But there are also other rewards. I have been privileged to meet a network of wonderful people who do this work throughout this country, and in the United States, Canada and England, whose dedication and passion for justice are truly inspirational. The [Griffith University] students, some of whom continue to volunteer their time on the Project, also make this work very rewarding.'

For the wrongfully convicted, the mere existence of these Projects must be a comforting thought – perhaps the only comforting thought. During the hardest of times, when most doors are closed, an Innocence Project will at least review your claim. And the goal of all Innocence Projects is simple – to release innocent people.

As Lynne Weathered says, 'Nobody wins by having an innocent person in prison. It just creates more victims: victims of crime and victims of the criminal justice system.'

An Uneasy State

Kathryn Deans

To paraphrase the Bard, it seems 'there's something rotten in the State of South Australia'. Known for the country's more bizarre murder cases, something odd also appears to be happening to justice in our mid-southern state.

In recent years, one man was handed a hefty sentence based on what was later discovered to be flawed and inadequate pathology results, while another was permitted to walk away from a terrible crime with few consequences, despite there being considerable evidence that he acted outside of the law. The former was charged with the murder of his wife; the latter escaped from the actions that resulted in the deaths of two of his children.

Convictions in both cases hinged on the testimony of expert witnesses – one for the prosecution and one for the defence – evidence that has been challenged by other experts since the coronial and trial results were handed down. Both cases refuse to go away; they represent a snapshot of all that appears to be wrong with a justice system that should be there to prosecute the guilty and defend the innocent.

South Australia has come under fire for its troubled forensic department, while its state prosecutors have had to defend their plea bargains more and more. So we have to ask the question: is the judicial system in South Australia failing victims *and* their families?

Henry Keogh: sentenced to 25 years

The Night She Died …

Friday 18 March 1994 had been an unexceptional day for Anna-Jane Cheney. It was, in fact, a day much like any other: Anna had been busy at work, putting in a full day at the Law Society where she was Acting Manager for Professional Conduct. Her position was to monitor the business practices of solicitors and she was good at her job.

She had lunched with friends, caught up with others for coffee, and had met up with her fiancé Henry for a few drinks after work at the Norwood Hotel, before they headed home together.

Henry Keogh, a senior banker who had just taken a position with a firm of financial planners, appeared to be in a mellow mood. He and Anna had been engaged for some time and their wedding date was looming. Anna had gone for the final fitting for her wedding dress on the Wednesday, and couldn't hide her excitement about her forthcoming nuptials.

Henry was planning on visiting his mother Eileen later on in the evening; Anna had arranged to meet her sister-in-law Susan, so they could walk their dogs together. After returning home from the pub with Henry, Anna changed into a tracksuit before heading out again. Susan was married to Anna's brother Marc, and the two women had always got on well. Anna arrived at their place at about 7.30pm. Henry arrived at his mother's around 8.30pm.

Anna and Susan took the dogs to the local park and chatted about the forthcoming wedding. Anna mentioned that she'd gone to the pub with Henry earlier on, and that she was skipping dinner because she wasn't hungry. When Anna left for home, just before 8pm, it was the last time Susan saw her sister-in-law alive.

Less than 90 minutes later Anna-Jane Cheney was dead, drowned in her bath.

So how could that happen? How did Anna die? There are only three possibilities:

The first is that she was killed by her fiancé, Henry Keogh.

The second is that she was killed by some unknown assailant.

The third and last possibility is that she was one of the unlucky few that make up the tiny percentage of seemingly healthy young people who die of natural causes every year.

Initially, the police attributed her death to accidental drowning but they were soon to change their minds.

Nobody reviewing the evidence can *really* know what happened that night. Any answers that Anna's body might have provided were destroyed when her remains were released for cremation by the State's pathologist. But the testimony of witness neighbours and the photographic evidence do indicate that there were some unusual circumstances that were never satisfactorily explained, or even investigated by the police.

Both of Anna's neighbours offered thought-provoking statements. On one side of Anna's house lived a lady who owned two dogs. She reported that around 7pm one of her dogs became agitated and began barking and running towards the front door, behaviour that was completely out of character. On the other side of Anna's place, another neighbour reported that she heard a car pull up and a horn sound three times, a highly unusual occurrence as she'd never heard her neighbours blow their horns before.

The last, and quite possibly the most inexplicable thing that happened that night, was the strange behaviour of Anna's car. This has never been explained but is certainly worth a mention. Pictures taken by the police at the scene on the night of her death indicate that it was missing, or rather not where it should be. It was not parked under the carport, and it wasn't in the street. And yet Anna drove home from Susan's place.

But hang on, because it gets stranger. Another police photograph taken two days later shows the car parked beside the house, under the carport, exactly where it should have been.

One thing was certain, on the night of Anna's death, and that was that the police were convinced her drowning was an accident, a tragedy, possibly brought about by the amount of wine she drank that evening. Although that said, she apparently showed no signs of intoxication when she met up with her sister-in-law.

But, as the death wasn't considered suspicious, the area was not cordoned off. Family and friends were allowed all over the scene, contaminating any evidence there may have been. Nobody took measurements of the depth of the bath water, nor were any samples of the water itself taken for bodily excretions or foreign matter.

When Henry Keogh discovered his fiancée, Anna was laying on her side, her face submerged in the water. Unable to pull the plug out, because she was lying on top of it, Henry managed to drag Anna over the side of the bath. When his attempts at resuscitation failed, he called an ambulance. It's on record that the service received the call at 9.33pm. The ambulance took only five minutes to get there, and the two attending paramedics performed CPR on Anna. All attempts to revive her failed, and Anna-Jane Cheney was declared dead.

Five months after the event one of the ambulance officers, Kerry Stevenson, made a statement regarding the events of the night. Nine months later she and Paul Murgatroyd, the other attending officer, were asked to make another one. Both claimed that there was no vomit beside Anna's body, even though Keogh had told them he tried resuscitation. (There should be vomit if someone tries resuscitation; even if the person is dead, the act of pushing on the chest will push air and fluids into the mouth.)

Both ambos claimed the body felt quite dry, as did the carpet Anna was laying on. Photographs of Anna's body taken by Technical Services on the night, however, show the carpet beneath her looking damp.

The conflicting evidence by those who were there on the evening is a recurring facet of the 'investigation'. The evidence of the two ambulance officers contradicts that of other witnesses, including attending police officers, who stated that the bathmat was saturated and the floor was wet.

If the scene had been secured, this evidence would have been recorded as a matter of course. It has never been suggested that any of the witnesses deliberately lied about what they saw that evening; but it does demonstrate how unreliable eyewitness evidence can be, and does make a reliable retrospective evaluation of the scene virtually impossible.

A parade of unsupervised people traipsed through the unsecured (by anyone official) premises that night. After the ambulance officers arrived, so did the police, and then Anna's family – around 20 people in total, each of them walking through the house, all looking at and occasionally touching Anna's body.

And what about Henry Keogh, in the midst of all this confusion? Everybody who was present was quite adamant that Henry appeared inconsolable; he was crying and visibly distraught. Even the police were sympathetic, thinking his grief was perfectly understandable for a man who'd arrived home to find his fiancée dead in the bath. Henry seemed unwilling to leave Anna's side, touching her hand while he wept over her.

Amongst all the police that appeared at the house that night were two officers from Holden Hill Criminal Investigation Branch, and Constable Walkley from the Coronial Investigation Centre. Following standard procedure, the CIB officers investigated the premises but the only thing of any note that they discovered was a bottle of Naprosin, an anti-inflammatory, in Anna's handbag.

Constable Walkley, who'd been with the CIC for 11 years and had attended many sudden deaths, examined Anna's body. Once again following standard procedure, Walkley used latex gloves as she went over the body, even including the scalp in her examination. She discovered no signs of bruising.

Senior Constable Jones, with police Technical Services, also scrutinised Anna at the scene and, like Walkley, he found no signs of bruising or physical violence anywhere on the body. After the examinations were complete, they took Anna away, carrying her from the house and placing her on a stretcher before loading her into the Coroner's van. Note that Anna's body was carried out of the house by two people – one who took hold of her under the arms, another who held her legs. (This rather odd handling might have resulted in post-mortem bruising).

Afterwards, both Henry's father and Anna's parents tried to get him to return home with them, rather than spend the night in the house. But Henry refused, telling them that he wanted time to himself. He intended to go to bed and try to get some sleep.

The Autopsy

Anna died on a Friday. On the Sunday, an autopsy was performed by the State's chief forensic pathologist, Colin Manock. Dr Manock had often given evidence, as an expert witness, in cases before the State and was used to facing a jury. He'd been featured in quite a few other cases, some of them very high profile, such as battered baby cases and the trial of Emily Perry.

Shortcomings in his analysis of data had been found in the past, so his 'expert' reputation was dubious, but he *was* the State's chief forensic pathologist. What turned out to be the case against Henry Keogh was the last that Dr Manock would give evidence in before his retirement. It has been said that, with Manock the subject of ongoing controversy, the police should have bypassed him as an eminent witness long before he handed in his damning findings on the Anna-Jane Cheney case.

Why? Because it was largely on the evidence compiled by Dr Colin Manock that, six weeks after Anna was discovered dead, Henry Keogh was charged with her murder. He was at a basketball game, with his children, when the police arrested him on Saturday 7 May 1994.

While nobody has ever claimed that the entire case against Henry rested on Dr Manock's findings alone, without the substantial weight of his testimony it is doubtful that there would have been enough evidence to prosecute, let alone secure a conviction.

Dr Manock claimed that, in his preliminary investigation, he found a 'grip' mark on the lower part of Anna's left leg. He immediately inferred that she had been murdered. He suggested that somebody had held Anna's legs over her head (in court, he likened this method to the famous 'Brides In The Bath' murders that occurred in England at the beginning of the last century), and indicated to the police that they should be looking for a killer.

By definition, a pathologist's job is to look for *every* possible cause of death. They must be open-minded and observant. They must look at each deceased individual who arrives before them without prejudice. Pathologists are, essentially, forensic detectives who must sift through a battery of test results to determine, with a weight of evidence behind them, the manner in which a person has died.

The responsibility they have, both to the dead and the living, is huge because the ramifications are far reaching. They affect not only how the police treat a death, but the kind of closure experienced by the family, friends and anybody who was close to the deceased. A pathologist plays a key role in the course of events that can follow a suspicious death, so it's reassuring that we can usually be confident that they have not only the right credentials, but also a dispassionate mind able to carry out their job with due diligence.

So what happened in the case of Henry Keogh?

Having discovered the 'grip' mark on Anna-Jane Cheney's lower calf, Dr Manock concluded that she had been murdered, and was therefore keen to assist the police in meting out justice – just as he had done in the past. Prior to doubts being cast upon his abilities, Dr Manock had been considered the 'unofficial' coroner of the police.

Manock's evidence was responsible for the conviction of Fritz Van Beelen, who was tried for the rape and murder of Deborah Leach in 1971. The case was the first time that forensic evidence had been used to obtain a conviction in Australia, and Van Beelen was given a life sentence. For years, however, other medical experts, including pathologists, have claimed that the evidence presented by Colin Manock was unsound, and that Van Beelen should never have been convicted on the strength of it. Consistently turned down for parole because of his insistence that he didn't do it, Van Beelen's claims were later substantiated by the confession of a psychiatric patient (also on the beach the day of the murder) who admitted to having raped and killed a young girl.

Two decades later, the same objections to Dr Manock's forensic evidence that have been levelled at the Van Beelen case, could be directed at that of Henry Keogh. Manock gave evidence that, after performing an autopsy on Anna on the Sunday 20 March (two days after her death), he later did a follow-up examination during which he claimed to have found 'further' bruising on the scalp.

Confusingly, the written evidence he submitted to the court put this second examination on the day after the autopsy, but in his statement to the court he said he performed it two days after, on the Tuesday.

On the following Monday, 28 March, the Coroner released Anna's body for burial and on the Wednesday she was cremated. It should be noted, perhaps, that the Coroner only released the body on the say-so of Dr Manock.

Anna's cremation ensured that no further tests could ever be done, which was unfortunate as much of the forensic analysis was later condemned to be substandard or non-existent. A review of the evidence that *was* collected indicated that Dr Manock had missed some fairly basic procedural steps, such as weighing and measuring the body. This is extraordinary when he was the one who decided Anna's death was suspicious.

All of Dr Manock's suspicions apparently derived from the grip mark on Anna's calf but his deductions about this bruising weren't actually entered into his autopsy report. The supposed grip mark is certainly a pivotal part of the case, however. Manock measured his own hand against it and found that it matched the pattern of his hand. He never attempted to match the grip mark to Henry Keogh's hand print, which seems just plain stupid given it was Keogh that the police would be looking at.

Errors in Evidence

In June 1994, nearly three months after his autopsy, Dr Manock visited the scene of Anna's death and gave a fanciful description of what he believed had happened that night. Manock linked the bruises he says he found on Anna's scalp to a fall, and even described the manner in which she'd fallen. A later re-enactment, however, proved that if one actually took into account where the bruise *was*, such a fall would be physically impossible.

Despite the fact that it is standard procedure to take colour photos during an autopsy, only black-and-white shots were taken of the suspect bruising, and only half a dozen or so, at that. Only two photographs were shown in court during the trial, neither actually identified the victim, and Dr Manock had to circle the 'thumb print' on the calf in red pen to highlight where it was.

A forensic photographer stated that he could barely make out anything in the shot, let alone that it was a bruise from a thumb. Later, an Associate Professor of Forensic Photography would testify independently that the photograph the Department of Public Prosecutions presented to the court as 'convincing evidence of murder' was unrecognisable as a bruise, and that all such photographs were considered notoriously unreliable. An Associate Professor in Anatomical Pathology – on examining the slide that Dr Manock took of the 'grip' mark – stated quite unequivocally that, while he could see fibro-fatty tissue, he saw absolutely no evidence of bruising.

This just gets more and more disturbing, as this 'mark' was presented as one of the most damning pieces of evidence against Henry Keogh in his trial. *If* there had been a clear grip mark on Anna's leg (as Manock testified) then clearly she 'may' have been held under the water until she drowned (as he believed). But what of the many other possibilities that were never taken into consideration?

Of course it is possible that Anna *was* killed but by somebody other than her fiancé; a stranger perhaps, or even someone else she knew. There was no evidence of forced entry that night, but there was the odd behaviour of the neighbour's dog and the horn blowing; and let's not forget the mighty peculiar reappearance of Anna's curiously missing car. While death at the hands of someone else is only an outside chance, the police never looked at any other suspect but Henry Keogh.

On the night in question they thought the death an accident; then Manock pushed in with his bruise theory, and from then the police never considered that foul play *wasn't* the cause of Anna's mysterious death.

But what about accidental death? Every year, a small percentage of young people die unexpectedly. We have no idea what Anna's state of health was at the time. She had visited the doctor on 37 occasions in the five years leading up to her death, quite a lot of visits for a healthy young woman, but as we have no idea why she made those visits (it wasn't investigated at the time) it's but another question mark over the possible cause of her death. If Colin Manock had done his job properly that question mark might have been eliminated – or even led to a logical explanation for her death.

Even if natural causes is ruled out, Anna could actually have died in a number of ways.

Anaphylactic shock is created by a severe allergic reaction to a bite, medication or food of some kind. Did the three or four glasses of wine Anna drank earlier in the evening affect her in some way? Could she have received some kind of bite while in the park with Susan and their dogs? Photos of Anna's body indicate that there was some swelling to her face, and discoloration to the upper left-hand side of her body. The make-up found in Anna's house was for people with allergies.

So, rather than immediately leaping to the conclusion that Anna was murdered, the pathologist should have investigated every possibility.

Oh, and getting back to the alleged 'grip mark' on her calf, another factor that wasn't considered was the way in which Anna-Jane Cheney was carried from the bathroom outside to the gurney that was then put into the Coroner's van. Her body was literally manhandled – one supporting her under the arms, the other carrying her by the legs.

The courts are quick to point out that Henry Keogh wasn't convicted solely on the evidence of Dr Colin Manock. But there's no denying that his findings played a large part in securing the guilty verdict that saw Keogh receive a 25-year sentence.

Since then, there's been an increasingly insistent demand for the case to go back to court. Expert testimony from numerous sources has discovered that Dr Manock's findings were suspect at best, utterly inadequate at worst.

With so much pointing to the verdict being 'unsafe' we have to wonder why the High Court is so reluctant to follow up on the matter. Henry Keogh is incarcerated for 25 years based on the evidence of a man who has been investigated for negligence. The same man who for decades has provided a similar, less than reliable, standard of service for the South Australian judicial system.

Scott Aitken: three-year suspended sentence

The Night They Died …
In the early hours of Sunday 9 January 2000, Scott Aitken, on a weekend access with his children, was returning home after a visit to the drive-in. In the Pajero with him were his four kids: Haley, Lauren, Callum and Hayden. Aitken, an Adelaide lawyer, had recently broken up with his wife of 16 years, and he and Karen were involved a heated custody battle.

Somehow, on the journey home that very early morning, Scott Aitken's vehicle managed to leave the road, travel approximately 15 metres across a grass verge, and over a 27-metre cliff.

Two of his children, Lauren and Callum, were killed.

The story that Scott Aitken told was that he was driving home at around 2am from the drive-in. This was a route he frequently travelled but there were roadworks and Aitken said he became confused as to the direction of the road. When a dog appeared out of nowhere and ran out in front of the car Aitken swerved to avoid it, dropping his cigarette in the process. He took his eyes off the road to search for the cigarette, and that's when disaster occurred. The 4WD left the bitumen, travelling some distance before plunging over the 27-metre drop.

This was a terrible tragedy, and not just because the lives of two children were lost that night. The most incomprehensible thing about the incident was that their father was allowed to bargain his way down from a murder charge to one of dangerous driving.

Both a Coronial hearing and the inquest cleared Scott Aitken of murder, their decisions influenced by the evidence of one Jeffrey Muttart, an American accident reconstruction expert. Muttart was sent the initial findings of the Major Crash Investigation team that examined the scene on the night; his subsequent report was given to the Coroner.

Taking into account a prior 'agreement of facts' that had already been worked out with the prosecutor's office, the Coroner concluded that Scott Aitken did not deliberately attempt to kill himself and his children that night. Aitken received a fine and a suspended sentence, a result that devastated his ex-wife and his eldest child Haley.

Dissenting Opinion
It's said that most eyewitness accounts are unreliable, but there is no doubt that one of the greatest victims of that 'accident' was the front-seat passenger who lived to bear witness to what happened that night.

Then 14 years old, Haley Aitken was sitting next to her father on the journey home. She disagreed passionately with the Coroner's verdict; she believed that her father had tried to kill them all that night. Her evidence at the time directly contradicts her father's statements.

Also there, at the scene that night, was Lewis Edgely, who saw the Pajero go over the embankment and stopped to render aid. He recounted a conversation he heard between father and daughter. According to him, Scott told Haley that he'd swerved to avoid a dog and had dropped his cigarette in the process. Haley, however, seemed bewildered, saying that she hadn't seen any animal, and she hadn't realised he smoked.

But why would somebody deliberately try and kill himself and his children?

Scott Aitken has been described as 'violent and controlling' by his ex-wife Karen. He was furious about the custody dispute, about losing control of his family, and his behaviour had become even more erratic. After three attempts, Karen managed to get a restraining order against him.

The children's custody visit with Aitken, during which the accident occurred, was the first since they had come back from a holiday with their mother.

Scott Aitken wouldn't be the first father who took the 'if I can't have you, no-one can' route in a custody dispute, and Haley Aitken's voice on the subject is certainly not a lone one in the wilderness.

Independent reconstruction experts, who have evaluated both the scene and the evidence since, disagreed strongly with the findings of Jeffrey Muttart.

When investigating the evidence, Muttart used a different vehicle to recreate the accident, a Ford Explorer SUV. Not a great start. He then decided to recreate 'the conditions' of the accident – of the road, the grass, the cliff – in a car park, using traffic cones. From this, the American expert somehow concluded that Scott Aitken did not deliberately drive off the road and across the grass, the night his Pajero plunged off a cliff and two of his children died.

Not surprisingly, Professor Jack McLean from the Centre for Automotive Safety Research at Adelaide University, a man who leads the field in crash analysis, disagrees with Muttart's findings. From his own reconstruction of the crash site he concluded that Muttart's report left many questions unanswered. For example, there was no evidence of braking at the scene; yet Aitken claims he tried to avoid a dog. Almost all drivers brake when attempting to avoid something; sometimes they brake *and* swerve at the same time. Aitken merely swerved, a very uncharacteristic action.

But assuming he did just swerve, according to McLean, even though Aitken might not have had time to stop after he'd gone through the gap in the concrete barrier, he would certainly have had time to brake *after* he'd done so. And yet he didn't, not once.

So, was justice served in the case of the Aitken children? Did 12-year-old Lauren and 10-year-old Callum get a fair deal?

Or did the South Australian judicial system let a man go free, when there was a body of evidence that said he should have gone to jail?

There are some other highly questionable aspects to Scott Aitken's version of events. Why, for instance, was he carrying cans of petrol in the car that night – not in the rear of the vehicle, but placed in the front and middle compartments?

Why, according to several witnesses, was Aitken *reversing* down the freeway?

Aitken claimed that he swerved to avoid a dog but his daughter Haley says there *was* no dog; nor does she remember her father smoking before the accident.

How does a man, travelling on a familiar road, manage to go through the *only* break in the roadside concrete barrier, continue on for 15 metres without realising that the road surface had changed, and *then* plunge over a cliff?

After reviewing the evidence, the police asked the very same questions before charging Scott Aitken with two counts of murder. A year later, those charges were plea-bargained down to those of dangerous driving.

Not forgetting for a second that Scott Aitken himself is a lawyer, *his* solicitor, Eugene McGee, had once been a State prosecutor and so knew a great many of the people in the office of the Director of Public Prosecutions. It has been suggested that he and the prosecutor, Paul Rolf, got together to sort out the case over a couple of beers; a suggestion Mr Rolf has always denied emphatically.

But there's also no denying that, under the circumstances, the decision to reduce Aitken's charges seems quite extraordinary, despite the DPP claiming a murder charge wouldn't stick.

Another troubling aspect of the case is that Aitken refused to answer 15 questions put to him that would have provided information on the events of that evening. This hardly seems to be in keeping with the behaviour of a man who had nothing to hide.

Given that Scott Aitken was going through a traumatic marriage break-up, that he'd had a restraining order taken out against him, that his bedroom looked like a shrine to his children, how – why – did those who were meant to be looking into the death of two young children allow their father to get off so lightly?

Scott Aitken walked from the Coroner's court a jubilant man. His lenient fine and suspended sentence meant that he could continue to practice law and could continue on with his life – although now without his entire family, not just the ones who died that night.

His remaining children want nothing to do with him; hardly surprising given the pain they must endure without their siblings, and with the unimaginable likelihood that the one man they should have been able to trust, had tried to take their lives.

Karen Chandler, the children's mother, has to deal with her own grief and the trauma that her two surviving children suffered. The knowledge that Scott Aitken walked away with next to no consequences for his actions must make her pain infinitely worse. As for Haley Aitken, she'll probably never be free of the past.

Expert Witness

The cases of both Henry Keogh and Scott Aitken received widespread attention and have raised serious questions about South Australia's judicial system. Both cases relied heavily on expert testimony.

Even though the High Court rightly pointed out that Keogh wasn't convicted on forensic evidence alone, there is no doubt that evidence was *so* flawed that much of it should have been subject to review. Dr Colin Manock, the expert witness, had been the State's chief forensic pathologist for nearly 30 years but his chequered reliability, and the numerous criticisms of his methodology and practices, should have ensured that somebody else was assigned to the Keogh case. Despite his findings being questioned by equally credible experts, the State continued to use him. Manock has seen himself over the years as something of a vigilante, joining in the pursuit of would-be murderers with enthusiasm, when his job *should* have been all about seeking the truth.

His findings in a number of battered baby cases – where he determined death as bronco-pneumonia when many of the babies' injuries clearly suggested they'd been abused – created a scandal. The man did not fulfil his brief in those cases, so the big question is: did he do what was required of him in the case of Henry Keogh?

Keogh's 25-year sentence has provoked growing unease within the South Australian community. In August 2006, the SA Governor declined Keogh's petition for mercy for a third time, claiming there was no miscarriage of justice. While the government itself is willing to admit that there is some reason to doubt the evidence presented by Dr Colin Manock, they insist that circumstantial evidence alone is enough to let the conviction stand.

As for Scott Aitken – the State Coroner, Wayne Chivell, freely admitted that he had placed considerable reliance on the evaluation of the accident by American crash reconstruction expert Jeffrey Muttart. Even so, in the case against Scott Aitken, there seems to have been *more* than enough other evidence to secure a trial. The man had ongoing custody issues with his wife, she'd taken out a restraining order against him, he was considered to be controlling and irrational, there were those two containers of petrol in the vehicle, witnesses observed his car reversing down the freeway, and he headed for a steep drop, making no attempt to brake.

Anyone can see all that probably points to at least a 'well-planned accident'. It was certainly enough to set off warning bells for the police who charged him with two counts of murder in the first place.

The Keogh and Aitken cases are but two in a series of ongoing judicial issues that are plaguing the troubled state of South Australia. The list includes Eugene McGee and Andrew Priestly, two hit-and-run drivers who left their victims to die. McGee walked free from court and Priestly received a four-year sentence with a two-year minimum. The public outcry was so loud that the sentence was increased. Then there's Paul Nemer, who shot out the eye of a newspaper delivery man. He, too, plea-bargained his way down to a suspended sentence and $100 three-year good behaviour bond. And Fritz van Beelen, Dr Manock's first real 'success', served a 17-year sentence which was based on evidence that has since been proved to be completely unsound.

So the question remains: does an uneasy state of injustice exist in South Australia? It certainly seems to be served up differently depending on the individual. Whatever the case, the only opinion that really seems to matter, in establishing a person's guilt or innocence, is that of the so-called expert witnesses.

But when the experts get it wrong, who is going to stand up and shout that an injustice has occurred? One thing seems certain: South Australia has got some explaining to do.

Wrongful Conviction

PD Martin

Often it takes the support of family and friends to help you get through something bad. Sometimes, though, the thing is so bad it takes more people than you know to fix it. It takes a team of strangers, working tirelessly, and fighting – for one goal – alongside the ones who love you. When you're in jail, for something you didn't do, that one goal – your freedom – is a fight worth fighting.

On Monday 23 May 1994 Pamela Lawrence was found bludgeoned to death in her Mosman Park jewellery store. The community was horrified by the brutal murder of the mother of two, especially in one of Perth's most elite suburbs, and in broad daylight.

Who would do such a thing? What could be the motive? The pressure was instantly on the police to find their man – and fast.

Pamela Lawrence's wallet was missing, so the Western Australian Police initially deemed the murder a robbery gone wrong, even though jewellery, there for the taking, was left untouched.

Over the next couple of weeks the police interviewed a variety of people: a witness who'd seen a man in Lawrence's shop; people who'd seen a man behaving strangely in the area; neighbours, customers, local shopkeepers etc.

The case was already daunting, with an overwhelmingly large pool of suspects – 136 'people of interest'. One such person was Andrew Mallard, a 31-year-old homeless man who was diagnosed with bipolar affective disorder (commonly known as manic depression). During initial interviews, Andrew was unable to give a clear account of his whereabouts on the day in question, confusing the days and giving police incorrect information. Because of these inaccurate accounts, Andrew climbed his way to the top of the suspect pile. The police, even though they initially interviewed Andrew Mallard at Graylands Psychiatric Hospital where he was a patient, felt that his behaviour was suspicious rather than simply a product of his mental state.

On 10 June 1994, the police picked Andrew up after his release from Graylands and took him to the police station for a formal interview/interrogation. From this point on the story, and the case against Andrew, is dogged with inconsistencies and discrepancies.

According to the WA Police, Andrew Mallard confessed to the murder of Pamela Lawrence. But according to Andrew, he was harassed and assaulted while in custody, strip-searched and aggressively questioned. Andrew has also always vehemently denied any sort of confession.

So who should we believe – a few high-standing police officers, or one mentally vulnerable homeless man?

Of course, if the videotaping equipment that the room was fitted out with had actually been used during the interview, it would never have been a case of Andrew's word against those of two cops.

But the video equipment was not used – and perhaps this is the biggest mystery of the case, except perhaps for the fact that Andrew's so-called confession was in one of the detectives' handwriting, and was unsigned by Andrew.

The problems with the first interview don't stop there, however. If Andrew confessed to murder during this interview, as the police claim, then why did they let him go? Were they really happy to release a killer back onto the streets of Perth?

Instead of arresting their murderer, the police engaged in a strange undercover operation for the next week (a fact that would be discovered later). It is alleged that during this time, an undercover policeman known as 'Gary' supplied Andrew Mallard with high-grade cannabis. On 16 June, several days into the drug binge, Andrew went on an all-night 'bender' that finished in a Perth nightclub. Later that night, he was severely bashed by several men.

On 17 June, following this week of constant marijuana smoking and in a state of sleep-deprivation – not to mention his vulnerable mental state and the fact that he'd just taken a beating – the cops took Andrew into custody for questioning.

Again, for reasons unknown, the first three hours of this interview went unrecorded. Then, finally, the VCR was switched on. What resulted was a 20-minute video that, although touted as a confession, is bizarre to say the least.

The video shows Andrew talking in third person about how the murderer could have killed Pamela Lawrence. Andrew even talks about and draws was he suspects was the murder weapon – a Sidchrome spanner.

As far as the police were concerned, Andrew Mallard had just fessed up to not only the crime, but the weapon he had used to brutally kill Pamela Lawrence.

In July 1994, Andrew Mallard was arrested and charged with the wilful murder of Pamela Lawrence. The police had their man; or did they?

This is when things went from bad to worse for Andrew Mallard, who was appointed a young, inexperienced legal aid attorney. Incredibly, the unsigned, untaped confession in the detective's handwriting was deemed to be permissible as evidence. The crux of the prosecution's case rested on this confession; in fact, they had little else – no DNA, no fingerprints, no actual murder weapon.

Andrew Mallard and his family believed in the system; they thought an innocent man would not go to jail. Because Andrew's life was on the line though, he applied for a QC, with the support of his legal aid attorney. That request was denied by the judge, Justice Murray.

On day one of the trial, the prosecution opened with a description of the spanner and how Andrew used it to bludgeon Pamela Lawrence to death. The evidence they presented included the detective's handwritten 'confession' by Andrew, and the 20-minute video of Andrew.

They also had witness statements. Kate Barsden saw a man at Lawrence's shop wearing what she described as a bandanna, but which the police alleged was a baseball cap turned backwards. Supporting this eyewitness ID (the revised police one rather than Ms Barsden's) was a statement from the woman Andrew was staying with at the time, Michelle Englehardt, indicating that Andrew owned a cap similar in colour to the 'bandanna'.

Police alleged that Andrew Mallard was wearing that cap when he killed Pamela Lawrence, and that it was Andrew who Kate Barsden saw at the crime scene around the estimated time of death.

Andrew's trial lasted 10 days, and included testimony from Andrew himself. Unfortunately Andrew's tendency to ramble and indulge in conjecture often got him into trouble; it had already landed him in court, where his testimony did more harm than good.

Despite everything, Andrew and his family were still confident that justice would prevail. This belief was dashed when, much to their astonishment, Andrew was convicted of wilful murder and handed a strict life sentence in a maximum-security prison. And there he would stay for many years, despite the best efforts of his sister Jacqui, his mother Grace, and his new lawyers.

After the initial shock verdict, Andrew and his family appealed the conviction on the grounds that the judge should never have allowed the detective's notes – Andrew's so-called confession – as evidence. The justices dismissed the appeal but warned police that in the future all interviews must be recorded.

Then another tragedy struck the Mallard family when Andrew's father, Roy, died of cancer. Andrew, however, had withdrawn into his own world; he refused to see any visitors – even his beloved mother and sister – and did not believe his father had died. He thought it was all part of a police conspiracy and even believed that all the letters he received from his family were being dictated by police.

Most people could not even begin to imagine how it would feel to be locked in a prison cell night after night, knowing you're innocent and that a real murderer is still out there. It should be such a remote and unlikely event that it could only be a worst nightmare. And being wrongfully imprisoned would test the mental strength of any person, so the toll on someone who is already mentally troubled would be magnified.

In 1998, appeal lawyer Mark Ritter lodged an application for the right to appeal with the High Court, but the application was rejected. The High Court is, as the name suggests, the highest court a convicted person can approach. Hope was dwindling and fast.

Desperate for a next step, desperate to do *something*, *anything*, Jacqui and Grace turned to Mark Ritter for advice. With no more legal avenues open to them, their only hope was to convince the Attorney-General to step in and order another trial. To do that, they'd somehow need to find fresh evidence; evidence that hadn't been presented to the court to date.

Ritter saw two potential options for this quest: hire a private investigator, or get an investigative journalist interested in their case. Jacqui and Grace had tried the private investigator route with no success, so they decided to try the media and were given Colleen Egan's name.

Colleen Egan was an experienced journalist with a keen interest in the justice system. She had covered high-profile criminal trials during a three-year stint on the national broadsheet, the *Australian*, and had just returned from London, where she'd reported from the famous Old Bailey courthouse.

'I was working as a researcher for a TV program and agreed to see them,' Colleen explained. 'They told me they believed Andrew was innocent and shouldn't be in jail. As this isn't unusual for a mother to say, I called the lawyer and he said they had a good case and that the evidence was pretty flimsy. He felt it was worth me looking at, so I got the trial transcripts and read through them. As I was reading I realised Andrew had been really poorly represented by a young legal aid lawyer who was clearly out of his depth.'

As we know, journalists look for angles when researching a possible story. And the angle that was crying out to Colleen Egan was that justice is only available for those who can pay for it.

'I felt Andrew and his family had been served very badly by the public system. At this stage I didn't know if he was guilty or not, but I knew he didn't get a fair trial. I certainly felt that if he'd had a top legal team he probably wouldn't have been convicted,' Colleen said.

From the transcripts, Colleen noticed anomalies in the case and realised Andrew had been convicted solely on the 20-minute video interview and the police officers' account of what had happened during the two unrecorded interviews. She found the video 'confession' bizarre and couldn't make sense of why Andrew would say the things he was saying.

Later, when Andrew's psychiatrist watched the video he could see that his client's responses were classic bipolar behaviour. The psychiatrist felt Andrew was manic during the interview and was theorising about what *might* have happened to the woman who was killed. He thinks that Andrew truly believed the police were interested in his opinion.

Now, this possibility probably wouldn't even cross the minds of most people in that situation, but for Andrew life was a completely different story; in fact, around the time of the interview, he'd been claiming to be an Interpol agent.

At this stage the case was not a story for Colleen's TV program – lots of people claim to be innocent, and most are not telling the truth. For the story to become newsworthy she'd have to find evidence of police misconduct, or fresh evidence that cleared Andrew's name or led to someone else.

Colleen phoned Mark Ritter again and when he agreed to spend some time on the case for free, she decided to do the same. Colleen was also drawn to the Mallard family's plight and had a lot of respect for Jacqui and Grace and their persistence and dedication to Andrew. She describes them as 'decent, lovely people who had been treated very badly by the system. They had a lot of faith in the police, lawyers and courts, and this faith was smashed'.

Colleen started working the case in her spare time, a couple of nights a week and on weekends. She was ultimately looking for the all-important fresh evidence; evidence that could free Andrew Mallard.

One of the first things she did was to contact renowned American false-confession expert, Professor Saul Kassin. She sent him a copy of Andrew's unsigned written confession (aka the police notes), the 20-minute video, a ledger of what Andrew had said (or what was attributed to him in the case of the unsigned confession), and the actual facts of the crime. For example, in his conjecturing, Andrew *said* Pamela Lawrence was wearing a skirt suit, when she was in fact wearing jeans. After reviewing this information, Professor Kassin said he believed it had all the hallmarks of a false confession. He even offered to testify if Colleen managed to get the case back into the court system.

While this mini-breakthrough strengthened Colleen's view of the case, it wasn't fresh evidence; rather it was something that was, or could have been, available to the defence at the time of the trial and the appeal. The definition of 'fresh evidence' is very narrow, legally defined as 'evidence that did not exist at the time of the trial or which could not have been uncovered with due diligence at the time of the trial' (Ratten v The Queen; Gallagher v R).

While Professor Kassin's opinion corroborated Andrew's account, it wasn't something Colleen and Ritter could take to the Attorney-General. 'Every time I found something wrong that happened in the trial, Mark Ritter said the court would say that the legal aid attorney should have addressed that. The system assumes you have a competent lawyer,' she said. In our current legal justice system, you can't go back and say that a question should have been asked, or a particular point should have been raised – it's too late once the original trial and the appeal are over.

The other problem Colleen found was that the lack of actual evidence – as in no DNA, no fingerprints, no forensic evidence at all – meant there was hardly anything to disprove or retest. She was at an impasse, compounded by the fact that Andrew himself wouldn't even see her. He wasn't even talking to his mother and sister at the time. So, after about a year's work, Colleen went back to the family; she said that, while she empathised with them, she couldn't move forward, not without Andrew's help.

A year later, that's exactly what she got. Andrew suddenly snapped out of his fantasy world and was ready to start the fight again – and accept his father's death. In 2000, Colleen was able to get him to sign authorities enabling her to get hold of important documents – his legal files. While Colleen didn't have access to the police files, at least Andrew's cooperation gave her something more to work with.

She assembled a team of people: Jacqui Mallard, Mark Ritter, various journalism students and prison chaplain Rob Devenish, who'd become an Andrew Mallard supporter. This core group – Team Mallard – met regularly at Colleen's place for a couple of years, and investigated people, witnesses, forensics, in fact anything and everything that was a possible line of inquiry. Colleen's spare room was piled high with boxes and boxes relating to Andrew's case.

Around this time, desperate to prove his innocence, Andrew Mallard suggested a lie-detector test. Coincidentally, Colleen had heard Bill Glare talking about his work as a polygrapher on talkback radio, so she contacted him. Not only was Glare 'Australia's leading expert', he also agreed to visit Andrew and conduct a lie-detector test for free.

'At that time I was convinced the evidence pointed away from Andrew,' Colleen explained, 'but emotionally I didn't really want to believe he was innocent because it felt like such a burden, given I wasn't having success getting the case back to court.

'But when he passed the test with flying colours, and the polygraph examiner was utterly convinced, I finally allowed myself to think that he was innocent. That's really when I crossed that bridge.'

But again, a lie-detector test wouldn't be enough for the Attorney-General so the search went on.

Next, Team Mallard found Michelle Englehardt (the woman with whom Andrew had been staying when arrested) and obtained some crucial information – something, finally, that would be instrumental to their case.

Michelle told them that she had been brought in by detectives many times and signed several different versions of her statement. She said she felt manipulated and confused by detectives, who had intimated that she would be let off a cannabis offence if she cooperated with the case against Andrew Mallard.

Colleen's team was later to find that Michelle's witness statement, the one submitted in court, was an *altered* version. In her first statement she had said that the cap that was used by the prosecution to place Andrew at the murder scene was hanging on a peg in her house at the time of Pamela Lawrence's murder. Andrew had not even been wearing it!

The reality of Michelle's evidence blew another hole in the so-called confession. The team also found the undercover policeman, the famous 'Gary', who'd been involved in the week-long undercover operation; but surprise, surprise, he didn't want to talk.

Although they'd achieved quite a lot, it still wasn't enough to convince the Attorney-General, and Colleen found this period very frustrating. 'Even though I was convinced that he didn't, and couldn't have done it, there wasn't anything significant enough to pursue. I was feeling quite disillusioned. I was feeling guilty; as in, "God, I'm going out to dinner tonight and he's behind bars." It was a very frustrating time.'

Team Mallard needed more and Colleen decided that finding an advocate with clout, preferably political clout, was a good option. She decided the man for the job was MP and ex-barrister, John Quigley, although she realised that asking for his help could backfire on them. Quigley had spent 27 years defending police officers, and was a lifetime member of the Police Union.

Colleen was worried that if they fed him information and he fed this back to the police or the Director of Public Prosecutions (DPP), then important evidence could disappear. He was a risky choice, but would be a powerful ally if they could pull it off because Quigley would be more than impartial; if anything, his natural leaning would be in favour of the police and the criminal justice system. Colleen approached him, in what she calls an act of desperation, hoping he'd become a voice for them in the public and political arenas, and that he'd eventually approach the Attorney-General on Andrew's behalf.

John Quigley felt it was his public duty as a Member of Parliament to review the case, and he proceeded to spend 14 weekends reviewing all of the documents. Later, Quigley would say: 'The conduct of the police has been both vile and repugnant.'

Obviously Quigley's reaction was good news for Colleen Egan. 'He was better than my wildest dreams really, because he didn't just advocate for us, he took the case and used his skills to further our efforts,' she said.

Quigley opened the case right up. Through his position he had access to information that Colleen didn't – such as the autopsy photos. Quigley talked to the forensic pathologist who worked the case, and discovered that they'd done tests *before* Andrew Mallard's trial that showed, conclusively, that the weapon Andrew had named and sketched – the Sidchrome spanner – could *not* have caused Pamela Lawrence's injuries. The pathologist took Quigley through the photos and explained the discrepancies between the supposed murder weapon and the shape of the injuries.

This was a significant breakthrough and supported Andrew's claim that the 20-minute interview, and his drawing of the spanner, were no more than hypotheses of what could have happened. Team Mallard wanted confirmation, so they purchased a pig's head and a Sidchrome spanner. The forensic pathologist completed another round of tests and confirmed, once again, that there was no way that 'weapon' could have caused Lawrence's injuries.

So why did the prosecutor lead with the weapon during the opening of Andrew's original trial? Surely he knew the spanner couldn't possibly have been the actual murder weapon?

The fact that the police and DPP had this information before the trial and at the time of the trial meant there'd been significant non-disclosure to the defence.

From there, Quigley managed to get the DPP to open up the case file and what Team Mallard found was, quite literally, a mess.

'When we had access to the files, we realised there was all this evidence that hadn't been disclosed.' Colleen said that part of the file included the original document about Pamela Lawrence's wounds – a document that was never shown to the defence (or the court!) and that would have gone a long way to clearing Andrew. Certainly it raised even more doubts about his questionable confession, putting more holes in the prosecutor's case and ultimately in Andrew's conviction.

The new stocktake looked pretty good. The prosecutor had used a handwritten confession that wasn't in Andrew's handwriting and hadn't been signed by him. On top of that, Andrew staunchly denied he had ever made the confession, and this was now backed up by a lie-detector test.

The prosecution had the 20-minute video interview, in which Andrew only talked about the case in the third person, distancing himself from the crime, and never once admitting that *he* did any of the actions he was describing. In fact, Andrew's mental condition led him to believe that the police were genuinely interested in his opinion of what the murderer would have done and how it would have played out.

Plus, one of the key elements of the 'confession evidence' had been proved wrong – the spanner. That Andrew had drawn the so-called murder weapon was not as incriminating as it had originally seemed because there was no way *that* spanner could have made the injuries inflicted on Pamela Lawrence. The drawing was no longer damning evidence.

Team Mallard had also uncovered the manipulation of Michelle Engelhardt's statement, and further witness-statement manipulation. Kate Barsden had 'drawn' the man she'd seen in Pamela Lawrence's shop and the drawing clearly showed a man with a full beard and no moustache – a fact that was deleted from the final report and from the evidence presented to the jury. Why? Presumably because Andrew Mallard had a moustache and no beard.

The team had also uncovered other inconsistencies. For example, the attack on Lawrence would have splattered blood on the killer's clothes, and while in his 'confession' Andrew said the killer would have washed his clothes in a salt river, forensics had found no evidence to indicate Andrew's clothes had ever been in salty water. This significant fact was also deleted from the forensic report presented in court. Again, his 'confession' was proved inaccurate, or nothing more than what it was – an elaborate hypothesis.

The non-disclosure and manipulation of evidence was a big leap forward. More than eight years after Andrew Mallard was jailed, things were looking up for him and his team of supporters. They finally had enough to approach the Attorney-General. They had the forensic tests on the pig's head, they had non-disclosure, they had the manipulation of witness statements, and they had the powerful voice of John Quigley.

'This was the big breakthrough and the Attorney-General almost immediately agreed to refer the case back to the courts,' Colleen said. 'At this stage we thought he'd be out of jail in months.'

Team Mallard was confident their appeal would be granted and Andrew Mallard would be a free man; finally his ordeal was coming to an end, they were going back for their day in court.

This breakthrough also marked the first time Colleen, who'd been working on the case in her own time for four years and had returned to the *Australian* newspaper, could write an article. She finally had a newsworthy piece about a miscarriage of justice – something she wanted others to hear about.

They had to wait 11 months until the appeal and while this gave Team Mallard plenty of time to prepare their case, it also meant another 11 months in jail for Andrew.

In preparation for the approaching trial, Team Mallard expanded. The jail's chaplain, Rob Devenish, who had known Andrew for six years and was convinced of his innocence, spoke with his friend and top-flight QC, Malcolm McCusker, who had already taken an interest in the case. As chairman of the Legal Aid Commission, McCusker had met with the devastated Mallard family in 1998 and encouraged them to search for fresh evidence. The eminent lawyer and his talented junior barrister, Rhodes Scholar James Edelman, immediately agreed to take the case on, pro bono.

A team of lawyers from the national litigation firm Clayton Utz also joined the fight, again pro bono. What Andrew Mallard lacked in his original trial – a strong legal team – he now had.

Quigley also approached former police officer and renowned investigator Peter Coombs. Coombs traced Andrew's movements on the day of the murder very closely, piecing together a detailed timeline of Andrew's whereabouts. What he discovered convinced him of Andrew's innocence.

On 23 May 1994, the day Pamela Lawrence was murdered, Andrew was being questioned by police. He was eventually released and a taxi driver testified that he dropped Andrew off in Mosman Park at 5pm, and waited outside a block of flats for Andrew to return with friends. (Andrew, in fact, didn't have any money to pay the driver and had done a runner.)

Given that Kate Barsden had seen 'the man' in Lawrence's shop at only one or two minutes past five, Andrew would have had to walk four blocks in around two minutes to get there in time, for *that* man to have been him. What's more, he was seen in an elevator, back at the block of flats where he was staying, at 5.10pm.

So, Andrew had only 10 minutes in which to get to the shop, kill Pamela Lawrence and get back to the apartment block.

The witness in the elevator also testified that there was no blood on Andrew's clothes – and forensic experts agreed that the attack would have caused blood splatter onto the perpetrator's clothes.

So, 10 minutes to walk four blocks, kill Pamela Lawrence, clean himself up, and walk another four blocks back to the apartment block. Things just didn't add up.

Andrew Mallard's appeal started on Tuesday 10 June 2003. His future was in the balance, but there was more at stake than that – there was a whole family whose lives have been irreversibly damaged by his ordeal. They had lost one family member along the way, with the death of Andrew's father Roy, and it was time they got another family member back – from jail.

During the appeal the judges decided to consider the polygraph as evidence, but the prosecution objected to the way the first test was conducted. Andrew submitted to another lie-detector test and again passed. This test was reviewed by America's leading expert in polygraphs, who stated that Andrew was telling the truth.

Andrew was also called to testify at the appeal – something that concerned some of his supporters, given the shambles of his first trial. But this time he was properly prepared by his legal counsel and kept his answers short and to the point, rather than entering into conjecture.

After 23 hearing days and six months, the judges retired to deliberate. Team Mallard was concerned that the parochial judges seemed hostile to their case even though they had so much evidence now, including the lie-detector test and Andrew's whereabouts on the day tied down to a 10-minute window.

After 10 days of deliberation, the three judges gave their unanimous decision.

To everyone's dismay, the appeal was denied. In their ruling, the judges said that they didn't feel the non-disclosure would have altered the jury's verdict.

John Quigley went on record expressing his shame of the system. QC Malcolm McCusker told reporters it was the most disappointing decision of his long and illustrious career.

'People in senior positions fought tooth and nail to keep Andrew Mallard inside,' Colleen said. Reputations were on the line; the key players in the case had now moved into the upper echelons of the WA justice system, occupying senior positions. The DPP at the time of the original trial was now a Supreme Court judge and two of the detectives were assistant police commissioners. They were powerful and had powerful friends.

When asked if she had believed in the justice system before her involvement in the Mallard case, Colleen said, 'Yeah, I did actually. I was always sceptical about taking the police's word for things – like unsigned confessions – but I always told the Mallards that I would help them get the case back to the courts and then I'd leave them at the door. I was positive that once the case was put back to the courts with a good lawyer, properly briefed, that it would result in his freedom.

'I still can't believe I was so wrong about that, I still have trouble trying to understand the attitude and approach of the WA judges. It certainly shook my belief in a fair judiciary.'

With the appeal unsuccessful, they still had one legal avenue left – the High Court of Australia (again). They lodged their application for an appeal, knowing that only five per cent of such applications were successful.

But in October 2004 their application was granted. Elation rippled through the supporters – it was about time they had something to celebrate. Yet again, however, there was a wait involved – this time 12 months; another year of Andrew Mallard's freedom taken.

On Tuesday 6 September 2005, the High Court case started in Canberra. Quigley was relieved to be out of the Western Australian system, and the team's hope was tantalised on the first day, when two of the judges commented negatively on the prosecution's behaviour and the issue of non-disclosure. But it would still be a little over two months before the High Court was ready to give its decision.

On Tuesday 15 November 2005, the Mallard family and supporters gathered in McCusker's office, waiting for a phone call that would reveal Andrew's fate. The long-awaited call came and the news was well and truly overdue – finally someone had ruled in Andrew's favour. Team Mallard had won and the High Court ordered a retrial.

Three months later the WA DPP announced that the case would not be retried because the prosecution had insufficient evidence to secure a conviction.

On Monday 20 February 2006, Andrew Mallard was finally a free man.

There were, however, repercussions still to come. In December 2005, following the High Court's decision, Western Australia's Corruption and Crime Commission (CCC) announced an investigation into the case. The Police Commissioner announced a cold-case review of the murder, and five police officers were stood down, pending the outcome.

Forensic evidence was re-examined, and the new investigators found a palm print that had never been disclosed to the Mallard lawyers. When it was run through the system, they found it matched a convicted murderer – someone Andrew had, coincidentally, shared the prison ground with.

British citizen Simon Rochford was serving time for murdering his girlfriend, a crime he committed seven weeks after Pamela Lawrence's death. What's more, both Lawrence and Rochford's girlfriend were bludgeoned to death, and both had blonde hair.

Criminal profiling indicates that some violent people displace their anger with a loved one by harming someone else. The classic example is the serial killer who targets women of a certain appearance, because they look like their girlfriend, sister or mother.

Could Simon Rochford have been displacing the violent anger he felt towards his girlfriend onto another blonde – Pamela Lawrence? Or was she simply in the wrong place at the wrong time?

Police visited Rochford in jail and questioned him in relation to Lawrence's murder. The palm print not only gave them another prime suspect, it also gave Andrew Mallard hope that the real offender would be brought to justice. Realistically, finding the real murderer was the only way to unequivocally exonerate Andrew in everyone's eyes.

But 10 days after the police interviewed Simon Rochford, he committed suicide in prison. Was he the man Kate Barsden saw in Pamela Lawrence's jewellery shop?

Andrew, Team Mallard and the public had to wait again – until the results of the cold-case inquiry were finally released on Wednesday 11 October 2006.

On that day, an official WA Police media release stated:

> *Andrew Mallard has been eliminated as a person of interest in the murder of Pamela Lawrence. The investigation has identified sufficient evidence implicating Simon Rochford in the murder of Mrs Lawrence such that were Mr Rochford alive today, a brief of evidence would be prepared for submission to the Office of the Director of Public Prosecutions for consideration.*

Andrew Mallard had spent 12 years behind bars for a crime he did not commit. He was taken advantage of by the police system and the justice system and a dozen years of his life in prison for a crime committed by Simon Rochford.

But in 2006 Andrew was finally officially and unequivocally cleared of the charges, and issued an apology by the Commissioner of Police.

The 11 October 2006 media release also points out: 'The Special Crime Squad was not tasked with examining the conduct of the officers involved in the original investigation. This is a matter to be considered by the CCC [Corruption and Crime Commission] inquiry.'

Could this happen again? Could someone else spend a decade in jail for a crime they didn't commit? Could it happen to anyone?

Colleen Egan says it is possible. 'If Andrew wasn't so mentally vulnerable I don't think he would have been charged in the first place, because he wouldn't have been so easily manipulated by the police. And then, once he was charged, if he'd had a good legal team I believe he would have got off.

'But I do think this can still happen to people, particularly in Western Australia, where there is a culture of police and prosecutors deciding who's guilty, instead of just presenting evidence fairly for the courts.'

Wrongful conviction is a risk in any system. Innocent people behind bars are also victims of crime – as are their families. Andrew had a team of dedicated supporters behind him, including his family, all working tirelessly to clear his name and to set him free.

Colleen Egan, who worked side by side with Jacqui and Grace Mallard, admits she became emotionally involved with their struggle, despite trying to remain objective.

'They're exceptionally decent people,' she said. 'Jacqui is the most amazing big sister that any person in trouble would want and Grace is just sweet and gorgeous. The whole time I've known them, in their desperate states, they've never lied to me once, never misled me.'

Colleen remains close to the family and is currently working on a book about the case, along with barristers McCusker and Edelman, to be published by ABC Books.

The Mallard family fought for Andrew all the way, but they also paid a big price. During the TV documentary, *Saving Andrew Mallard*, Grace Mallard said: 'This case, this injustice, killed my husband. I not only lost my son through a system that is faulty, I lost my husband as well.'

The Truth is Out There

Liz Filleul

Parents should never outlive their children.

A child's death, at any age, goes against all expectations; against the proper order of things. Parents expect to see their children grow up – for them to attend school and maybe university, to have careers, to form relationships, and perhaps to have children, even grandchildren of their own. They expect that when they die, their children will be established and happy; that they'll be there to organise *their* funerals.

So when sons or daughters die before their parents – perhaps through illness or car accident – the grief of those who brought them into the world is immense. Bereaved parents grow older and older wondering what their son would have been like, what their daughter might have achieved; indeed what they'd be doing at *any* given time, had they lived. They grieve on never-to-be-celebrated birthdays, especially big ones like 18, 30 or 40. And when friends' children turn 21, get married, have their first child, the milestones are sad reminders of what might have been.

Coping with untimely death is hard enough at any time, but imagine how much worse that sense of loss would be if your child was murdered.

Living on, beyond that, would be soul-destroying.

How much more unbearable then if, over a decade after her murder, you still had no idea who took your daughter's life, or why?

Worse still – what if, after more than 13 years of searching, of public appeals and publicity, you still had no idea of the whereabouts of your daughter's body.

Imagine you've never been able to hold a funeral; there's no known final resting place to visit; no place to leave flowers in remembrance; no place from which their spirit was freed; no place to feel a sense of them.

How could *anyone* cope with all of that? And, with all of that, the awful knowledge that somewhere, out there, a brutal killer had got away with murder.

How would you deal with it?

I've been a mother for only six years but know I wouldn't cope with my child's death, no matter what the circumstances. I've talked with other mums from my son's preschool about losing loved ones and, while we agreed we'd be devastated by the loss of parents, partners, siblings or friends, we know we'd be able to move on. But, none of us could imagine ever getting over losing our children. It wouldn't matter what age they were when they died, they'd still be our 'baby' – the precious child who'd kicked in our womb; who we'd nursed, played with, potty trained, taught to walk and talk; who we'd laughed with and cried over. None of us felt we'd ever even begin to cope.

But for 13 long years now, Joy and Roger Membrey have had to do just that – cope. They've lived with the truth that their only daughter was violently murdered; with the distress that no-one has ever been arrested for killing her; with the fact that no motive for it has ever been established; with the anguish that they still don't know where her body is, so they've never been able to say goodbye; and with the harsh reality that despite a lengthy investigation, public appeals and even a $1 million reward for information, justice has never been done.

From the time 22-year-old Elisabeth Membrey disappeared from her Melbourne unit in the early hours of Wednesday 7 December 1994, Joy and Roger Membrey have appeared in the press and on television and radio at regular intervals talking about her life and her death. Each time, they have appealed for anyone who has information relating to her murder to step forward.

Now in their 60s, they're a kindly looking couple, with a reputation among the press for being polite and gracious; although there's no mistaking the sadness in their eyes in even the smallest of newspaper photographs.

Their interviews over the years usually stemmed from renewed media interest in the investigation owing to sudden developments, like the posting of a big reward, a tip-off to police or Crime Stoppers or the uncovering of a questionable alibi.

But more often than not, Joy and Roger have given media interviews because they wanted to maintain public awareness of their daughter's murder. They always hoped the publicity would trigger a memory or prick a conscience and lead to an arrest, to the discovery of Elisabeth's body, to some kind of resolution. They were determined to find out what really happened.

'For our peace of mind we have to find some truth and justice,' Joy Membrey told Melbourne's *Age* newspaper in December 2005. 'If the tables were turned she would be fighting for us.'

When I began researching Elisabeth's story, I had hoped to be able to talk to Joy and Roger Membrey about their daughter. However, my request to speak with them was met with a polite and friendly refusal. Given their previous relationship with the media this seemed strange; although, personally, I completely understood.

Detective Senior Sergeant Ron Iddles, who has headed the investigation into Elisabeth Membrey's death since August 2000, and who speaks to her parents about the case every week, explained their concerns about talking to me.

He said that every press interview and every article publicising the case has led to increased hope for Joy and Roger that their daughter's body might be found and her killer brought to justice. But instead of resolution, the publicity has too often led only to further, bitter disappointment as potential leads from tip-offs fizzled to nothing, compounding their grief. While Joy and Roger still hope that publicity about Elisabeth's murder *will* one day lead to justice, for the moment, after years of raised and dashed hopes, they feel the need to step back from all forms of media involvement. They can't bear to keep talking about Elisabeth's death; to keep going over the same ground in the vain hope that someone somewhere will read the article and ring the police with vital information, with a clue or a name that will lead to the answers they crave.

In any case, the Membreys might well feel that there is nothing more that they can say that they haven't already said. They have talked at length to the media – and via them to the public – about their love for their precious daughter. They have tried to give journalists an impression of what she was like, by showing them a short video featuring Elisabeth as a baby, as a little girl, as a teenager and finally as a young woman – all to the tune of *The Impossible Dream*. Some journalists who watched it have admitted in print to crying.

Joy and Roger have always emphasised to the press that Elisabeth is not just a story or a case; she is their daughter, whom they love and miss. The press, to their collective credit, have respected this.

The Membreys, parents of two sons as well as Elisabeth, have talked about how they try to deal with the ever-present grief – Roger, a retired company secretary, by taking long walks along the beach; Joy, a retired nurse, by punching a boxing bag in the backyard until her fingers became permanently damaged by pounding.

They've spoken about the anger and frustration, and the total exhaustion they feel as the years pass by with no sign of justice being done; and how comments from well-meaning psychics became destructive. They explained how they have supported each other through the long, grief-ridden years, how if one of them is depressed, the other will try to remain optimistic; and how they've planted a garden of remembrance for the families of those missing in violent circumstances.

The Membreys recently decided to move to Gippsland from their long-time family home in Vermont, in an attempt to move on in their lives and not have the persistent reminder of 'Elisabeth's room'. And perhaps also because they've observed too often how others react to them – how people, whether long-time acquaintances or total strangers, can feel uncomfortable around them and shy away; knowing about the dreadful tragedy that has befallen them but not knowing what to say. Ordinary death is sadly still a conversational taboo in our society, so violent death, beyond the understanding of most people, is a subject too difficult to even broach.

When they were communicating with the public, through the media, Joy and Roger talked about the night they discovered Elisabeth was missing and the realisation that something awful had happened to her; that their daughter, part of their lives for 22 years, had suddenly been snatched from them in the most violent of circumstances.

'For the first time in our lives, we were involved with police,' Roger told *The Australian Women's Weekly* in May 2006. 'For the first time in our lives, we had a daughter who was presumably murdered. For the first time in our lives we were in the media. We've never got used to it.'

A couple of years ago, Lindy Cameron and I were asked by Sisters in Crime Australia to plot and present an event entitled 'How to commit the perfect murder'. The idea was that two crime *fiction* writers should be able dream up a murder that two real-life experts – Melbourne forensic pathologist Dr Shelley Robertson and Homicide detective Narelle Fraser – would not be able to solve, in the time allotted; and all before an audience, who'd also be encouraged to have a crack at guessing whodunit, how and why.

Lindy and I began hatching our 'perfect murder' plans over lunch at the Dorset Gardens Hotel in Croydon, in Melbourne's outer eastern suburbs. We opted for a *Strangers on a Train* scenario, whereby two people commit murder for each other, and therefore have no connection to the victim they have killed. We conspired over methods, so that the two murders couldn't be traced back to us: an ice bullet for one victim; aggravating the other victim's rare Addison's disease by depriving them of medication and salt.

As we plotted our perfect murder event, we started to worry – not that we were engaging in something morally questionable because, as writers of crime fiction, imagining murder and mayhem is 'what we do'; but that the two experts might work it all out within minutes rather than the event's scheduled two hours. You see, our biggest reality check, was that we knew most murders aren't perfect, and that thankfully, most killers do get caught – through forensics, through mistakes, through thorough police investigation.

Detective Senior Sergeant Ron Iddles has, for example, during his 16 years as a Homicide cop, investigated about 250 murders, only 15 of which remain unsolved. And, of all the suspects he has charged only two have been acquitted.

The ironic thing then, about me writing this story, is that about 15 minutes' drive from where Lindy and I cheerfully made plans for our hypothetical perfect crime, a real and shocking, so far unsolved, perhaps unsolvable murder *had* taken place. And Elisabeth Membrey's homicide is one of Ron Iddles' 15.

Despite his awesome track record for putting murderers behind bars, Detective Iddles admits they have 'hit the brick wall' in the Membrey case; that after 'an enormous amount of work', Victoria Police is, in effect, still at square one. After 13 years, there's still no identified killer, no motive, no discovered body. Whoever murdered Elisabeth Membrey took great care to make sure they never got caught. To date, they appear to have committed the perfect murder.

Elisabeth Frances Membrey was murdered in the early hours of Wednesday 7 December 1994. At the time of her death, she was 22 years old; an attractive young woman, with cascading dark curls. She had graduated from La Trobe University with a degree in politics in 1993, and had aspirations to be a journalist. As a precursor to her career she'd written many letters to Melbourne newspapers on topics she felt passionate about: women's issues, human rights, animal welfare.

She was about to start work as a journalist for Channel Ten in November 1994, the month she died.

To fill the gap between finishing her studies and starting her career, Elisabeth had taken on casual part-time bar work at the Manhattan Hotel – a large hotel complex complete with a somewhat startling (as seen from the road) in-your-face replica of the Statue of Liberty – on Canterbury Road in Ringwood. She had also moved out of the family home in nearby Vermont and was sharing a rented unit with a girlfriend, Viv Crump. The unit, also in Ringwood, was in Bedford Road, a busy thoroughfare between Canterbury Road and Maroondah Highway and a convenient short drive from the Manhattan.

On the Tuesday night, 6 December, Elisabeth worked a double shift at the hotel. She left work at 11.45pm, got into her red Mazda 323 to drive home, and was never seen again.

On that night, remembered by everyone connected to the case as 'stinking hot', she was to be, unusually, home alone. Her housemate Viv had broken her ankle in a horse-riding accident and had gone to stay with her boyfriend for a few days at Safety Beach on the Mornington Peninsula. Viv's car, however, remained in its customary spot next to Elisabeth's outside their unit. For this reason, Detective Iddles is adamant that Elisabeth must have known her murderer.

'The killer knew that Elisabeth was going to be alone that night,' he says. 'Viv Crump's car was parked outside the unit, but the killer was confident that Viv wasn't there and that she wouldn't be returning … The killer was confident enough to back Elisabeth's car up to the front door and then to drive it away. And he had the confidence to later return Elisabeth's car and to try to clean the unit up without fear of being disturbed.'

It was almost 24 hours after she finished her shift at the Manhattan Hotel that Elisabeth was discovered missing. Her parents and her boyfriend Jason met up outside her unit on the evening of Wednesday 7 December, having exchanged concerned phone calls as to her whereabouts. She hadn't answered her home phone, and confirmation that she wasn't working a shift that night was provided by a quick visit to the Manhattan Hotel.

When Joy, Roger and Jason arrived at her unit, they found her car parked in the driveway, next to her flatmate's. But Elisabeth did not answer the door. A quick check in the shops on the opposite side of the road verified that she wasn't out shopping.

Earlier in the week, Elisabeth had mentioned that she'd been feeling unwell, so now her parents and boyfriend feared that she might have collapsed inside the unit. Jason forced his way in via a window and let Joy and Roger into her home.

'In the passageway outside her bedroom was a big pool of blood. But the unit didn't look ransacked. It was neat and tidy,' Roger recalled in the interview with *The Australian Women's Weekly* in May 2006.

Now thinking that she might have fallen and then called for help, Joy and Roger checked with local hospitals and ambulance and taxi services. When none of them reported having seen Elisabeth or being summoned to the unit, the Membreys then phoned the police.

The police brought in detectives – and it was then that the nightmare of Joy and Roger's life began.

The killer had devoted quite some time to cleaning up the unit, obviously trying to convey the impression that Elisabeth had disappeared of her own accord. The Membreys recalled that their shoes stuck to the tiles when they entered, 'as if Handy Andy had been used'.

Somehow, strangely, the killer had missed the blood outside her bedroom. Forensic tests revealed other blood that the killer had tried to hide: on the walls, on the tiles, on Elisabeth's mattress, in her car.

DNA would later confirm that the blood found on the back seat of Elisabeth's car came from a child of Joy and Roger Membrey; and, in 2000, Coroner Jacinta Heffey found that the pool of blood in the passageway alone was big enough to indicate fatal blood loss.

Elisabeth Membrey had been murdered in her own unit, wrapped in her own doona, which had been taken from her bed, and driven in her own car to – where?

Trace evidence indicates that Elisabeth's car was driven from her Ringwood unit either 38 kilometres to Kinglake or 17 kilometres to Silvan. The sandy soil found under her car and under the car doors was consistent with the soil in those areas.

'The car had been driven for some distance and at some speed for the soil to billow up under the door sill the way it did,' Detective Iddles says.

But knowing just 'where to look' for her body, and in which of the two extensive areas, was the problem. Detectives believe that whoever hid Elisabeth's body knew Kinglake and Silvan well; that perhaps it was somewhere they had spent time exploring as a child or as a teenager, or somewhere they'd camped or bushwalked a lot. The killer must have felt confident that the spot they had chosen to conceal Elisabeth would be impossible to find.

Using the victim's car to transport her body indicates careful planning too – and perhaps even some knowledge of forensics. Had the killer used their own car, and police had found traces of Elisabeth's blood in it, then justice would most likely have been done a long time ago.

From the various statements given in the wake of Elisabeth's death, detectives have been able to piece together some of the events of her final hours. On the Tuesday morning Elisabeth had gone for a swim at Ringwood Aquatic Centre, where an old school friend had spotted her talking to a man described as 'athletic, tall, about 25, Australian'.

At around 1.30pm, a neighbour of Elisabeth's in Bedford Road saw her arguing with a man, fitting that same description. Elisabeth and the man were carrying plastic shopping bags from Elisabeth's unit and placing them in the boot of a 1970s blue Gemini.

About an hour later Elisabeth exchanged a greeting with a postal worker, en route from the milk bar across the road, and at 4.30pm she headed to the Manhattan Hotel for her shift, after which she was never seen again.

At 1.30am, a woman who lived directly behind Elisabeth's unit was woken up by the barking of her own pet dogs. She went outside to try to calm them down and noticed a white car parked outside Elisabeth's unit.

At around 3.30am, a passing milk-truck driver noticed the red Mazda 323 backed right up to Elisabeth's front door. (The killer must have been about to, or had just, placed Elisabeth's body in her car.)

When the neighbour with the dogs rose at 7am, she noticed that the white car had gone and that Elisabeth's Mazda was parked in its customary position.

Police appealed for the man – or men – fitting the description of the person seen with Elisabeth at the pool and outside her unit to come forward. They also appealed for the driver of the white car to contact them. But no-one fitting the description has ever come forward and said they knew Elisabeth or spent time with her on the day that she was killed. The driver of the white car is also still unknown.

So the questions remain: were the man at the pool and the man seen outside her unit one and the same? Did the owner of the white car also have access to a 1970s blue Gemini? And if the man, or men, weren't responsible for her death, why haven't they come forward?

The police are no closer to answering these questions now than they were in the immediate aftermath of Elisabeth's death in December 1994. Nor are they any closer to understanding why she was killed. Had the man – or one of the men – she'd been seen talking to earlier in the day felt rejected by her and killed her in revenge? Had she, as a budding journalist, perhaps stumbled across something she thought might make a good story – a story someone didn't want her to tell?

Despite years of digging, no-one knows quite what went wrong for Elisabeth Membrey.

Although the investigation into Elisabeth's death had been ongoing since 1994, it appeared to gain new momentum with the setting up of the Cold Murder Squad in the spring of 2000. Appointed coordinator of the Cold Murder Squad was Detective Senior Sergeant Ron Iddles. Now in his early 50s, he has been in the police force for 30 years, Victoria's Homicide squad for 15 years, and has worked in a variety of other divisions, including general police duties and drugs.

People who know Detective Iddles, or of him or his work – from my local copper through to an anonymous writer on an internet forum for those who have been bereaved through violent circumstances – readily described him as 'a good bloke'. He has been commended four times by the Chief Commissioner of Police for his dedication and commitment, has received a Chief Commissioner's Certificate for bravery, and in 2000 was awarded the Australian Police Medal.

And despite the fact that he has investigated so many crimes both before and since Elisabeth Membrey disappeared, Iddles possesses an amazing memory for detail about her case. When he talks about Elisabeth's murder, he appears to know the details backwards, easily recollecting the names of the witnesses who gave statements, and vividly recalling the tiniest details.

Detective Iddles therefore came to the Cold Murder Squad in 2000 with a reputation for tenacity, for being someone who would keep working and never give up until he had uncovered the truth. He was also known as a policeman with a deep sense of moral obligation to the families of victims. When he was appointed as the squad's coordinator, he was optimistic that the renewed investigations into some 280 unsolved murders would be worthwhile.

'I've always got this thing that it doesn't matter what homicide – somebody in the community will always know the answer,' he told ABC reporter Geoff Hutchison. 'You know, maybe they've been in a relationship with somebody that's broken up and they find ... that finally they can pick up the phone and ring; or it's something which has played on their conscience and eventually they ring.'

For a while, as far as the Elisabeth Membrey case was concerned, it looked as if Detective Iddles' optimism might bear fruit when a girlfriend of one of the long-time suspects was charged with trying to pervert the course of justice. Now, seven years later, the detective can still 'only hope' that if someone in the community does know something about Elisabeth's death, they will finally talk.

Away from the job, Ron Iddles is married with three children, is passionate about education and has long been active on school councils. As a parent, he can understand how desperate the Membreys are for closure. Since heading the investigation into their daughter's death, he has been something of a 'lifeline' to Joy and Roger, speaking to them regularly even though he knows he has nothing to report, no hope to offer them. 'It's terrible,' he says, not to be able to provide them with the information they so desperately desire.

For nearly 11 years, the police had two suspects in mind for Elisabeth's murder. The name of one has never been made public, but Detective Iddles says he was someone who 'drank at the Manhattan Hotel, swam at Ringwood Aquatic Centre and lived for a time in Bedford Road'.

The other one's name was made public at the time his girlfriend was charged with giving him a false alibi, but for legal reasons he cannot be named here. At the time of Elisabeth's death he worked as a bouncer at the Manhattan Hotel, was known to be obsessed with her, and bore a physical resemblance to the description of the man (or men) seen with her at the Ringwood Aquatic Centre and later at her unit.

For a brief time, in 2002, it looked as if the police might have garnered enough evidence to charge this man with Elisabeth

Membrey's murder. His girlfriend, with whom he had lived in 1994, was taken to court accused of trying to pervert the course of justice. The police claimed she had lied about her boyfriend's whereabouts in a statement she had given in the days following Elisabeth's death; that she had in fact provided him with a false alibi. In her original statement, she had claimed he had been at home at on the night of 6–7 December, and hadn't gone out at all.

That alibi seemed to crumble, however, when the suspect himself admitted that he'd gone out at 1am to buy drugs from his supplier. He had later allegedly returned with marijuana, which the couple had smoked before going to sleep in separate rooms. The drug dealer had declared the story as 'bullshit', saying he'd been playing darts in the Manhattan Hotel until 2pm and had not sold drugs to the suspect.

A breakthrough appeared on the horizon when the girlfriend went to live in London. One of her friends there became suspicious not only about the suspect's involvement in the murder, but also the girlfriend's.

Detective Iddles flew to London to interview the friend, who told Melbourne Magistrates Court via a video-link from London in February 2003 that she had 'formed a view that [the suspect] was responsible for Elisabeth's disappearance and [his girlfriend] either knew about the circumstances or was present'.

The girlfriend was charged with attempting to pervert the course of justice for giving the suspect a false alibi. 'She got off on a legal technicality,' says Ron Iddles. 'To be perverting the course of justice, she needed to know that he was the only person considered a suspect when she gave her statement.' At the time she gave that statement, she hadn't realised that he was a suspect – and in any case he was not the only suspect in the investigation.

For Joy and Roger Membrey, the ruling of Deputy Chief Magistrate Jelena Popovic that there was insufficient evidence for the suspect's girlfriend to stand trial on the charge – that the information brought by the prosecution was in the realm of conjecture – was an enormous blow. More than a decade had passed since Elisabeth was murdered, and this had appeared to be the breakthrough they yearned for. The magistrate sympathised with them in court but said she had to 'discharge her duties according to law, irrespective of her feelings or the feelings of others'.

Detective Iddles now says that he believes that the evidence that this particular suspect had killed Elisabeth Membrey was 'circumstantial'.

'He fitted the description; they worked together; she'd been to his place. He said he'd been out the front of her house, but denies ever having been inside. Gut instinct,' Iddles explains, tells him that this man wasn't responsible for Elisabeth's death. He is also 'confident' that the other suspect in the case didn't kill her either.

'By the end of 2005, I was completely satisfied that neither of the two suspects did it.'

For 13 long years, the Membreys have waited for closure. The collapse of the case against one suspect's girlfriend was just one of numerous disappointments and hurts they have received since the night they discovered their beloved daughter had disappeared.

In September 2000, Joy and Roger stood beside Ringwood Lake while police dragged it, acting on a tip-off given in the wake of renewed publicity about the case with the establishment of the Cold Murder Squad. A month and another tip-off later, they waited again while detectives combed some 44 mine shafts at Warrandyte State Park, about eight kilometres from Elisabeth's Ringwood home. Both searches were in vain.

In 2005 Joy and Roger's hopes of resolution were raised, and dashed, again when an anonymous email was sent to Crime Stoppers claiming that someone had privately confessed to murdering Elisabeth. The apparent confession was a new twist even though the person's name was known to the police, but nothing came of investigation into the claim.

Then, in January 2006, Victoria Police announced a reward of $1 million for information leading to the arrest and conviction of the person responsible for the death of Elisabeth Membrey. (It was only the seventh such reward offered by the force for unsolved crimes in the State.) Detective Iddles said at the time that, in addition to the reward, the Office of Public Prosecutions would consider indemnifying any person who was an accessory to the murder, though not the principal offender.

The announcement of the reward again built up the Membreys' hopes. Joy believed confession would bring peace to the killer, as well as to Elisabeth's family. According to Australian Associated Press she said: 'Whoever did this brutal murder, it's in the back of their mind all the time. No matter how hard they try to suppress it, it's still there, and it's something they have to live with ... The sooner they can come forward, it will give them some peace of mind as well as us.'

Sadly, as yet, even the lure of the dollar – all one million of them – has not resulted in a resolution. 'We've had about 50 or 60 leads,' says Detective Iddles, 'but they haven't led to anything.'

If the loss of their daughter in dreadful circumstances, and the years and years that have gone by with every hope of an answer or justice thwarted, wasn't enough, Joy and Roger have also found themselves having to battle bureaucracy in the wake of Elisabeth's death.

The *Sydney Morning Herald* reported in September 2004 that when Elisabeth had taken out her superannuation fund, she had named her father as the beneficiary. Roger put in a claim for the benefit in 1995, but had to wait nearly six years before Hannover Life Insurance of Australasia finally honoured the policy. They had refused to pay up until the Membreys had 'proof' that their daughter was dead.

The issuing of a death certificate by the Coroner in 2000 finally gave the company the 'proof' it demanded but then, amazingly, Hannover Life refused to pay the interest it had accrued on the money since Roger first put in his claim. Roger had to take the case to the Superannuation Complaints Tribunal and later to the Federal Court before, finally, in 2004 – ten full years after her death – the Federal Court settled the matter. It found that Hannover Life should have paid the interest. It is worth noting that the amount of superannuation paid out to Roger Membrey was not exactly huge. For an insurance company the cost of the interest accrued would surely have been minimal.

We live in a world in which murder is entertainment. A quick scan of TV listings on any given week will reveal the public penchant for crime shows: *Wire in the Blood*, *CSI: Crime Scene Investigation*, *Criminal Minds*, *Midsomer Murders*, even bloodless old favourites like *Marple* and *Poirot*. So too a scan of the bestseller shelves in your local bookshop will expose the reality that many of the world's favourite writers – Val McDermid, Michael Connelly, Patricia Cornwell, Tara Moss – all write crime. Even children's favourite Harry Potter contains more than its fair share of murder. Fictional crime is everywhere and the public can't get enough of it. The hypothetical 'How to commit the perfect murder' that Lindy Cameron and I presented in Melbourne attracted one of the best crowds of the year to a Sisters in Crime Australia event.

True crime for most of us, especially violent crime, happens at a comfortable distance. We read about real murders in the newspapers, express horror at the violence and sympathy for the victim and their families, but then we forget about it – because, thankfully, it hasn't touched us directly. Then, in our safe personal space, we can happily 'relax' by watching our favourite TV crime shows or reading mysteries from a host of imaginatively twisted crime writers. We enjoy watching and reading crime fiction, secure in the knowledge that it *isn't* real. And even when we read or watch something about a true crime, a real violent incident, we can just move on, secure in the knowledge that it doesn't affect *us*.

But think for a moment how awful it would be to be the parents of Elisabeth Membrey. Imagine too, the ongoing lives of the loved ones of Jane Thurgood-Dove or Sarah MacDiarmid, two other Australian women whose lives ended violently and whose families are still seeking answers and justice?

Could you go on with your life day after day, not knowing what had happened to your child or why? How would you deal with the frustration of knowing that the murderer was still out there, walking about freely, while you still don't know where your daughter's body lies? Even in cases where there *has* been resolution, it must be hard for the bereaved families of crime victims to pick up the pieces and move on in their lives – witness, for example, the separation of Lindy and Michael Chamberlain; or, in the UK, the parents of Jamie Bulger, the toddler murdered by other children in the early 1990s.

How much worse then for the Membreys, who've had no closure, who've not even been able to give Elisabeth a funeral. There must never be a moment's peace for them – especially in a world where crime is entertainment. For Joy and Roger and others who have lost a loved one through violent crime, murder is real; an unimaginable horror that has happened to them and torn their lives apart.

It's been 13 years since Elisabeth Membrey was murdered; 13 long years for her parents who have clung to every hope, and tried every step of the way to make sure that Elisabeth was not forgotten. For over a decade they've done everything they could to help the investigation along in the hope of bringing her killer to justice – and in the hope of finally being able to give their treasured daughter a funeral. As recently as May 2006, Joy told *The Australian Women's Weekly* that 'we're getting older and we're battle-scarred and weary.

You get to the stage where you've had enough, but you know you can't give up.'

It's also been 13 long years for the detectives on the case, who have worked tirelessly only to see every lead fizzle to nothing. The Cold Murder Squad, established in 2000, was disbanded three years later in a police restructuring.

Homicide detectives now investigate cold cases alongside contemporary crime, and Detective Iddles continues to head the investigation into Elisabeth's death. Despite feeling confident in eliminating his two suspects, he does believe it is 'possible' that he has already interviewed the killer.

'I always say the answer is in the file,' he says. Over the years, the file on Elisabeth's death has grown to 'mammoth' proportions, containing some 30 to 40 ring-binders full of statements.

It has presumably, hopefully, been 13 *long* years for Elisabeth's killer as well. While, on one hand they're probably confident that they got away with murder, on the other, they must always be waiting for that tap on the shoulder; for the news that Elisabeth's body has been found and that justice has finally caught up with them.

Will the case ever be solved? Detective Iddles hopes so, hopes that someone somewhere will one day come forward with a piece of vital information that will lead to the discovery of Elisabeth's body or to the identity of the person who killed her.

But, for the moment, the chances of successfully closing Elisabeth Membrey's enormous case file look bleak.

Detective Iddles admits, 'I said to Roger Membrey the other day, "Roger, I told you that one day I'd tell you if we hit the brick wall; well, that day's about here."'

Old Injustices

The Case of Mary Fortune

Lucy Sussex

> *You must have led an unhappy and roving life, to know how hard it is to be still, and to go quietly through the world like the people – the tame nothingness of people around you.*
>
> Mary Fortune, *The Bushranger's Autobiography*

On Christmas Day 1868, a woman writer and her son visited the Melbourne Waxworks, and cast a critical gaze over its version of the Chamber of Horrors. She was unimpressed, finding it more dusty than scary, with the figures unreal and dressed in second-hand clothes. Moreover, she told her readers later, it was inauthentic. In the tableau depicting a sensational 1866 murder in New Zealand appeared one John Sullivan, whose waxen image had 'an unknown visage and unlike figure, with both of which it was my hap to have been acquainted'.

Not many Victorian-era women would have casually admitted to knowing a murderer; far fewer would have commented on his figure. It was a prudish age, whose ideal of womanhood was pure, passive and dependent. Women who departed from these norms were treated harshly – as was the aforementioned writer, Mary Helena Fortune.

Mary is best known as the author of *The Detective's Album*, the longest-running detective serial of the 19th and early 20th centuries, for which she wrote over 500 stories from 1867 to 1908. A selection from the serial, with the same title, was the first book of crime fiction published in Australia, in 1871. Yet she was never recognised for her pioneering writing – an injustice in any author's book.

The story of Mary Fortune's life (c. 1833–1909) is even more unjust. The full facts have only recently emerged, and provide an instance of crime both being lived and written, by someone very well qualified to judge the Chamber of Horrors' authenticity. While Mary paid an appalling price for this inside knowledge, no doubt a modern crime writer and their publicity people would kill for the same access.

Mary's life provides ongoing lessons: on attitudes to gender, which still prevail; on how little Australia values its authors; and on how easy it is to forget aspects of our past that do not conform to the national mythologies – the secret, ratbag histories of real people.

Mary Fortune did not conform, being a professional at a time when women were expected to be domestic helpmeets. She took pride in being self-supporting. In the same article chronicling her 1868 Christmas excursion, she boasted that her tea tasted all the better because 'I have earned every penny of the money that bought it myself'. She added, 'God bless ye all, my dear friends, and grant me continued independence!' An unusual wish for a Victorian woman.

But although her writing, some of which is autobiographical, appeared regularly in Australian periodicals over a 40-year period, Mary Fortune, as such, was totally unknown to her public. She hid behind pseudonyms – Waif Wander and WW – as was conventional for contemporary women writers, such as the Brontës and George Eliot.

But Mary was not a conventional woman. If anything, the pseudonym shielded her – and protected her dearly won income – from her reading public and their Victorian values.

Until the 1980s, Mary Fortune had been largely forgotten, with even her gender uncertain – because of the pseudonyms. Research showed she was born in Belfast, Ireland as Mary Wilson, and as a child emigrated to Canada with her father George. There she married Joseph Fortune, a Quebec surveyor, in 1851, and the couple had one son, Joseph George. She and her child migrated to Australia in 1855, to rejoin her father George Wilson, on the Victorian goldfields.

It was on the goldfields that Mary would have met the New Zealand murderer John Sullivan. He was a seedy character who, among other things, operated a wayside grog shanty. Although, quite probably, so did Mary. Her father George had a goldfields general store, and followed the diggers from rush to rush. Storekeepers selling liquor without a licence were a motif in Mary's writing, liquor being the one commodity always in demand on the rushes.

Mary also, in a partly fictionalised memoir, refers to the family stove being put to illegal use, a remark that boggles the imagination but suggests a still. She wrote authoritatively of stills in her fiction, and also of women liquor-sellers attracting the romantic attention of young policemen, with names like Percy Butt. In October 1858 Mary married a goldfields mounted trooper named Percy Brett.

By his second marriage, Brett became the great-grandfather of Dr Judith Brett. (Judy Brett is a political historian at La Trobe University, and author of *Menzies' Forgotten People* and other books.) There was no evidence of a Fortune/Brett divorce; such things were expensive and difficult at the time. Bigamy was indicated, but whether by Fortune or Brett it wasn't known for some time.

In addition Mary's second son was born in Australia in 1856, prior to her marriage to Percy Brett. The boy's father was given, on his birth certificate, as Joseph Fortune; but there was nothing to suggest that Mary's first husband emigrated to Australia with or after her, nor that he died here – the biographical facts that would have made her, to the Victorians, a respectable woman.

A death record for Joseph Fortune could not be located here; neither could Mary's, though she lived into the 1900s. The latter remains elusive, despite the efforts of various researchers.

Recent research in Canada by members of Joseph Fortune's family solved not only the issue of where he died, but also the question of bigamy. Joseph Fortune died in Quebec in 1861, three years after his wife married Percy Brett in Australia. Thus Mary Fortune is apparently situated in the Victorian-era category of Scarlet Woman, with a child born out of wedlock. But this image of Mary is not the whole story, nor an explanation of her life.

The title of Mary's newspaper series, *The Detective's Album*, referred to a collection of police mugshots. In a case of life imitating art, it would come to have an unpleasant biographical resonance.

Mary Fortune's first son, Joseph George, born in Canada and son of Joseph Fortune, died on an Australian goldfield at the age of five. The second son, Eastbourne Vaudrey Fortune, known as EV or George, lived to adulthood. His life is well documented by prison mugshots over a 20-year period, during which he was jailed for offences ranging from vagrancy to robbery under arms.

EV was first arrested as a teenager in 1871, the year his mother's one book was published. The 15-year-old was found to be a 'neglected child' – which, at the least, meant he was on the streets unsupervised, then grounds for relegation to an institution.

An issue in his sentencing (or not) was his family's perceived respectability. When a parent appeared to plead for their child, they would be closely scrutinised by the magistrates. Should the parent be known to the police, or appear 'incapable, slovenly, or inarticulate' then the child would be deemed neglected.

Mary Fortune was highly articulate and, in the *Children's Registers of State Wards*, EV was described as clean and literate. And yet he was committed to the Industrial School (i.e. Reform School) in Sunbury for two years, which was the usual procedure for children considered at risk. Why? The most likely grounds were because his mother was not a model Victorian woman. Thus EV was regarded as being 'at risk' but was unwittingly put at more risk by being sentenced. By entering Reform School, he entered upon a career trajectory familiar, still, to modern social workers and probation officers. EV made bad associations, and was set upon a course of crime that would ruin his life.

It is not known whether Mary's employers, the *Australian Journal* (then edited by Marcus Clarke), tried to help her or not. She certainly made her own efforts to get EV out of the Industrial School, by writing to the authorities. A discharge was approved but something happened, and EV remained in Sunbury. In January 1872 he absconded, together with three other boys, but was picked up again (this time under an alias) early the following year, for stealing tobacco. He was re-committed, but further absconding and petty thieving followed, the records indicating EV had basically become a larrikin, or street kid. In 1879 he received his first sentence as an adult, for feloniously receiving. His last sentence, of 10 years' hard labour for burglary, was given in 1890.

Ultimately I have no great interest in EV himself – I leave him to other researchers, such as the several PhD students currently at work on Fortune – for my interest is his mother. And EV does not, apparently, feature in Mary's fiction. Her crimes are the big melodramas of murder and bushranging, rather than the theft of £4 from somebody's house (one of his actual offences). He is, if anything, a minor case study in a history of Melbourne's lowlife. But, because he figured in the records of juvenile crime, he does provide a snapshot of his mother; albeit an unflattering one.

EV's initial entry in the *Children's Registers* stated that his mother was 'at present an inmate of the Melbourne Home'. This was the Melbourne Immigrants' Home in St Kilda Road, which (writes Suzanne Davies) was 'little better than a British workhouse' providing accommodation for the 'ill, old and destitute' and 'disreputable'. The home would, five years later, attract the attention of journalist John Stanley James, who wrote for *The Argus* as 'The Vagabond'.

Unlike The Vagabond, Mary – who wrote some very good articles about Melbourne's street life – was not slumming in the Immigrants' Home as part of a journalistic investigation. She may have been a regular inmate, defined as someone unable to find work, or just a casual, as James wrote, 'admitted for a night's lodging and a meal of bread and tea'.

Either way, Mary Fortune was homeless despite being, at the time, arguably the most published author in Australia, having contributed four serialised novels, poetry, journalism and over 60 short stories to the *Australian Journal* and other magazines.

Given Mary's homelessness, it has to be wondered whether her pseudonym of Waif Wander was another case of art into life. She was often self-referential in her writing, perhaps emboldened by her anonymity. Percy Brett, for instance, makes various recognisable appearances in her fiction. Waif Wander was certainly an odd nom de plume for a woman in an era where femininity comprised domesticity; though perhaps it was precisely this separation from the woman's place, the home, that she denoted.

In an 1872 article, 'Our Colonial Christmases', she referred to herself as a rolling stone; and unlike The Vagabond, she actually lived her pseudonym. Additionally, Waif is a legal term signifying, among other things, lack of ownership. A woman without a 'legal owner' in the Victorian era was single – beyond the control of husband or father. Delving into the dictionary even further, waif also has the meaning of outcast, which, for a woman in Victorian society, usually meant loss of virtue. So did Mary's pseudonym hint at her errant status? Most probably yes.

In 1898 the magazine *Table Talk* described Mary Fortune as 'probably the only truly Bohemian lady writer who has ever earned a living by her pen in Australia'. It praised her as 'the best detective story writer' in the country, but added 'she is very old now and lives from hand to mouth' despite still publishing regularly in each monthly issue of the *Australian Journal*.

'Truly Bohemian' was truly apt. In March 1873, when EV was convicted for a second time (under his alias James Davidson), the *Children's Registers* record that Mary Fortune was seemingly living in a de facto relationship: 'Father James Davidson, Mother Mrs Mary

Davidson … is stated to be a writer for the *Australian Journal.*'

His third conviction, from October 1873, noted: 'Father Joseph Fortune dead. Mother Mary Fortune, a governess … East Melbourne, is in poor circumstances. Mother is a drunk.'

Indeed, one of the few things remembered about Mary at the *Australian Journal* office was her alcoholism. But if she was a drunk in 1873 yet survived, writing hundreds of stories until the early 20th century, then she presumably dried out, to relapse again.

Drunken women were regarded with particular horror by Victorians. In her own writing, Mary echoed the conventional attitude, being rigidly censorious. Her first detective story, *The Stolen Specimens* (1865), contains a young woman called Ellen who becomes 'more and more addicted to the cursed liquor … it at length became no uncommon thing to see her staggering up the street, still carrying the unfortunate child, with its clothes, as well as her own, the picture of neglect and untidiness'.

Mary was writing, on that occasion, from the narrative viewpoint of a male detective and his prejudices. Poor Ellen ends by hanging her child and later dying herself in an asylum: 'victim to the curse of intemperance so prevalent in our colony'.

An 1868 piece of journalism is even more evocative and similarly scathing. Waif Wander has gone looking for lodgings. She meets a prospective landlady, Mrs Rash, with a partiality for Lime juice (gin). Later that day she encounters Mrs Rash again, now legless drunk, stuck in a mud hole and being taunted by urchins.

> *A number of angry ducks that her slip had dislodged from said hole were quacking and flapping their dirty wings behind her, and she herself propped up against the fence, with her hair hanging in disorder, and her scarlet jacket displaying a deplorable rent, was abusing, to the best of her ability, the dancing, and screaming, and halloing children.*

Waif Wander helps Mrs Rash to her feet, and through her gate home. Despite the kind act, she is quite unsympathetic. She finds the spectacle ludicrous, and it cheers her up after a long day's trudge after accommodation. But she herself was no better; in 1874 the *Police Gazette* of Victoria noted:

> *Information is required by the Russell-street police respecting Mary Fortune, who is a reluctant witness in a case of rape. Description: 40 years of age, tall, pale*

> *complexion, thin build; wore dark jacket and skirt, black hat, and old elastic-side boots. Is much given to drink and has been locked up several times for drunkenness. Is a literary subscriber to several of the Melbourne newspapers. Stated she resided with a man named Rutherford, in Easy [Easey] Street, Collingwood.*

This APB is the only known visual record of Mary Fortune. Were this article a fiction, like my own novel *The Scarlet Rider* (1996), which partially fictionalised my (re)search for Mary, I'm not sure I would add the detail of Easy Street, coincidentally the site of a notorious 20th century murder. Sometimes life is too neat even for art.

What could produce a female, 19th-century version of Charles Bukowski? Certainly EV would have been enough to drive anyone to drink.

Ron Campbell, a detective writer and 20th-century editor of the *Australian Journal*, thought he knew why. He wrote in 1952: 'God knows, she probably had every reason, as she wrote more, and doubtless got less for it, than any other Australian writer of the time.'

Campbell wrote *The First Ninety Years* (1949), the history of the Massina firm, the publishers of the *Australian Journal*. He had access to a wages book (now lost) from the early years of the periodical. It is possible Waif Wander's pay was recorded within, given Campbell's comments. In the *Bulletin* of 1953 he described her as 'one of the first women freelance-writers of these parts ... she supported herself entirely by writing, though apparently only just'.

Other writers also found the *Australian Journal* a hard paymaster. Mary's crime fiction collaborator, James Skipp Borlase, publicly complained that the magazine 'did not pay its writers a quarter as high per page' as its English equivalent, the *Family Herald*.

It perhaps should also be recalled that another *Australian Journal* writer, the poet Adam Lindsay Gordon, famously shot himself on Brighton beach. However, the magazine was probably not unusual in its poor pay for writers. Borlase wrote: 'Australia is, in fact, at present, the last place that the professional man or the man of letters should emigrate to. Many [are] at present enduring semi-starvation in every Australian city [because their wages] are lower than that of the compositor who sets the copy.'

Some simple, brutal economics of 19th-century Australia: the reading market was tiny, there were no local book publishers, and the overseas market was months away by ship; only those with steady day jobs or private means, or who had the money to return to the northern hemisphere (as Borlase, but Fortune never did) had any degree of financial stability, and it's probable that, as a woman, Mary's pay was even more reduced. (And we modern authors complain about the GST!)

Australian feminist journalist Alice Henry complained in 1901 that: 'Women writers of more than ordinary ability receive less than half the remuneration given to men whose writing is of far inferior merit.' By 1901 women were entering the professions, and had far more rights, such as suffrage. It seems unlikely Henry was describing anything new regarding women journalists' pay.

The injustices of Mary's life multiply: no due recognition as a pioneering detective writer, poor pay, the punitive nature of Victorian sexism, the tragedy of her son.

But I want to introduce another area of life, where it seems she was faced with injustice and reacted decisively against it. Most analogous situations are modern ones, usually involving the Family Court. But if true, then the following is even more extraordinary – from a woman who, in so many ways, defied the mores of her time.

In 1855, Mary Fortune travelled to Australia from Canada, with her two-year-old son Joseph George, leaving her husband Joseph Fortune behind. What happened?

The year, 1855, is significant in the history of Canadian law. In that year, the separate Canadian provinces began to reform their marriage, divorce, alimony and child custody legislation – to be slightly more in line with the American states, on the other side of the border. Metta Victor, Mary's contemporary and the first author to write a detective novel in America, had married under the relatively liberal Michigan law and was able to divorce and remarry without complication.

In Canada, there was one exception to the reforms: the state of Quebec. Mary Helena Wilson had married Joseph Fortune in Melbourne, Quebec, in 1851. Quebec was strongly Roman Catholic, and it followed the Napoleonic and patriarchal code of law, which did not permit divorce, although it recognised legal separations.

The Fortunes, as Protestants, had slightly more options than a Catholic couple. A few Protestants were able to divorce under Quebec law by Parliamentary decree, something involving expense and difficulty, even assuming both were of agreement that the marriage had broken down. An alternative was to cross the American border and divorce there, although the divorce would still not be legally recognised in Canada. Such actions were known as 'migratory divorces'.

It is possible Joseph and Mary Fortune did obtain an American divorce. But it's not likely because at issue was the issue: Joseph George, born 1852, the only son of an only son, of a family who were of some significance and standing in the community. (They had, however, gone down in the world since the 18th century, when they'd been substantial land and slave owners in South Carolina.)

Canada's 1855 reforms did liberalise custody, with the father's absolute patriarchal rights being modified. From that year the courts would examine the child's welfare, and make discretionary rulings, but the double standard still applied. Maternal custody was dependent on good character and, most importantly, the presence of male relatives of respectability and with sufficient money to house and keep the mother and her children. This applied both to Upper Canada and Quebec, where judges ruled on *separation de corps*. The tendency, though, was still to favour the father in granting custody.

In 1855 Mary Fortune was only 22. She had no brothers and her father, George Wilson, had migrated to Australia. She thus had no male relatives in Canada, something crucial if she wanted to get out of her marriage and take her child with her. If their marriage broke down, it is possible that the couple parted by mutual agreement. But would a father have consented to his only son being taken to the other side of the world, never to see him again? I do not know for certain, but I think not.

One of the modern-day Canadian Fortunes emailed me: 'Mary must have been very unhappy.' I think this is *one* thing not in dispute. We can postulate a young woman, in a failing marriage, with a small child, aware of geographical inconsistencies in the marriage laws and, from reading newspapers, that they were changing. But she would also have been aware that, even in the case of a divorce or a legal separation, custody decisions would have gone against her.

So a drastic option, for the unhappily married in the 19th century, was simply disappearing – what, in Australia, was known as the Poor Man's Divorce. It was practised by Mary Fortune's crime-writing collaborator James Skipp Borlase, by Daisy Bates and by who knows how many others.

Mary's father, George Wilson, was on the goldfields in Australia. Perhaps he had a lucky strike and sent her money. Joseph Fortune, a surveyor, worked in a rural area where townships were being created, and his job could have taken him away from home for long periods.

And, where they lived in Knowlton Falls, Quebec, was close to the American border. Once over it, Mary and Joseph junior would be out of the reach of Canadian law. She could then very quickly have taken ship, in Boston or New York, for England and then to the Australian colonies.

The above is conjectural, but I have run this scenario past several Canadian legal scholars, and the consensus is: it looks like Mary did a runner with the child. Sue Martin commented: 'But how brave for the period!' It was certainly daring but with the particular bitter irony that within three years the contested child was dead, of meningitis contracted on the goldfields.

The voyage to Australia may have turned Mary Fortune into a writer, but her personal life apparently condemned her to an existence of anonymous, underpaid literary drudgery. It was not really possible for a woman without money or title to be a colourful literary identity in the era of the Angel in the House (the then popular concept of the ideal wife, devoted and submissive to her husband, from a poem by Coventry Patmore.) Moreover, the economics of colonial Australian publishing were heavily weighted against the writer. At least Mary did not die in complete poverty; around 1909 she successfully applied to the Massina firm for an annuity, when she was apparently suffering from poor eyesight, and unable to write anymore.

She may have had additional health problems. After his final release from prison EV went to Tasmania, seemingly reformed, but where he eventually died in 1907. And yet, two years later Mary Fortune wrote to her friend Minaille Furlong and mentioned having received a letter from her son. The possibly exists that she had a third son, but it is more likely she was simply suffering from senile dementia, one symptom of which can be false memories of the beloved dead, where they apparently live again.

Indeed she commented to Furlong, somewhat ambiguously: 'There is a want in that brain somewhere nothing else can possibly account for the muddle.'

So, in the end who do we have: sinister or shady lady; scarlet woman; drunk; the long-suffering mother of a jailbird; the only truly Bohemian lady writer in Victorian Australia; or the mother of Australian detective fiction?

Perhaps Mary Fortune was all of these; or simply just human – and a singularly unfortunate one.

Did Ken Kill Barbie?

Shelley Robertson

They made such a handsome young couple; they could have come straight out of a catalogue – a toy-shop catalogue.

She was a petite blue-eyed blonde, her features a perfect backdrop for showcasing the costume jewellery she sold as a home-based business. He was very good looking too, a prerequisite for his job as a photographic model. Life sure seemed perfect in Barbie-and-Ken-land. Baby daughter Bonnie had arrived, showing all the signs of inheriting her parents' looks; the family had recently moved into a new house in one of Melbourne's ever-expanding south-east suburban 'McMansion' estates.

But was there trouble in Toytown; was their toy-story life not quite so perfect? I only ask because this toy story does not have a fairytale ending.

Barbie's case – for that's what her story became – is a sad, but not terribly uncommon, example of a police investigation failing to result in a satisfactory outcome.

Nothing went wrong, the investigation was thorough, there were no scientific errors, and nothing was overlooked. There was also no conspiracy, corruption or negligence. It is just an unfortunate fact that a killer is not brought to justice in every murder case, no matter how hard everyone involved tries.

Unlike crime fiction or television shows, there is not always a neat solution to murder. The high-technology machines and clever computers do not always provide the answer. They certainly did not in this case.

Following an evening out visiting friends with baby Bonnie, Ken returned home to find his front door ajar. Entering the house via the rear door, he ran upstairs to find Barbie lying dead in the hallway outside the bathroom.

That's what he told police who attended shortly after he'd made his horrific discovery.

Police officers must obtain statements from all persons involved, when a dead body is found and the circumstances suggest sudden unnatural death. And it didn't get much more sudden or unnatural than the case of Barbie's battered and bloodstained body.

On finding Barbie's body, the first thing that Ken did was telephone his father. This could be considered to be a little strange, as most people would dial 000, the emergency services number. But, for whatever reason, Ken chose instead to call his father who told him to contact the police.

Ken then drove to the local police station, only to find it closed for the evening. He then rang the emergency number posted on the door of the closed station.

The first officers to arrive on the scene knew immediately that this was a matter for Homicide detectives, the police trained to investigate suspicious deaths. They notified police headquarters, requesting the squad's attendance, and that of crime-scene analysts, forensic scientists and a police photographer.

The necessary personnel all arrived quickly, in the early hours of the morning. One of the early priorities was taking photographs of everything exactly as it was, before being touched, moved or trodden on by one of the many investigators now present.

Ken was interviewed by Homicide detectives as soon as they arrived. He was a 'person of interest' to the police, not only as the person who discovered the body, but as the deceased's husband as well.

Ken stated that the whole family had been to the movies that day, returning home late in the afternoon. After an early dinner, Ken went to visit some friends who lived several suburbs away, taking baby Bonnie with him. Barbie had elected to remain at home, saying that she was tired, and needed to do some bookwork for the jewellery business.

As a Senior Pathologist with the Victorian Institute of Forensic Medicine, I was called to attend the scene of Barbie's death a short while later. It is important for the forensic pathologist to see first-hand how and where the body was found and what the surrounding area looked like, and to attempt to identify any objects that may have been used as weapons or caused specific injuries.

The pathologist also observes other features relating to the body, such as any pattern of bloodstains and spatters. Blood spatter pattern analysis is a science based on the behaviour of droplets of blood when subjected to the laws of physics. Interpretation of blood spatter can yield much useful information, such as the exact location of the victim at the time the fatal injuries were received, the number of blows delivered, and even the type of weapon that may have been used.

When I arrived at Barbie and Ken's 'McMansion' in the early morning, there was plenty of blood around. Barbie's body lay crumpled on the floor of the hall leading to the upstairs bathroom and bedroom. Curiously, a man's leather belt loosely encircled her lower legs. Her hair was wet, the blonde streaked and matted with blood. A damp towel lay nearby. She was wearing a pink lace teddy and matching panties. The outfit was in true Barbie style – the blood everywhere was not.

Blood was spattered on the wall and the ceiling of the hallway, indicating that this was where the assault had occurred. The pattern of spatter suggested 'cast-off' blood; that is, droplets of blood flung from a bloodstained weapon as it is being forcibly swung back and forth, inflicting more than one blow.

I don't routinely, even now, do the blood spatter analysis; that is the job of the crime scene people from the Victorian Forensic Science Centre (run by the police). But Barbie's case *was* one of the first where I saw blood spatter pattern analysis being used. It's why I became interested in doing a course in it, and how I came to be a member of the International Association of Bloodstain Pattern Analysts.

After I had briefly examined Barbie's body, I accompanied a Homicide detective on a walk around the house. It sometimes helps to get a 'feel' for a crime scene – asking it questions, in a sense. For instance: what were the people like; what did they normally do; was there anything out of place, or blatantly wrong about the surrounds of the crime scene? These questions can sometimes be answered by looking at the area adjacent to the actual scene.

It didn't take the detective and me very long to get a feel for this household. Everything was clean and neat. A lot of things were pink; obviously Barbie's signature colour.

'I've found the motive,' announced the seasoned detective. He pointed to a guest toilet and powder room, where every stationary object bore a pink frill, toilet seat and all. 'If my wife put pink frills on everything, I'd probably kill her, and the jury would call it justifiable homicide.'

I was inclined to agree with him; the Barbie thing really was going a bit too far. But all levity aside, there were other things to see besides pink frills.

In the main bedroom, the bedspread and bedclothes (pink of course) had been turned back. A television set had been knocked off its stand, drawers had been ransacked and the contents strewn over the floor.

Ken stated that video equipment was missing, along with some of Barbie's own jewellery (but not her sales stock). He also said that a number of items were missing from the tool shed in the backyard. This was a bit puzzling, as there didn't seem to be any signs of forced entry. Ken said he recalled seeing the front door open when he arrived home, but had let himself into the house through the back door, which he unlocked with his key.

A picture was emerging of a weary young woman who had opted to stay in while her husband took their small child out with him to visit friends. She had showered and washed her hair, wrapping it in a towel turban, then put on her night attire. She had planned on doing some paperwork for her business, after getting into bed, when she was disturbed.

So the question was: who disturbed her? Was it a stranger knocking on the door? Surely she would have donned a dressing gown of some sort to answer a doorknock in the late evening; but Barbie was not wearing a gown when her body was found.

Perhaps it was someone she knew, was even expecting, so there was no need to don a gown. But who was that person?

Later enquiries failed to reveal any of Barbie's friends who may have dropped around and there was no suggestion that she might be expecting a lover that evening. On the contrary, Barbie's friends, relatives and Ken all stated categorically that she was not having an affair.

Did she disturb a burglar who, thinking everyone had left the house for the evening, was taking the opportunity to break into the premises?

Maybe, but this would be a burglar who was not put off by lights in the upstairs rooms, the sound of the shower running, or a car sitting in the driveway. This would be a burglar with a key, who let himself in the front door, killed Barbie when she confronted him, then had a bit of a rummage around the bedroom, taking two VCRs and a bit of jewellery. He then just walked out the front door again, this brazen burglar, or he left the house through the back door, carefully locking it behind him, and stopping to pinch a few tools from the toolshed before disappearing into the night. Must be a pretty cool customer, this burglar; he'd just murdered a beautiful young woman, and yet he takes a detour to nick a spanner set from the shed on the way out.

Barbie's body was removed from the scene and taken to the mortuary by undertakers. The crime scene could now be studied in detail without risk of disturbing physical evidence relating to the body. Homicide detectives also commenced 'doorknocking' the neighbourhood in the quest for information, and the huge amount of paperwork that documents a homicide investigation began to accumulate.

Back in the mortuary later that day, I performed the autopsy on Barbie. Members of the Homicide squad watched the procedure through the glass windows of the 'viewing room' of the autopsy suite. The police photographer was in the autopsy room with me, along with the technician who would assist me, and of course, Barbie.

The autopsy room is set up along the lines of a hospital operating theatre. Overhead lights illuminate the 'operating table' or trolley that is locked into position and on which the body lies. The dissection is carried out on stainless steel benches using surgical instruments.

An autopsy really is like a surgical procedure, albeit a very major one, and similar principles apply. Obviously the subjects don't need anaesthesia, for they will never feel pain again, but we forensic pathologists still treat them with the same respect that doctors afford their patients during life. Our job is to examine them and document all findings, normal and abnormal, so that we can diagnose the cause of death and reconstruct the circumstances surrounding death.

Barbie's autopsy began with the photographer taking pictures of her body to display all of her injuries, while I documented them. She had quite a few injuries, some of them relatively minor bruises, and two black eyes. There were no injuries to suggest that a sexual assault had taken place.

The cause of death was the head injury. Barbie had been forcefully struck on the head with a blunt object. There was nothing specific about the injuries that could have pointed to a particular weapon; just something heavy, with no sharp edges. The blow had split her scalp, which was the source of all the blood around the body at the house, fractured her skull and damaged her brain. She would have died very quickly.

Barbie also had some small bruises to the back of one hand. This is the type of injury typically seen when the hands are struck while the victim is attempting to ward off an attacker, or protect more vulnerable parts of the body such as the face and head.

I found no other abnormalities. Barbie had been in excellent health and she had not been drinking alcohol or taking any drugs. Unfortunately, I didn't have much additional information to give the Homicide investigators in the viewing room.

What were they left to deal with? Here was a lovely young woman with a stable family life, seemingly bashed to death with a heavy blunt object while her husband and small child were out for the evening. No weapon was found at the crime scene. There were no signs of forced entry. There had been a rather 'half-hearted' burglary.

Despite their impression that the burglary may have been staged, police concentrated enquiries on burglaries and known criminals in the area, with the assistance of the media. There was no record of similar burglaries having been carried out in the area, and no information regarding the identity of any burglar ever came to light.

It was obvious a different approach needed to be taken.

Let's consider Homicide Rule No. 1 – learnt from experience by those people involved in the investigation of murders in our society. Quite simply, Rule No 1 is the spouse (or partner or close relative) did it.

Statistics show that most people are murdered by someone they know. The rule is based on the straightforward premise that no-one other than a person very close to the victim feels strongly enough about them to commit murder. And who usually has the strongest motive, and usually the best means, to carry out a murder? Who indeed, but the partner or next of kin.

Of course, there are exceptions such as gangland murders and fights in pubs, but the random or unknown killer is very rare. Rule No 1 is always tucked at the back of the investigator's mind, even though there may be evidence pointing elsewhere – as it did in Barbie's case. Or did it?

Take Ken's alibi that he had gone to visit the friends, at their place, with baby Bonnie in tow. The friends would no doubt corroborate Ken's visit, along with his arrival and departure times.

But, as it turned out, Ken had rung them, supposedly en route, stating that he was running a bit late. Was he just getting a bottle of milk like he told them, or was he engaged in something a lot more sinister? Was it possible that Barbie was already dead before he went out?

Which brings me to the timing, because ascertaining the exact time of death is almost impossible. Quite unlike our counterparts in popular TV shows or crime fiction novels, real forensic pathologists are reluctant to commit themselves to a precise time of death. The fictional pathologists glance at a body and say with authority, 'He's been dead three-and-a-half hours. He was killed between 2 and 2.15pm.'

If only! There are just too many things that influence the estimation of the 'post-mortem interval' – or the time between death and discovery of the body. The real forensic pathologist has no way of knowing what all these things were. Sure, some of them (like temperature) can be measured, but factors like air movement and humidity are harder to determine. Then there are other influences such as the type of clothing worn; the size, shape and age of the deceased; previous state of health; and even the cause of death itself. Was the body killed somewhere else, with a different set of conditions, and then moved to where it was found? Was it stored somewhere for a while, again with a different set of conditions, like the boot of a car or even a fridge? All these things can affect determination of the time of death.

I could not be more precise about the time of Barbie's death than the time frame given by Ken – the last known person to see her alive. He said that she was alive when he went out at around 7.30pm, and he found her dead when he got home around 11.30pm.

I could find nothing to suggest that she had not died between 7.30 and 11.30pm. But I also couldn't exclude the possibility that she had died a bit earlier in the evening.

Then there was the motive. Who could possibly have wanted Barbie dead? There were any number of possibilities, starting with the brazen and cold-blooded burglar, disturbed during his robbery attempt. But the burglary theory didn't quite ring true.

Was it the work of a rapist who sought out his victims in the south-eastern suburbs, waiting till they were home alone before breaking in to rape and murder them? Almost certainly not. No similar incidents had been reported to police, and Barbie was not sexually assaulted.

How about a disgruntled lover, visiting Barbie while Ken was out? Again, no – we have no reason to believe that Barbie had a lover, let alone one who came around that evening while she was alone and killed her in a fit of murderous rage.

We also didn't have any serial killers lurking around the McMansion estates looking for victims, nor did any come to light in the weeks or months following Barbie's death.

Rule No. 1 was starting to look good.

It was with a sense of frustration that I finalised my report relating to Barbie's death. I had described her body, documented her injuries and established her cause of death. I had commented on her general state of health and her negative toxicological analysis results.

I thought that there had been more than one blow to her head by the blunt weapon but I could not say exactly how many blows had been struck. I could not positively state what the weapon was.

I had no explanation for the leather belt around Barbie's legs, except that I was certain it had not been there while the blows to the head were being inflicted. Why? Because there was a tiny spatter of blood within the imprint of the belt on Barbie's leg. If the belt had been there *while* she was being struck, the droplet would have landed on the belt itself, not on the underlying skin of her leg. I wondered briefly if the belt was used to drag the body somewhere. But the blood spatter pattern in the hallway indicated that she had been killed right there; and there were no drag marks or anything of that nature to indicate that the body had been moved. I could offer no explanation for the belt.

The police investigation also seemed to grind to an unsatisfactory halt. No burglar or other suspect was ever identified. Despite the extensive investigation, which left no stone unturned, no evidence led to the killer.

No-one was ever charged with Barbie's murder. The life of a lovely young woman, mother and wife, was just taken suddenly and brutally one night, changing forever the Barbie and Ken story of eternal perfection.

Many years later, a coronial inquiry was held. The role of a Coroner's inquest is to ascertain the cause of death and the circumstances surrounding that death. The Coroner does not have the power to 'blame' someone for a death; that lies within the criminal justice system. The Coroner can only find that someone has caused or contributed to a death.

In a case such as the brutal death of Barbie, where a Homicide investigation has failed to result in anyone being charged or convicted of murder, a Coroner will make a finding of 'death caused by person or persons unknown'. In doing this, the Coroner is effectively providing some form of closure for everyone, particularly family and friends of a deceased person, but also those involved in the investigation of the death.

Additional information may come to light in a Coroner's inquest. Information that may not be considered to be of evidentiary value in a criminal court, but interesting information nevertheless, may be admitted. Like, for instance, the information that Ken was having an affair at the time of Barbie's death. Interesting? Yes. But that doesn't make him guilty of murder.

So it was that Barbie's case was laid to rest – with more than a few lingering doubts, and questions that will probably never be answered.

Questions like, *why* was Barbie murdered? Who murdered her? Did Ken kill Barbie?

Contributors

Robin Bowles – *Due Process*
In 1996 Robin read a newspaper report about the alleged suicide of Victorian country housewife Jennifer Tanner. Guessing there might be a book in the 'story behind the news', she closed her PR consultancy business for a year and wrote her first book, *Blind Justice* (now in its eighth reprint). She's written a bestseller almost every year since, including the definitive books on the Jaidyn Leskie murder, *Justice Denied*, and the disappearance and alleged murder of British tourist Peter Falconio, *Dead Centre*.

Robin is not bound by legal or journalistic conventions, which upsets both lawyers and journalists at times. (Not to mention the police!). During her new career as an investigative writer she also obtained a Private Investigator's licence. Widely recognised as Australia's foremost true crime writer, Robin is also a national co-convenor of Sisters in Crime Australia.

Kathryn Deans – *An Awful Truth, An Uneasy State*
Kathryn has written short stories in a variety of genres, mainly science fiction and fantasy, and is currently working on *Shine*, the third novel of the *Troll's Tale* series, a young adult fantasy trilogy published by Pan Macmillan. It follows *Shimmer* (2005) and *Glow* (2006).

Kathryn lives in Victoria's Dandenong Ranges, has three children, a variety of animals and far too many bookshelves.

Liz Filleul – *The Truth is Out There*
Liz was born in the English Midlands, was educated on the Welsh coast, and now lives on top of an Australian mountain. She currently works as a freelance editor, journalist and writer, and her articles and stories have appeared in magazines in both Australia and the UK.

In 2004 Liz won the Sisters in Crime Scarlet Stiletto Award for short crime fiction, having previously been shortlisted twice. Her first novel, *To All Appearance, Dead*, was published in the UK in 2007.

Kerry Greenwood – *And Justice for All*
An advocate in the Magistrates Court for Victorian Legal Aid, Kerry has written 39 novels: 16 featuring the fictional sleuth Phryne Fisher, and three so far starring Corrina Chapman. She wrote the Delphic Women series and many novels for young adults, and was also editor of both editions of *On Murder* (2000 and 2002).

She lives with a registered wizard and two imperious cats, and in her spare time stares blankly out of thc window.

PD Martin – *Champions of the Innocent, Wrongful Conviction*
Phillipa's debut novel, *Body Count* (2005), has already gone into several reprints. Its sequel, *The Murderer's Club*, was released in Australia in late 2006. *Body Count* hit the shelves in Germany (2006) and the USA (2007). Her short story, 'Missing', featured in the March 2006 issue of the *Women's Weekly*.

Phillipa has studied psychology, criminology and writing, and has worked in the corporate field as a writer and editor for over a decade.

Susan Metcalfe – *Australia's Pacific Borderlands*
Susan is a writer currently doing a PhD on 'Australia and Asylum Seekers: Nauru and its consequences'. In recent years she has been supporting and advocating for many of the asylum seekers detained in Nauru under Australia's Pacific Solution. Susan has been fortunate to gain access to Nauru where visas are hard to obtain, making six visits to the camps since the beginning of 2005.

Leigh Redhead – *Bad Bad Big Brother*
The author of *Peepshow* and *Rubdown*, Leigh has worked on a prawn trawler and as a masseuse, a stripper and an apprentice chef. *Peepshow*, which introduced her fictional series character Simone Kirsch – full-time stripper, part-time private eye – won the *Sydney Morning Herald* Best Young Novelist award. Both books won the

Davitt Readers' Choice Award presented by Sisters in Crime Australia.

Shelley Robertson – *The Truth, the Whole Truth, and Nothing But the Truth, Did Ken Kill Barbie?*
Dr Shelley Robertson MBBS (Melb), LLB (Melb), FRCPA, DMJ (Path), FACLM, DAvMed (Otago) MHealSc (AvMed) is a specialist forensic pathologist based in Melbourne with over 18 years' experience in murder investigations. She is Senior Pathologist at the Victorian Institute of Forensic Medicine; a Senior Lecturer in Forensic Medicine at Monash University; and Honorary Senior Fellow, Department of Pathology, University of Melbourne. She also has a law degree and frequently gives evidence in court. Shelley contributed true crime essays to both editions of *On Murder* (2000 and 2002).

Lucy Sussex – *Old Injustices*
Lucy was born in New Zealand, and is a Senior Research Fellow at Melbourne University. She has published editions of the crime writers Mary Fortune and Ellen Davitt, and edited four anthologies, including *She's Fantastical* (1995), which was shortlisted for the World Fantasy Award.

Her award-winning fiction includes five books for younger readers and one adult novel, *The Scarlet Rider* (1996). She has written two short-story collections, *My Lady Tongue* and *A Tour Guide in Utopia* (2005), with another, *Absolute Uncertainty*, published by Aqueduct Press (Seattle, USA).

Currently she reviews weekly for the *Age* and *West Australian* newspapers, and is also completing a book on early women and crime fiction.